PRAISE FOR
FOOD SUPPLY CHAIN
MANAGEMENT AND LOGISTICS

This book offers a comprehensive analysis of logistics and supply chain management in the food industry. Given the criticality of food supply chains, and the risks if not managed properly, managers in the food and adjacent industries will greatly benefit from the thorough analysis. The end-to-end view of food supply chains is well-covered. The topical case examples relate the discussion to practice and are a great source for teaching.
Professor Stephan M Wagner, Chair of Logistics Management and Director Executive MBA at the ETH Zurich

Samir Dani has provided a perceptive overview of food supply chains and their operations, including topics on innovation and sustainability. This book contains interesting case studies and is an essential read for anyone involved in food and drink production, distribution and retail.
Praful Talera, Managing Director, Dynamics Logistics India

A comprehensive text covering food supply chains from all perspectives, including logistics, technology, regulation and safety as well as innovation and sustainability.
Professor Samir K Srivastava, Chairman of Research Strategy and Policy Committee, and Professor of Operations Management at the Indian Institute of Management, Lucknow

International food supply chains are complex and fraught with risks. This book provides an end-to-end examination of food supply chains and logistics, and highlights the challenges faced by international food supply chains. The comprehensive treatment of relevant topics and recent case examples will be extremely beneficial to both practitioners and academics.
Priyesh Patel, Managing Director, Cofresh Snack Foods Ltd

Food Supply Chain Management and Logistics

Food Supply Chain Management and Logistics
From farm to fork

Samir Dani

KoganPage

LONDON PHILADELPHIA NEW DELHI

First published in Great Britain and the United States in 2015 by Kogan Page Limited

2nd Floor, 45 Gee Street	1518 Walnut Street, Suite 1100	4737/23 Ansari Road
London	Philadelphia PA 19102	Daryaganj
EC1V 3RS	USA	New Delhi 110002
United Kingdom		India

www.koganpage.com

© Samir Dani, 2015

The right of Samir Dani to be identified as the author of this work has been asserted by him in accordance with the Copyright, Designs and Patents Act 1988.

ISBN   978 0 7494 7364 8
E-ISBN   978 0 7494 7365 5

British Library Cataloguing-in-Publication Data

A CIP record for this book is available from the British Library.

Library of Congress Cataloging-in-Publication Data

Dani, Samir.
   Food supply chain management and logistics : from farm to fork / Samir Dani.
      pages cm
   ISBN 978-0-7494-7364-8 (paperback) – ISBN 978-0-7494-7365-5 (ebk)   1. Produce trade–
Management.   2. Produce trade–Marketing.   3. Food supply.   4. Business logistics.   I. Title.
   HD9000.5.D155 2015
   338.4'7664–dc23
                                                                                            2015015894

Typeset by Graphicraft Limited, Hong Kong
Print production managed by Jellyfish
Printed and bound in Great Britain by CPI Group (UK) Ltd, Croydon CR0 4YY

To
my parents
Suresh and Sarita

CONTENTS

PREFACE

Food is a very important part of human life. It pervades our waking time – breakfast, lunch, dinner, snacks, drinks, puddings. When I was growing up, snacks, or for that matter chocolates, were not often available. The shops were convenience stores, but they were unlike the retail ones we find now. There was less advertising of food and the reliance was on a staple diet that one received at home. The culture of snacking had not yet arrived. Fresh fruit and vegetables were available in a market where they were sourced locally, so that the produce was seasonal. We can still find these markets in India (although the retail sector has started changing the scope), but in the West these vegetable markets are more wholesale markets that are open very early in the morning for traders and individual shop owners to purchase their supplies. The retail environment has changed the way food is available to us and in turn has modified our eating styles and regimes.

Food is everywhere around us. As a species, today we are nearer to food than the hunter-gatherers were. However, the irony is that more than half of the world's population lives below the poverty line and cannot afford to have one decent meal every day. The bigger irony is that small farmers who produce the food and contribute to the world's food security and the complex food supply chain are also in a terrible state. It is sad to hear that in the developing world, farmers take their own lives because they are unable to sustain their livelihoods and hence unable to pay their debts.

The food sector has changed rapidly in the past decade. The movement of people for work and migration has led to a demand for food products from across the globe and retailers are keen to oblige. The style of retail environments, the technology advancements in tracking, operations management and packaging have made it possible to import a food item from any part of the world at the right quality specifications. Companies and countries around the world have been working very hard to get a share of the pie. This is not an easy task and it needs a lot of effort to create capability within the system to manage international trade. Specifically within the food sector, the one factor that plays a very important role in the success or failure of a food supply chain is 'food safety'. This one variable supersedes all other challenges within the chain. It is also the number-one risk that companies will be concerned about when dealing in food. Recent cases have demonstrated how it can go horribly wrong if food safety is not taken seriously. Food fraud and food crime are important topics being discussed in the West since the horsemeat scandal, leading to policy discussions and an investigation into methods to stop it.

Food supply chains criss-cross the world, with two aims:

1 satisfy the consumer as per the requirements; and

2 by carrying out (1) efficiently, become economically sustainable.

Food supply chains are becoming increasingly complex. For example, fish caught in the North Sea or off the western coast of the United States is frozen and shipped to China where it is defrosted, filleted, packed and refrozen before reaching retail shelves in Europe and the United States. The only reason for the supply chain being this complicated is to save on operating costs, but this also brings more risks into the chain.

A major discussion worldwide concerns food security and the capability of feeding nine billion people in 2050. Many initiatives have been formed to try to find a viable solution to the challenge. There are many local initiatives in play, both in developed and developing countries, to solve food security problems. As the developed world looks towards utilizing local produce and creating local supply chain capabilities for regional economic development, the initiatives in the developing world are directed towards building the capability of the farmer. The farmers, who are predominantly smallholders, need to get a fair price for their produce, infrastructure for their sector, individual financial instruments, skills and training regarding modern methods of agriculture and, in general, their rights as humans. A lot of good work on this is currently being conducted in South America, Africa and Asia. Along with food security, which is about securing the future supply of food, sustainability within the supply chain and the sector is a topic that has garnered a lot of attention. Considering the triple bottom line concept, the food sector needs to work hard on the social front, which will provide incentives to producers and processors to maintain environmental bottom lines which will provide economic sustainability in the long term. Scarcity of arable land and water, and uncertain climatic patterns, put a lot of stress on the food system. However, there are many positive things happening within the food sector. One of the characteristics of the food sector is its ability to innovate. There is a consistent process in the industry with regard to innovations in food products, business models, packaging, technology and so on, which adds value in the supply chain.

When I thought about writing this book, I knew that it was going to be a daunting task and that when I had finished writing it I would feel that I had just scratched the surface. This is exactly how I feel now that I have finished it. Food as a topic is so multidisciplinary that it is very difficult to comprehend all the literature that covers it. Hence, it needs a focus, and the focus in this book was to understand the supply chain and the operations and factors that surround it. As you read the book, you will notice that it does not go into great detail but that it points you towards important processes and topics that can be looked at in detail. The additional reading list at the end of the book provides a lot of good information. As the focus of the book is to simplify the process and discuss new developments, it also refers to information from newspapers and magazines, including academia.

The book covers various aspects of food supply chains in detail. The basic premise is to cover the food supply chain from farm to fork, taking into consideration the various challenges and supporting mechanisms to make sure that the food reaching our plates is safe. It is important for the food industry to innovate with regard to both demand management and the sustainability of food sources for a growing population. This book covers various aspects of food supply chains from a management and social perspective.

Figure 0.1 shows how the book is structured. The book is divided into three sections. The first section sets the scene and discusses the different entities in the food supply chain. Section 2 is about operational challenges and hence discusses topics that are relevant for the efficient operation of the chain. Section 3 is about sustainability and food security challenges. This section also looks at innovation in the food chain and how food supply chains can bring about economic regeneration.

FIGURE 0.1   Outline of the book

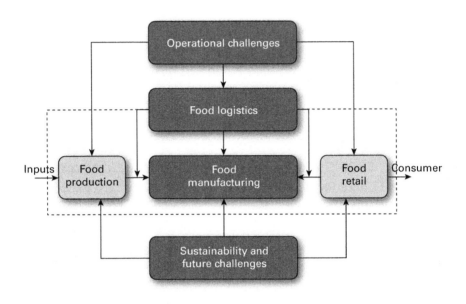

ACKNOWLEDGEMENTS

I would like to take this opportunity to thank Julia Swales and Jenny Volich at Kogan Page for their continued support and trust in me. Julia saw the opportunity and the gap for this book. Jenny has been extremely supportive during the writing, and very helpful by reading the chapters and providing excellent feedback. I also take the opportunity to thank Géraldine Collard at Kogan Page for her support in the initial stages of the book.

I am extremely grateful to Uday Dholakia OBE, Chairman of the National Asian Business Association, UK, Chairman of the Leicestershire Asian Business Association, UK, and Brand Ambassador, Birmingham Airport Limited, for introducing me to the domain of international food supply chains.

I would like to thank Babso Kanwar (Permedia Foods Pvt. Ltd, India) and Sudarshan Rao (Honey R Us, India) for their continued discussion regarding food supply chains and the food sector in general. The discussions have been fascinating and I look forward to the future ones.

Also many thanks to Aman Deep, Abhijeet Ghadge, Roman Buck, Stella Despoudi and Liam Fassam, who have worked with me at various stages on projects regarding food supply chains. The discussions we have had have filtered into the book.

A special thanks to my friends Anil Puntambekar and Savita Puntambekar, who have been another source of discussions regarding food retail.

Kogan Page and I also gratefully acknowledge the involvement of Steve Osborn and thank him for his valuable review of the manuscript for this book.

Finally, a very big thank you to my wife Shilpa and kids Harshita and Anshul for their unwavering support during the writing phase and for giving up their weekend time with me so that I could finish the book.

Introduction to food supply chains

Food supply chains are the lifeline for human existence on the planet. Whether these chains are local or international, the availability of food at the right time, right quality and right quantity is paramount. The recent United Nations report *World Population Prospects: the 2012 Revision*[1] projects that the population of the world will be 9.6 billion by 2050, and one of the biggest challenges to mankind will be to feed this growing population. Another school of thought insists that although the challenge is great and food production needs to be ramped up, we are currently producing a sufficient amount of food to sustain the population. If this momentum continues, there will be sufficient production for the future. If this is the case, why does half of the world's population go hungry every day, or have only one meal a day? Food poverty is rampant in the developing world and this has led not only to covert supply chains in food fraud and food crime, but also to a change in social environments where individuals move towards a life of crime to bank the necessary food rations for the day. International agencies such as the United Nations and the World Health Organization promote programmes to combat child poverty. These programmes focus not only on the availability of food but also on the quality and the nutritional aspects of food. Time and time again, history has shown that wars have been lost and won by controlling food supply chains. It is essential to study food supply chains from an operational perspective, as they not only influence everyday life but also affect businesses and livelihoods. This chapter considers the food supply chain and introduces the actors within food supply chains. It sets the scene for the remainder of the book. The detailed discussion on each actor will follow in the subsequent chapters.

The actors in a food supply chain

The series of processes, operations and entities that help to take the food from its raw material state to our plates is known as the food supply chain. It is not a singular chain of certain entities but a complicated web of interconnected entities working to make food available. The food supply chain starts with the producer (an agriculture-focused organization) and the food sourced at this stage moves through various methods of processing. The movement is facilitated by a host of logistics and transportation companies. These companies make sure that the food reaches us on time and at the right quality. The actors involved in a generic food supply chain are shown in Figure 1.1. The role of these actors is discussed briefly below.

Producers

As the world's population continues to grow, there is increased pressure on the food system to double food production by 2050.[2] To add to the population challenges, the rapid industrialization of developing countries has increased lifestyle and consumption patterns in these

FIGURE 1.1   Actors in a food supply chain

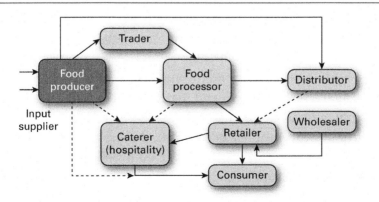

countries. As populations in the developing world receive a higher wage through employment, their food consumption preferences move from grain to meat and other protein-based diets. This provides additional challenges to the meat supply chains. The food supply chain starts at the producer end, which supplies food in its raw form – grains, fruits, vegetables, meat, fish, poultry and so on. The producers are farmers who are a part of the agriculture industry. Farming businesses range from small firms to very large corporates. Some are new to the business while others may be family farms that have been producing food for generations. Every country requires a strong food production sector as it affects both food availability for the population and economic sustainability for the food sector. There are entities in the supply chain that supply raw material (seeds, farming machinery, pesticides, fertilizers and so on) to the producers. These 'input suppliers' are generally large global companies with a lot of power in the chain. The producers also have to deal with increasingly uncertain climatic weather patterns, scarcity of water, land grabbing by unscrupulous agents in developing countries and soil degradation caused by industrialization and urbanization. As margins for producers within the food supply chain are getting smaller and smaller, an increasing number of farmers are now growing what they can sell at a good price in order to have economic sustainability. Although this is fair, as long-term economic sustainability is needed for the sector, it has an impact on the availability of core food products.

Processors

Processors are the entities in the food supply chain that transform the food products supplied by the food producers into products that meet consumer requirements. This process is also known as food manufacturing. This stage in the food supply chain will either prepare fresh food from the producer in a ready-to-eat format for consumers, or use it as a raw material to create other food products demanded by consumers. Food-processing companies are diverse in nature and will process products at different stages: for example, meat slaughtering and processing; preservation of fresh fruits and vegetables either by freezing, puréeing or juicing; milling of grains; making confectionery and bakery products; and other types of food manufacturing. Food-processing is an extremely important process, as it not only sustains the food sector economy by catering to the demands and requirements of consumers, but also helps to reduce waste and increase food availability by increasing the shelf life of raw food products that cannot be immediately consumed. Food processors need to work very closely with the downstream supply chain, which comprises the entities that take the processed food to the consumer. Food processors will need technology insertion, changes to distribution channels and innovation in order to keep pace with environmental changes and changing consumer demands. Another set of challenges that food processors are facing now and will face increasingly in the future is scarcity of resources such as water and energy and the availability of raw fresh food from the producers.

Retailers and distributors

This stage comprises two entities in the food supply chain: distributors and retailers. Distributors are companies that act as the link between producers, processors and markets. The distributors source either fresh produce or processed food from the processors and then distribute it through various channels to reach the final consumer. These channels are either retailing companies or other processing companies (for example, restaurants) which provide the product to the consumer. Distributors will generally buy in bulk and use an infrastructure of warehouses and distribution centres to deliver the products as and when required downstream in the food supply chain. Distribution companies are very important entities, especially when the supply chains are global and have to cross international boundaries, as distributors have to deal with local regulations.

Retailing is a process that showcases the product for the consumer. This can be in the form of local corner shops or large hypermarkets and supermarkets that deal with hundreds of thousands of stock-keeping units (SKUs). The retailer stage in the chain provides the consumer with the variety of core and innovative products that the food sector has to offer. It is a highly competitive industry where food processors compete for shelf space in the retailer environments and the retailers compete among themselves to attract more consumers through their doors. Consumers have a wide choice of retailers, retail channels and formats. Retailers try to differentiate themselves from their competitors and are increasingly creating innovative business models that provide a good-value proposition to consumers based on price, quality and service. Retailers are experimenting with a variety of fulfilment channels and formats, ranging from physical infrastructure (shops) to e-retailing. As large global retailers prospect for markets in the developing world, the food supply chains in developing countries are undergoing a transformation. As the retail environment in developing countries moves from an unorganized sector (corner shops) to a more organized sector (supermarkets), the food supply chains and distribution channels have to innovate and change their processes to respond to retailer requirements. There is an ongoing debate within developing countries regarding the introduction of large-scale retailers and the impact on small shops.

Hospitality sector

The hospitality sector is a key entity within the food supply chain. Although it is not directly a retailer or distributor as such, it is an important link between the producer/processor and the consumer. Food service agencies, hotels, restaurants and takeaway places will source raw material from the producers or processors and transform the food to suit the requirements of the final consumer. These entities provide a 'made to order' service function and are an important entity within the food sector, as they comprise millions of small and medium enterprises, sometimes one-person organizations delivering a very high value within the food system.

Consumers

The consumer is the final entity in the food supply chain. The economic sustainability of the chain depends upon the consumers buying the products and providing the necessary cash to travel upstream through the supply chain. Food is a staple necessity for every person on this planet and hence competition within the food supply chain concentrates on variety and value addition and not on core produce. Recently, in the UK, food supply chains have been subjected to a tussle between regular grocery supermarket chains and discount grocery retailers. This has led to squeezing of margins and prices upstream as the retailers try to outdo each other to offer the lowest-priced food products (for example, most large supermarket chains in the UK are offering four pints of milk for £1, which is greatly affecting the returns to dairy farmers and hence their sustainability).[3, 4] Although this is good for consumers, it leads to another debate about food sustainability and food wastage, as food is looked upon as a very cheap resource. Ironically, as the competition to sell more within the organized sector increases, the excessive variety of food products (with little or no demand) and cheap food available in large quantities creates more food wastage at the consumer end. Reducing food wastage at the consumer end has been a major focus among governments and food-sector organizations in Europe. Food safety is a major concern for consumers and all food supply chain entities have to take the necessary steps to avoid food contamination. This can range from an excess of pesticides in produced food to microbial contamination in processing to improper food handling within the distribution and retail environment.

Types of food chain

Food supply chains can be broadly discussed as those serving markets (as industrial products) and as those serving the final consumer. The first type works through the trading of agriculture produce in bulk or as a commodity. The second type works towards the fulfilment of the consumers' needs.

Commodity- and producer-focused chains

The output from farms moves downstream in two formats, either directly as fresh produce to the consumer (fresh fruit and vegetables, milk, grain and so on) or in bulk as a raw material within food-processing plants. The bulk purchase of raw food material can be done through strategic partnerships with the producers, through traders or by buying it as a commodity item. A commodity is an item that is subject to futures contracts. In a futures contract the two parties in the deal sign a contract to buy or sell an item (in this case food, for example cocoa) for a (future) price agreed today, with delivery and payment happening in the future. The buyer speculates whether the price of the food item will go up or down in the future and hedges the risk by signing a contract in the present for a future price. This process is conducted at the 'futures exchanges'. The commodity chains deal in products such as palm oil, cocoa, coffee, sugar, cereals, grains and so on. The supply chain model works with few buyers and many sellers. The process works as a spot market, and price determines the movement of the product. Commodity systems keep information flow between trading partners to a minimum. The processors, when buying in bulk, utilize this to buy quickly, reduce costs by hedging and maintain flexibility in product availability. Since the purchasing between the processor and producer does not happen directly but through the futures contract, the demand signals from consumers cannot be sent to the producers as there is a disconnect in the relationship. The prices of major commodities are influenced by climate change and uncertain weather patterns, variations in global demand and supply, and political processes such as trade agreements. Demand and supply volatility provides the required incentive to the futures trading environment. Traders tend to use flexibility in having diverse sources of the products to gain some profit, as profit margins are low. Volumes in bulk will tend to provide the returns rather than the actual trading price.

Consumer-driven value chains

Food traceability and identity are very important within consumer-driven chains, as this is the last stage of the food supply chain and has a direct impact on the well-being of the consumer. Food products within the retail environment are processed, branded and work effectively on the basis of uniformity in processing and high quality. Products traded in the commodity market, for example coffee, are now moving into the retail environment as branded, gourmet coffee, with close cooperative relations between processors and suppliers. Unlike the commodity chain, the consumer-driven chain is more regulated, sometimes vertically integrated, and works more on the principle of cooperation and collaboration. The consumer-driven chain has barriers to entry, such as 'voluntary' standards, codes and benchmarks, international regulations and phytosanitary certification, which can affect the entry to markets. There is a need for consistency, which is achieved through processing and on-time delivery. The application of management systems for quality (for example, ISO 9000) or environment (ISO 14000) or production system (for example, organic) helps to maintain the credibility of the food supply chain. Tracking and tracing are very important, and technology insertion is required in the chain for this to be effective. Stringent traceability and intense scrutiny by retailers are conducted through production site visits. It is necessary to check compliance with buyer codes and standards and especially sustainability performance.

Factors influencing food supply chains

The food sector is a very complex environment influenced by industrial, technological, economic, social and political factors that shape the availability of food, the nature of the food product and the delivery of the food to our plates. Entities within the food supply chain aim to improve the functioning of the chain, from the perspective of quality, competitiveness and pricing along with the necessary requirements for absolute food safety.

These complexities in the food supply chain are derived from within a number of areas:

- agriculture production;
- involvement of various governmental/non-governmental actors;
- processing and maintaining quality;
- consumer and market choices;
- local authorities;

- logistics companies; and
- a host of other small companies actively involved in this food supply chain and providing secondary value.

The world around us is constantly changing. Technological innovations, new business models, globalization and the movement of people have made food supply chains rethink fulfilment and effectiveness parameters. Innovations in processing and transport have made products more suitable for global distribution, and innovations in management and information and communication technologies (ICT) have allowed supply chains to become more responsive to the increasingly sophisticated food demands of consumers. Some other factors that influence and affect the food supply chain are as follows.

Consideration as value chains

Food supply chains should be viewed as 'value chain systems' in which the raw material (from an agro-based source) is transformed for final consumption as it moves through the chain and increases in value. Considering the food supply chain as a value chain also means that entities along the chain can aspire to move up the value chain, thereby increasing their share of the return. In some cases, operators across the supply chain integrate vertically to appropriate a larger share of the total revenue, though at the cost of lower flexibility in supplier selection. Transformation of food systems can influence market power along the chain. The food value chain is the network of stakeholders involved in growing, processing and selling the food that consumers eat – from farm to table. The stakeholders include:

- the input suppliers to the food production process;
- the producers involved in growing food;
- the processors, both primary and value-added, involved in processing, manufacturing and marketing food products;
- the distributors, including wholesalers and retailers, involved in distributing, marketing and selling food;
- the consumers involved in shopping for and consuming food;

- government and non-governmental organizations (NGOs) involved in creating policies and programmes for food sustainability and security;
- regulators involved in monitoring and regulating the entire food value chain from producer to consumer;
- logistics companies involved in moving, storing and managing food throughout the value chain;
- financial organizations involved in providing funding to the entities within the food value chain.

The food value chain is also an important vehicle to address global poverty. The value chain provides opportunity to alleviate poverty and increase food security by investment and employment within the food sector. Increased trade within the sector allows people in developing countries to improve their livelihoods and get access to essential services. The value chain, when focusing on food production and food processing with the aim of reducing food wastage and increasing food security, should also pay attention to food accessibility, food safety and food nutrition.

Legislation

The movement of food across international borders is subject to an agreement on the application of the Sanitary and Phytosanitary Measures (SPS Agreement) of the World Trade Organization (WTO). Other international standards will focus on varied topics related to food hygiene, labelling requirements and so on. These agreements and laws create a greater transparency when dealing in international trade. The EU food law focuses on risks and traceability in the 'farm to fork' supply chain, placing equal importance on human health, animal and plant health, and the environment. The principle is to have a precautionary approach and hence the European Commission, through general food regulation, established the 'one step backward – one step forward' approach, which requires operators to identify by whom and to whom a product has been supplied. Food labelling is a key focus within EU food regulation.

Consumer choice

Global food consumption patterns have shown two diverse scenarios. The developed world has seen an increased propensity towards consuming processed food, led by demand from a time-starved working population. The preference for ready-to-eat or microwaveable food products has led to innovations within the retail and packaging environments to service this demand. However, this produces a strange phenomenon in which fresh fruits and vegetables are more expensive than value-added processed food. One of the reasons for this is the economies of scale that the food industry achieves when processing food for the retail environment. Consumers in the developing world are moving from a cereal, grain-based diet to a protein- and meat-based diet. However, an increase in meat production requires increased animal feed and more input raw materials. To increase the availability of animal feed, food production has taken over intensive farming. With a focus on growing animal-feed-based crops rather than crops required for human consumption, this will have an impact on food security.

Sustainability

The global food chain is a significant contributor to global greenhouse gas (GHG) emissions. GHGs are produced at all stages in the chain, from food production (and its inputs) through food processing, food distribution and consumption to the disposal of waste. Sustainability within the food supply chain must be considered on a number of fronts. These include:

- energy consumption;
- carbon emissions;
- water usage;
- food availability;
- ethical behaviour;
- economic sustainability.

The food supply chain should be mapped with a systems perspective in order to understand the links and the locations that are non-sustainable.

Mapping the chain also provides a map of energy usage across the chain and an opportunity to reduce energy consumption. This can be utilized for other resources too.

Collaboration

Collaboration among the various stakeholders along the food value chain is extremely important. The interdependencies between stakeholders in the chain and the wider network should be considered as potential locations of collaboration. The recent global cases of food recalls, food safety and traceability have become a major concern within the food sector. Collaboration between the entities in the chain provides the entities with confidence in the sourcing, handling and quality control of food. Collaborative platforms help supply chain partners to have an end-to-end view of the chain. Collaboration between producers and processors (with the use of appropriate technology) can help reduce post-harvest food losses.

CASE EXAMPLE   The milk-processing value chain

Figure 1.2 depicts a brief schematic of the milk-processing value chain. A detailed mapping of the milk supply chain will include all the relevant entities, along with the primary milk-processing supply chain entities. These will be input suppliers to the dairy-farming process, raw material suppliers for packaging, logistics providers, technology providers and so on. However, the focus of this example is to show the value chain path of milk as a farm product and how it travels through the value chain to reach the final consumer in diverse forms.

Dairy farming is a very important sector for any country. This does not always have to be milk from cows, but includes milk from buffaloes, goats and sheep. Milk features as a staple product on the shopping lists of most consumers and hence sufficient availability of milk within the supply chain is of concern to governments and retailers alike. As seen recently in the UK, price wars between supermarkets have tended to focus around the price of four pints of milk. Milk, although much of it is consumed fresh, is also a major raw material in many food-processing industries. This can be in the form of fresh milk or a processed value-added product used instead of fresh milk. Figure 1.2 starts with the dairy farm as the

FIGURE 1.2   The dairy value chain

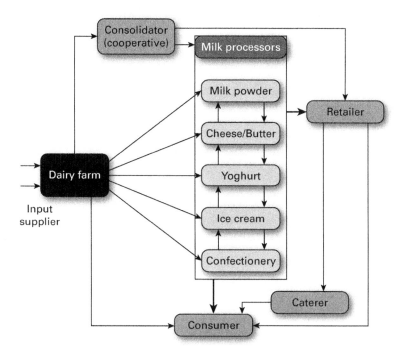

source of milk for the value chain. The dairy farm will have an upstream supply chain with input suppliers to the milk-producing process; however, this is not discussed here. The milk as an output of the dairy-farming process can progress to a number of destinations:

- the consumer;

- milk consolidators, which collect and consolidate milk from small dairy farmers on a local, regional basis – these could be private companies or a cooperative;

- milk processors;

- own farm-based processing;

- retailers and caterers.

Following each path depicts the nature of the business and the value chain.

The consumer: Dairy farms will provide a service to the final consumer by supplying milk directly to the consumer's door step. Generally, in the UK these are the milk rounds which take place every day, very early in the morning. However, as the price of milk in supermarkets has reduced, farms find it difficult to match prices and hence have seen a fall in demand.

Milk consolidators: These are companies which provide a local or regional collection centre for small dairy farmers to sell their milk. The consolidators act as distributors of the milk through the downstream value chain. Sometimes, dairy farmers will come together and form a member-based cooperative to consolidate and distribute the milk produced by its member farms. This is done with the intention of providing a fair price to the farmers and having a more equitable relationship. Sometimes, large food processors will form a cooperative to strengthen their supply chain and create better relationships with farmers. At other times, dairy cooperatives will integrate vertically in the value chain to become food processors (for example, Amul cooperative in India). The cooperatives will supply milk to food processors and retailers.

Milk processors: These are food-processing companies that use milk in its various forms to create further value-added products. Some of the common milk-processing companies are:

- further milk processing – for example, milk powders, evaporated milk, condensed milk;

- yoghurt, cheese, butter manufacturing;

- confectionery and bakery manufacturers – for example, chocolate, biscuits and so forth.

- baby milk powder.

Within this value chain, there will be another link that connects one processor to another as a raw material supplier. For example, further milk processors will act as suppliers for confectionery manufacturers, supplying milk powder, butter, yoghurt and so on as raw materials.

Own farm-based processing: Dairy farms that have a surplus of milk or that find it difficult to supply at very low margins integrate vertically in the value chain to begin processing. Individual dairy farms will manufacture cheese, yoghurt, butter and ice cream to sell individually as a local farm-based brand or in the retail environment. Not all farms have the capability and financial backing to become processors; however, some farms, such as Rachel's Organic in the UK, have been successful in this venture. Moving up the value chain is also discussed in the wider literature as a means for small farmers to become economically sustainable in the long term.

Retailers and caterers: These are classed together in this example as they are the entities closest to the final consumer. Retailers will stock a variety of milk-based products, both as fresh milk from individual farms or cooperatives and value-added milk-based products from farms and food processors. These will include: cheese, butter, yoghurt, ice cream, milk powder, all types of confectionery and bakery products, snacks and so on. The retail environment is not restricted to large supermarket chains but also includes corner shops and off-licences.

Caterers in this case are entities in the hospitality business, restaurants, street food vendors, cafés and so on that source fresh milk or milk-based products to fulfil the final consumers' bespoke demands.

Summary

This chapter has provided a brief introduction to food supply chains. It has discussed the different actors in the food supply chain and their roles. The main actors are:

- producers;
- processors;
- distributors;
- hospitality;
- retailing;
- consumers.

The chapter has also discussed the various factors that influence food supply chains. Along with technological innovations, new business models, globalization and the movement of people, the chapter also discussed the following factors:

- value chains;
- legislation;
- consumer choice;
- sustainability;
- collaboration.

The remaining chapters in this book focus on the key points discussed within this chapter.

Notes

1 World Population Prospects: The 2012 revision, Department of Economic and Social Affairs, Population Division, Population Estimates and Projections Section, United Nations

2 Food production must double by 2050 to meet demand from world's growing population: innovative strategies needed to combat hunger, experts tell second committee, panel discussion, Sixty-fourth General Assembly, Second Committee, United Nations [Online] http://www.un.org/press/en/2009/gaef3242.doc.htm (accessed 24 February 2015)

3 *Daily Telegraph* (2015) Milk cheaper than water: supermarket price war drives down pint of milk, 11 January

4 Smithers, R (2014) Supermarkets' milk price war leaves a sour taste for dairy farmers, *The Guardian*, 7 March

PART ONE
Food production

Food production

02

The agriculture sector or food-producing sector is a major generator of employment and income worldwide. The majority of people within the agriculture sector work at the level of small farms within largely rural areas of the world. As the world's challenges continuously grow on account of population and climatic changes (to name a few), the importance of the agriculture business sector or the food supply chain has grown significantly. The focus of the chain has moved to utilizing the food production stage of the supply chain as a stepping stone to create value-added products and innovations with the goal to 'feed the world'. However, this requires food to be safe and traceable right from the seed and to move safely through the stages to reach consumers' forks. As the world's governments debate food security and sustainability, most countries are forming national policies and strategies to promote investments in agriculture value chain development. This requires a deeper understanding of the elements that affect the sector and the steps being taken by various world organizations (United Nations, Food and Agriculture Organization, Organisation for Economic Co-operation and Development), national governments and private businesses to facilitate efficient operation of the food value chain. This chapter presents the food production or agriculture supply chain. It explains the entities involved in the agriculture supply chain until it reaches the processor. The chapter also discusses the challenges faced by the agriculture sector and the factors that will enable future development. A few case studies demonstrate how entities in the agriculture sector are working with each other to add value in the chain.

Entities in the agriculture supply chain[1,2]

The major entities in any agriculture system start with the input suppliers and end with the processor. However, an agribusiness chain (farm to fork) will end with the consumer. This chapter considers all the entities in the chain until it reaches the processor. The main entities are:

1 *Input supplier*. For the production process to work effectively and efficiently, the inputs to the process have to be of sufficient quality and delivered in a timely manner. These inputs are in the form of seeds, fertilizers, pesticides, machinery, labour and so on. Any disruption to the input supply chain can cause issues with food availability. The input suppliers are large international companies which have invested in food innovation (seeds, pesticides, etc).

2 *Landowner*. This is the entity that owns rights to the land on which food is produced. In most developing countries, land is an important resource and farming will take place only if a suitable piece of land has been identified. In developing countries, individual farmers have very little land holdings and hence controlling production is difficult. On the other hand, someone who has lots of land could subcontract or lease the land for a short period.

3 *Food production/farmers*. This is the most important stage in the agriculture supply chain, as it is the stage in which food is grown or managed (livestock, fish, meat etc) as per the inputs and availability of resources. There are around 450 million farmers globally, who can be segmented by farm size, crops grown and level of sophistication of the production process. Farm sizes vary considerably and the majority of the farmers in the supply chain are smallholders. Farming is a very risky process within the agriculture value chain. It is subject to uncertainties of weather conditions and market volatility.

4 *Traders*. Traders occupy the position between the producer and the processor. Traders could be small businesses or very large corporations. Some also have significant food-processing

capabilities. Within the agriculture supply chains, traders have both a positive image (as they maintain continuity of the chain and in some cases also invest heavily to make it efficient) and a negative image (some traders will use their buying power to reduce considerably the prices paid to farmers).

5 *Direct markets.* These are the markets that connect the farmer or producer to the consumer directly, without the need for any middlemen. These markets tend to operate when produce is plentiful. They could be an open platform, where two entities engage in the purchasing process or the produce reaches the small farmers' market.

6 Within the Indian context, some states in India permit the distribution of farm produce only through the *mandis* (markets) under the Agricultural Produce Market Committee (APMC)[3] Act. These are markets or traders who are certified within the APMC and have a licence to operate. These markets will purchase the produce from the farmer (through an auction) and then distribute it through the supply chain. Currently, the effectiveness of the APMC Act is under debate in India on account of food waste and farmers getting low prices for their products. Food processors have to buy the farm produce through the traders and cannot purchase directly from the farmers.

Along with these entities, logistics companies or transporters are very important for moving the raw food produce to either warehouses or to the trader/processor. The agribusiness or agriculture supply chain hence refers to any business related to agriculture, including farming, processing, exporting, input suppliers, trading, logistics and retailing.

The agribusiness sector is an important generator of employment and income worldwide, as even smallholders can participate in this activity and earn a livelihood. As the pressure on the sector to feed an ever-growing population has increased, mechanization and modernization of the sector have led to a change in the performance and organization of the sector. This is happening to a larger extent particularly within the developing world. Operational efficiency, food safety, food quality, innovation and new business models are helping the sector to reach the consumer faster and in a number of ways. Globalization and consolidation of agriculture produce put pressure on small farmers as they have to compete in a buyer-driven market without recourse to sufficient finance and funding to upgrade their capabilities.

The agribusiness sector deals with a product that is highly perishable and starts losing value as soon as it is harvested. Various processing and packaging techniques are implemented post-harvest to increase the longevity of the product so that the consumers can avail themselves of these. The products will vary in quality, depending on a number of external factors (such as climate, pests etc), and are also seasonal. This provides additional complexity for supply chain planning and requires coordination and integration across the chain.

The risks involved in the production process and the uncertainties in the post-harvest scenario create a risky investment environment for the agribusiness sector. This presents an entry barrier to the sector, especially for smallholders and micro-businesses that have neither the required financial backing nor the ability to manage risks. However, since the sector is directly responsible for 'food security', these barriers need to be studied and solutions need to be identified.

Agriculture and poverty alleviation[4]

Size of the farm

Small-farm agriculture has been encouraged as a solution towards alleviating poverty challenges within developing countries. However, small farms will require updated skills and training in order to manage their businesses efficiently and also have the ability to compete in a very volatile environment. Lack of financial products and cash-flow issues complicate the situation. The new models of retailing and public policy overlook the challenges within the rural sector and work towards cost minimization and highest quality, both of which will need a considerable change in the operational capabilities of the small farmer. However, the opportunity to produce food for the chain is still a very positive step towards creating employment and livelihoods. Future strategy should focus on upgrading small producers so that they can become members of global buyer-driven food chains.

Trade liberalization, commodity chains and concentration of corporate players in the chain can compromise the potential of the sector to act as an effective route for small producers to exit poverty and contribute to and benefit from broader economic growth. Small producers in developing countries find it difficult to stay on top of national product and process standards, demands for traceability and private standard certifications as demanded by international supermarkets. This can exclude them from global supply chains and hence they need support and facilitation mechanisms in order to upskill.

Agriculture and reduction of poverty

The Department for International Development (DFID) conducted a consultation on 'New Directions for Agriculture in Reducing Poverty'.[5,6] Among its conclusions about the future of agriculture were:

- The potential growth of agriculture as a sector will be in non-staple production.

- The prosperity of agricultural enterprises will depend upon the ability to provide high-quality produce which is predictable and traceable. The interaction of these enterprises with market agents and changing retail business models will influence their future.

- As the complexity and requirements in the food supply chain increases, farms will need to supplement their cash flows through non-agricultural sources; for example, setting up farm visitor centres or processing. This will have an impact on small farms.

- As farms move up the value chain through processing models, there is a requirement for upskilling and training.

Contract farming

Contract farming can also bring significant benefits to producers. With a reasonable contract the farmer is assured of a buyer, a fixed price (reducing the risk of price volatility), negotiated credit terms and reduced marketing costs. In the medium to long term, 'relationship marketing' and vertical coordination can lead to better relationships and a position of interdependence. The strategic relationships set up with the aim of enhancing traceability, quality assurance, security of supply and price are faced both with benefits (support of the buyer in times of need) and with the risk of having a single buyer, which can be detrimental to the business if the buyer pulls out.

Small farmers who do not have sufficient scale of production to sell directly to the buyer will lose their place in the strategic partnership. Also, small farmers will find it operationally difficult without access to finance, and the strategic relationships will require investment in technology and improvement in capacity so that they can benefit from economies of scale. Contracts could provide a vehicle for small farmers to get access to finance from the buyers.

The barriers to the development of the agri-industry

The extensive literature on this topic identifies similar factors that affect the development of the agriculture sector (Figure 2.1). This is even worse in developing countries. The barriers to overcome are:

- *Availability of finance.* The widespread view is that there is a lack of adequate finance available within the agribusiness and the agriculture industry as a whole. There is a lack of investment within the sector. The most finance-deprived stage within the sector is agriculture production. The lack of finance is attributed to the production sector being dispersed geographically, increasing transaction costs, and unavailability of sufficient banking facilities within rural areas. This is coupled with a lack of tailored products for the sector.

  The challenge of accessible finance can be overcome by:
  - developing better financial and risk management systems that are accessible to entities within the chain;
  - increasing accessibility of financial services within the rural environment;
  - the possibility of government grants for the sector to offset risks;

FIGURE 2.1   Barriers to developing the agri-sector

- expanding microcredit programmes and rural community banking (eg Grameen Bank);

- developing specific agro-risk finance and insurance products.

- *Food safety and quality.* New consumer preferences in food consumption are emerging across the world. The requirement for high-quality, safe and healthy food has increased the importance of features such as product differentiation, added value and consumer confidence. Food safety regulations and certifications are extremely stringent and entities within the developing world struggle to cope with the requirement. Improved coordination between producers and traders leads to increased fulfilment of consumer expectations. Investments in technology to monitor traceability and visibility will be required in order to ascertain the safety and quality of the food products in the chain. Infrastructure to train and upskill producers and processors within the supply chain will ensure that they are ready to meet the requirements of the export environment.

- *Regulatory environment.* The food supply chain works effectively in stable legal and regulatory environments. These are important for attracting business, leading to increased investment and employment. The challenge within this scenario is that different countries will have different perspectives on market liberalization and protectionism. Some countries may not compete on the basis of innovation and competitiveness but may do so for protection of their national interests. Countries will need to shape and refine proposals to attract foreign direct investment that will promote their own economic interests and also protect small farmers and emerging sectors in order to achieve a competitive advantage in local, national and international markets.

- *The role of public- and private-sector organizations.* The will and ability of national governments in developing countries is required to facilitate public investment in strengthening relevant government institutions. The governments should focus on the agriculture sector and work towards building the appropriate infrastructure for improving opportunities within the agriculture sector. There is also a need to promote good governance and the incorporation of accountability mechanisms in the institutional and governance systems, in order to guarantee efficiency in public expenditure.

- *Collaboration within supply chain entities.* Effective and efficient coordination is considered necessary for creating competitive advantage within the agri supply chain. Coordination among producers, processors, distributors and other stakeholders in the supply chains is necessary to meet consumers' demands. Collaboration and strategic partnerships will ensure meeting quality, quantity and on-time delivery performance indicators within the chain. Better contracts and regulations that promote competition and ensure market transparency should be facilitated in order to grow the sector. The setting up of chambers of commerce, farmers' organizations, export promotion councils and advocacy groups will provide additional support to the sector. Creating links among production, processing and consumption through technology that enables partnership mechanisms will improve integration and coordination between the supply chain entities.

There are other common barriers across different countries. However, not all of these will be valid for every country:

- efficient land markets and tenure systems for producers;
- access to appropriate rural and agricultural finance and risk management products;
- specific regulatory provisions;
- consistent trade policies for international trade;
- access to global markets and support for achieving this;
- availability of skilled human resources, training and capacity-building resources;
- improved technologies for all aspects of the chain;
- adequate infrastructural facilities and utilities (particularly rural roads and storage facilities).

The requirement for these enablers will differ on a regional basis, as some regions will be ahead of others. The requirements of each region and the capability of the agriculture supply chains within these regions must be analysed in order to create the required solutions and policies.

Future steps for the agriculture sector

A report submitted by a joint commissioning group, which included representatives from each of the Agriculture and Horticulture Development Board (AHDB), the National Farmers' Union (NFU), NFU Scotland, the Royal Agricultural Society of England (RASE) and the Agricultural Industries Confederation (AIC), and supported by the Technology Strategy Board (TSB), investigated the research and development priorities for the UK agriculture sector for the next

20 years. This report was submitted in 2013 and was titled *Feeding the Future – Innovation Requirements for Primary Food Production in the UK to 2030*. The report sets out the innovation requirements for primary food production in the UK in eight priority areas for research:[7]

1 Use modern technologies to improve the precision and efficiency of key agricultural management practices.

2 Apply modern genetic and breeding approaches to improve the quality, sustainability, resilience and yield-led profitability of crops and farm animals.

3 Use systems-based approaches to understand better and manage interactions between soil, water and crop/animal processes.

4 Develop integrated approaches to the effective management of crop weeds, pests and diseases within farming systems.

5 Develop integrated approaches to the management of animal disease within farming systems.

6 Develop evidence-based approaches to value ecosystem service delivery by land users and incorporate these approaches into effective decision support systems at the enterprise or grouped enterprise level.

7 Extend the training, professional development and communication channels of researchers, practitioners and advisers to promote delivery of the targets above.

8 Improve the use of social and economic science to promote the development, uptake and use of sustainable, resilient and profitable agricultural practice that can deliver affordable, safe and high-quality products.

CASE EXAMPLE   Cargill works with producers on finance and risk management[8]

Cargill is a large organization with 143,000 employees in 67 countries that provides food and agriculture products along with financial services. It also has businesses and products in varied sectors such as pharmaceuticals and energy. Within the agriculture area, Cargill deals in grain, oilseeds and other agricultural commodities along the different stages of the supply chain. The company sources, processes, transports and distributes grain and oilseeds around the world. The core products that Cargill handles are wheat, corn, oilseeds, barley and sorghum, as well as vegetable oils and meals which have full traceability. The company leverages efficiencies in its supply chain through logistical flexibility and economies of scale. Since the products are commodities and are subject to volatile prices and climate-change risks, Cargill has created a range of financial and hedging products taking into account financial and risk challenges within these supply chains.

CASE EXAMPLE   Nestlé works with dairy farmers[9]

Nestlé works with 600,000 dairy farmers across the globe, in roughly 30 countries, to source milk for its operations. This is in excess of 12 million tonnes/year of fresh milk equivalents, of which almost 7 million tonnes are sourced locally as fresh milk. The majority of the farmers in the supply chain are small businesses and Nestlé runs the Milk District Model to help and support the farmers to improve milk nutrition and quality and in general to run the business efficiently.

The Nestlé Milk District Model involves the following activities:

- milk collection centres featuring payment systems, quality and safety controls, electronic weighing equipment and cooling tanks;

- free technical and animal husbandry support to improve milk quality;

- free veterinary services;

- transportation and infrastructure networks;

- $25 million of microfinance loans each year;

- prompt payment to farmers for each milk delivery.

Along with these activities, the company also helps social development in developing countries by providing safe drinking water, tree plantation programmes and health clinics.

CASE EXAMPLE   ITC Ltd India empowers farmers through technology[10]

ITC's Agri Business Division is India's second largest exporter of agri-products. It currently focuses on exports and domestic trading of:

- feed ingredients – soyameal;

- food grains – wheat;

- marine products – shrimps and prawns;

- processed fruits – fruit purées/concentrates, individual quick freezing (IQF)/ frozen fruits, organic fruit products;

- coffee.

ITC Ltd has created extensive backward linkages with farmers to build a cost-effective procurement system. The company invested in a web-based technology to empower farmers with data related to the weather, crop conditions, best practices in farming, ruling international prices and a host of other relevant information. ITC has made significant investments in web-enabling the Indian farmer. This system is named 'e-Choupal' and consists of internet kiosks in villages. Farmers use these kiosks to access online information from ITC's farmer-friendly website, **www.echoupal.com**. This initiative now comprises about 6,500 installations covering nearly 40,000 villages and serving over 4 million farmers in 10 Indian states. This network is also supported by ITC's procurement teams, handling agents and contemporary warehousing facilities across India.

Along with this innovative platform, ITC also runs a programme of 'demonstration plots' or 'Choupal Pradarshan Khet' (CPK) to demonstrate the best agriculture practices to farmers. Another initiative, 'Choupal Saagar', comprises collection, storage and hypermarket facilities in the rural environment. This infrastructure also incorporates farmer facilitation centres, with services such as sourcing, training, soil testing, a health clinic, cafeteria, banking, investment services, and a fuel station. So far, 24 pilot projects have been implemented. With the intention of moving farmers up the value chain and reducing food waste, ITC is working on creating value-added products such as frozen agri-foods, frozen fruits, baby-food-quality purées and high-Brix pulp and organic purées. (The Brix scale measures the sugar content of an aqueous solution.)

CASE EXAMPLE   Microfinance models within the food sector[11-15]

Finance and the appropriate agriculture-sector-based financial products are scarce. This challenge is amplified within the rural environment in developing countries where access to banking facilities is difficult. Since a large proportion of the producers are small farm holders based in rural areas, the majority have great difficulty in accessing finance and managing their agribusiness. They need finance to create the required cash flows within the supply chain. The idea of having a rural-based microcredit finance initiative was piloted by Professor Mohammed Yunus in 1976 in Bangladesh. He named it the Grameen (Rural) Bank. The bank lends to the poorest in society so that they can invest in materials required for production. This also develops local rural enterprise. A large majority of the clients of this bank are women who use this initiative to start a source of livelihood. Although there have been criticisms of the initiative on account of the high interest rates and operational issues of using the money once it is provided, the initiative is still largely a very successful one and has spurred similar initiatives in many countries (especially in Africa). The Grameen Bank uses a group lending model in which a group of individuals are provided with finance and they are accountable as a group for its return. This model can be used very effectively within a small farm holder scenario, but the level of finance available will be rather less.

A number of institutions have tried out similar models within the agriculture sector, with some modifications. These organizations package credit loans with other products such as insurance and savings schemes, as well as training programmes.

The *One Acre Fund* was launched in Kenya in 2006. It supplies smallholders in East Africa with asset-based financing and agriculture training services in order to reduce hunger and poverty. The model provides help on four fronts:

- It provides financing for farming inputs.

- It helps to distribute seeds and fertilizer to the farm.

- It provides training on agricultural techniques.

- It provides a market facilitation service to sell the produce competitively post-harvest.

Opportunity International is a non-profit organization that provides microfinance, training and micro-insurance to farmers in 22 countries. The organization has built 45 regulated microfinancing local institutions and 9 banks. In 2002, it offered the world's first micro-insurance product, named MicroEnsure. This provides weather-indexed crop insurance for rural farmers and affordable health insurance within the rural communities.

Along with providing microfinance and insurance, the organization also helps the farmer navigate the food supply chain to the markets.

International Finance Corporation and the International Bank for Reconstruction and Development: The Global Index Insurance Facility (GIIF), which is a programme offered by the World Bank Group's Finance and Markets Global Practice, works by providing agricultural and disaster insurance in rural communities within the developing world, where such products are largely unavailable.

The bank provides an insurance product, known as 'index insurance', which pays out benefits on the basis of a predetermined index (for example, rainfall level, seismic activity, livestock mortality rates) for the loss of assets and investments resulting from weather and catastrophic events. Along with this, it provides microfinance, which is generally bundled with the index insurance. It also works on raising awareness through public education campaigns and provides grants for capacity building to train local insurers and financial institutions.

Summary

This chapter has briefly explained the different players within the agriculture/producer side of the supply chain. The discussion also focused on how the agriculture sector will help small farmers in the developing world in terms of livelihood and poverty alleviation. This discussion considered some of the challenges with this scenario. Further, the chapter considered the barriers within the agriculture sector and the ways to enable better environments. Finally, a few case studies examined the relationship between the entities in the producer–processor supply chain. Some of the challenges for the agriculture sector in regard to food sustainability and security are discussed in Chapters 6, 13 and 15.

Notes

1 Chandrasekaran, N (2014) *Agribusiness Supply Chain Management*, CRC Press, Boca Raton, FL

2 KPMG (accessed 13 February 2015) The Agricultural and Food Value Chain: Entering a new era of cooperation [Online] http://www.kpmg.com/Global/en/IssuesAndInsights/ArticlesPublications/Documents/agricultural-and-food-value-chain-v2.pdf

3 NDTV (accessed 13 February 2015) Why Abolition of APMC is a Good Idea [Online] http://profit.ndtv.com/news/economy/article-why-abolition-of-apmc-is-a-good-idea-532601

4 Vorley, B and Fox, T (accessed 13 February 2015) Global Food Chains—Constraints and Opportunities for Smallholders, OECD DAC POVNET, Paper for the Agriculture and Pro-Poor Growth Task Team, Helsinki Workshop, 17–18 June 2004 [Online] http://www.oecd.org/dac/povertyreduction/36562581.pdf

5 Maxwell, S (accessed 13 February 2015) Launching the DFID Consultation 'New Directions for Agriculture in Reducing Poverty' [Online] http://dfid-agriculture-consultation.nri.org/launchpapers/simonmaxwell.html

6 Department for International Development (accessed 13 February 2015) Growth and Poverty Reduction: The role of agriculture, A DFID policy paper [Online] http://dfid-agriculture-consultation.nri.org/launchpapers/roleofagriculture.pdf

7 Joint Commissioning Group (accessed 13 February 2015) Feeding the Future: Innovation requirements for primary food production in the UK to 2030 [Online] https://feedingthefutureblog.files.wordpress.com/2012/11/feedingthefuture2013-web.pdf

8 Cargill (accessed 13 February 2015) Agricultural Commodity Trading & Processing [Online] http://www.cargill.com/products/commodity/index.jsp

9 Nestlé (accessed 13 February 2015) Working with Dairy Farmers [Online] http://www.nestle.com/brands/dairy/dairycsv

10 ITC (accessed 13 February 2015) Agri Commodities & Rural Services [Online] http://www.itcportal.com/businesses/agri-business/agri-commodities-and-rural-services.aspx

11 Murray, S (accessed 13 February 2015) Food and Microfinance: Helping farmers reap rewards, *Financial Times*, 2 June 2010 [Online] http://www.ft.com/cms/s/0/073a641e-6d0c-11df-921a-00144feab49a.html#axzz3RcpnCUaP

12 Opportunity International (accessed 13 February 2015) Who We Serve [Online] http://opportunity.org.uk/what-we-do/who-we-serve/

13 IFC (accessed 13 February 2015) Global Index Insurance Facility [Online] http://www.ifc.org/wps/wcm/connect/industry_ext_content/ifc_external_corporate_site/industries/financial+markets/retail+finance/insurance/global+index+insurance+facility

14 One Acre Fund (accessed 13 February 2015) Program Model: A business solution for smallholder farmers [Online] http://www.oneacrefund.org/our-approach/program-model

15 Grameen Bank (accessed 13 February 2015) Home page [Online] http://www.grameen.com/

Food manufacturing

03

This chapter presents the next stage of the food supply chain, which is food processing. This is an important stage in the chain as it transforms the raw food produced within the agriculture environment to reach consumers' forks. This could be just packaging the raw food to facilitate movement within the logistics environment, or something more complex such as transforming the raw food into ready-to-eat meals for the retail environment. The chapter takes the reader through the various processes employed by the food-processing industry to transform raw food from the agriculture process into retail and consumer requirements.

The importance of food processing

The aims of food processing are:

- to extend the life of the food product post-production using relevant processing and preservation techniques;
- to change the form of the food to allow further processing (eg the milling of grains to flour);
- to increase dietary variety by providing a range of attractive flavours, colours, aromas and textures in food without losing the nutritional quality of the food;
- to generate sufficient income for the sustainability of the processing function;
- to make food accessible when fresh food is not an option.

Each of these aims will exist to a greater or lesser extent in all food production, but the level of processing of a given product will differ according to the requirement. All food processing involves a combination of manufacturing procedures to achieve the intended changes to the raw materials. These operations will have an effect on the food, leading to a permanent change. The nature of the final product will depend upon the combination and sequence of processing.

Changing market conditions

In developed countries the market for processed foods has increased exponentially. Changes in working patterns, family lifestyles and an interest in trying out different types of food has created a demand for food that is frozen or chilled and can be easily prepared in a microwave oven. However, just as one group of consumers prefer ready-to-eat food with a lot of processing and additives for preservation, another group of consumers are increasingly against additives or foods that have been excessively processed. They prefer foods that are 'natural' or processed for convenience of handling without losing the original properties. However, this group will prefer to eat fresh pineapple chunks out of special packaging instead of buying a fresh pineapple and cutting it at home. There has been a growth in demand for organic foods and hence the regulations around organic foods have become more stringent over the years. A quick glance at the supermarket shelves displaying ready-to-eat microwaveable dinners, soups and packed salads shows the variety and innovation behind creating these products. Not only do they have to look very professional (like restaurant food) but they also have to be packaged securely in eye-catching colours to attract the consumer. These pressures are an important influence on changes that are taking place in the food-processing industry, and manufacturers are responding by reducing or eliminating synthetic additives from products (particularly colourants and flavours) and replacing them with natural or 'nature-equivalent' alternatives. They have increasingly introduced new ranges of low-fat, sugar-free or low-salt products. New innovative products that are fortified with vitamins, minerals and probiotic cultures (or 'functional' foods) and products containing organic ingredients are now widely available. Improvements to food quality have also been achieved through changes in legislation, including legal requirements on manufacturers and retailers to display due diligence in protecting consumers from potentially hazardous foods.

Operational change within food-processing companies

The growth of the food retail environment and changing consumer demand have influenced food-processing companies to change their operations in four key respects:[1]

- Increased investment in capital-intensive, automated processes to reduce labour and energy costs.

- A quality management system that produces high-quality products consistently without the need for inspection.

- A more proactive approach to creating demand, using sophisticated marketing techniques and large advertising budgets and social media. There is also a trend of large food companies buying out competitor brands or smaller companies to increase their brand portfolio.

- A shift of power in the food supply chain to the retailer.

The changes in technology have been influenced by substantial increases in the costs of both energy and labour and because of public pressure and legislation to reduce negative environmental effects of processing, particularly air/water pollution and energy consumption. Food-processing equipment is designed to reduce processing costs and enable rapid changeovers between shorter production runs, to improve product quality. The aim is to be lean by eliminating non-value-adding activities. Increasingly, the food-manufacturing process is fully automated, from receiving raw material to end-packaging, as this reduces interference from the process and reduces risks of contamination. However, to achieve the benefits of improved quality assurance and a reduction in costs and wastage, a high level of capital investment is required.

Food processing[2,3]

Food is processed for the following reasons:

- preservation;
- food safety;
- creating variety;
- creating convenience;
- fortification for nutrition.

Some people have concerns regarding food processing as they believe that highly processed foods are unhealthy. These are high in sugar, salt and fat and do not provide any nutrition. Owing to the nature of the food supply chain, concerns regarding the control of processors within the chain are valid. Industry consolidation has occurred within the food sector and a few companies have a larger stake within the food supply chain.

As shown by Figure 3.1, food processing can be divided into four types of method:

- processing at ambient temperature;
- processing by application of heat;
- processing by removal of heat;
- post-processing.

Processing at ambient temperature

Processes are conducted at ambient temperature to improve the quality and functionality of the food produced. Food at the end of the production stage is in a form that has variable physical characteristics. This food will require further processing to make it ready for immediate consumption or for further processing. It is therefore necessary to perform operations of cleaning, sorting, grading or peeling to ensure that foods with a uniform quality are prepared for subsequent processing. High-quality raw material will produce high-quality processed foods. The operations mentioned above are a cost-effective

FIGURE 3.1   The dynamics of food processing

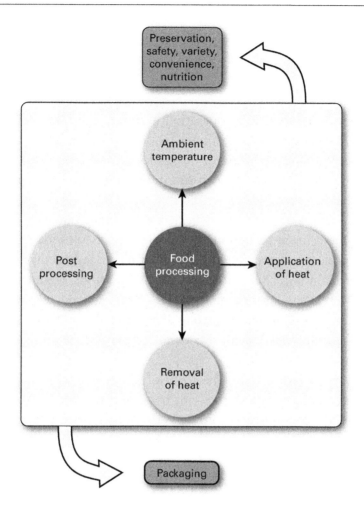

method of improving the quality of the raw material before processing. Size reduction or 'comminution' is the operation in which the average size of solid pieces of food is reduced by the application of grinding, compression or impact forces. Emulsification is a process that improves the eating quality or suitability of foods for further processing and will increase the range of products available. The processes during size reduction may cause degradation of the product as the surfaces are exposed and cellular tissue is damaged. This can be overcome to some extent by employing preservatives with the food.

Different methods of size reduction are classified according to the size range of particles produced:

1 chopping, cutting, slicing and dicing;

2 milling to powders or pastes;

3 emulsification and homogenization.

Mixing (or blending) is an operation in which a uniform mixture is created from two or more components, by combing or dispersing one within the others. The process of mixing has no preservative effect and is intended solely as a processing aid or to alter the eating quality of foods. It has very wide applications in many food industries where it is used to combine ingredients to achieve different functional properties.

Fermented foods are among the oldest processed food. Fermented food products are present in major sectors of the food-processing industry, including baked products, alcoholic drinks, yoghurt, cheese and soy products, among many others. During food fermentation, selected micro-organisms are used to alter the texture of foods, preserve foods by production of acids or alcohol, or to produce subtle flavours and aromas.

Ionizing radiation takes the form of gamma-rays from isotopes or, commercially to a lesser extent, from X-rays and electrons. It is permitted in 38 countries to preserve foods by destruction of micro-organisms or inhibition of biochemical changes.

Processing by application of heat

Heat treatment remains one of the most important methods used in food processing. Application of heat has extremely desirable effects on the quality of the food. This also increases the value of the final product from the perspective of the consumer. Application of heat (for example baking) cooks the food creating flavours and textures that are attractive to consumers. Application of heat also provides a preservative effect on foods by the destruction of enzymes, micro-organisms, insects and parasites.

Blanching, pasteurization, heat sterilization, evaporation and de-hydration are heat-treating processes, each having a specific objective as regards the food product. Other, more severe heat processes, in-cluding baking, roasting and frying, are intended to change the sensory characteristics of a product, and preservation is achieved either by further processing (for example, chilling or freezing) or by selection of suitable packaging systems. Evaporation and dehydration, that is, the removal of water, inhibit microbial growth and enzyme activity and thus achieve preservation.

Processing by removal of heat

Preservation by lowering the temperature of food helps in maintaining the sensory characteristics and nutritional value of the food product. Increased demand for fresh food and ready-to-eat meals has increased the need for chilling as a process for preservation. Ready-to-eat chilled foods, which are packed in modified atmospheres, have been an important development in the retail environment. In general, the lower the storage temperature, the longer foods can be stored, and freezing continues to be an important method of processing to produce foods that have a long shelf life. Although micro-organisms and enzymes are inhibited at low temperatures, they are not destroyed as in heat processing. As the temperature increases, the rate at which foods can spoil will increase due to the growth of the micro-organisms. Careful control is needed to maintain a low storage temperature and prepare foods quickly under strict hygienic conditions to prevent spoilage or food poisoning. Although the need to maintain chill or frozen temperatures throughout the distribution chain is a major cost to producers and retailers, it is an important factor when considering food retail chains. It is an important process as it impacts on food efficiency and food safety.

Post-processing

As food is prepared for final consumption, processors have to meet the requirements of the consumers in terms of appearance, taste and variety. Processors put a variety of coatings on food products to create additional value for the food consumers. Coatings of batter or breadcrumbs are applied to fish, meats or vegetables. Chocolate or compound coatings are applied to biscuits, cakes and confectionery. Coatings of salt, sugar, flavourings or colourants are also applied to snack foods, baked goods and confectionery.

Packaging is an important part of all food-processing operations and with some canning and modified-atmosphere packaging (MAP) it is integral to the operation itself. There have been substantial developments in both materials and packaging systems over the past 10 years, which have been instrumental both in reducing packaging costs and in the development of novel and minimally processed foods.

Food packaging

Packaging is the operation of enrobing the food item in a protective cover that keeps the food item safe, secure and with the intended characteristics.

The functions of packaging are:[4,5]

- Containment – to hold the contents and keep them secure until they are used.

- Protection – against mechanical and environmental hazards encountered during distribution and use.

- Communication – to identify the contents and assist in selling the product. Shipping containers should also inform the carrier about the destination and any special handling or storage instructions. Some packages inform the user about the method of opening and/or using the contents.

- Machinability – to have good performance on production lines for high-speed filling, closing and collating (1,000 packs per minute or more), without too many stoppages.

- Convenience – throughout the production, storage and distribution system, including easy-opening, dispensing and/or after-use retail containers for consumers.

The main marketing considerations for a package are:

- the brand image and style of presentation required for the food;

- flexibility to change the size and design of the containers;

- compatibility with methods of handling and distribution, and with the requirements of retailers.

The package should be aesthetically pleasing, have a functional size and shape, retain the food in a convenient form for the customer without leakage, possibly act as a dispenser which opens easily and recloses securely, and be suitable for easy disposal, recycling or reuse. The package will hold the barcode and/or RFID (radio-frequency identification) tags to facilitate better logistics. The package design should also meet any legislative requirements concerning labelling of foods.

Inventory management[6]

Raw materials (for example food ingredients) purchased for processing but not immediately used represent a significant portion of operational expense. It is important to maintain inventory levels high enough to ensure that food products can be produced in the right quantity, but low enough not to have excess product left over. This is called inventory control and also has an influence on controlling processing costs. Excess inventory can result in increased waste and costs, as food has a certain shelf life and will go off if not utilized. High levels of inventory in the supply chain create difficulties in tracking usage. Excessive inventory increases the requirement for storage space leading to increased operational costs. Unutilized inventory ties up capital and creates cash flow challenges. This is true for both raw ingredients and finished products.

On the other hand, not producing enough to satisfy demand, whether due to lack of raw ingredients or inadequate forecasting, leads to customer disappointment and may result in loss of market share. The goal is to have sufficient products to satisfy consumer demand but not an excessive amount of inventory causing monetary loss. This requires careful planning, standardized operating procedures, and regular monitoring to achieve desired results.

Producers, manufacturers and distributors experience excess costs and loss when anticipated sales do not materialize, resulting in excess inventories of product. This cost is passed along to consumers. Predictability in buying patterns will lower food costs for consumers. Retailers will use 'loyalty card' schemes to follow the buying patterns of their customers in order to achieve some control over inventory. Effective inventory management can help to maintain levels of consumer satisfaction.

Customer service

One important aspect of good customer service is to control stock-outs. When stockouts occur customers are disappointed. Processors and retailers will try to use substitutions to meet customer requirements. But this is not always successful as some customers may not like the substitution or have allergies or dietary restrictions. Substituting peanut oil for vegetable oil in the processing stage, as is done in some parts of South Asia where peanut oil is a staple product, can be harmful for certain customers in the international food supply chain. Good customer service also requires the delivery of product that is of excellent quality and within its due date. Some companies such as Subway utilize agility and product flexibility to provide a product mix to the consumer. With sufficient inventory of a few standard ingredients, Subway offers a mass customization service to the consumer whereby every consumer can design the sandwich that they feel like eating using the standard ingredients provided, thus offering enough variety to maximize participation.

Efficiency

Another aspect of inventory management is efficient product handling. The design of the facility, especially the location and arrangement of storage areas, can affect the availability and security of the inventory. It is essential for processors to locate inventory to facilitate its delivery to the processing areas.

Financial management

Inventory management leads to improved financial control within processing operations. The financial goal of inventory management is to ensure that the maximum value is generated from the processing of the raw material to fulfil consumer requirements. In addition to the actual cost of acquiring inventory, costs are associated with transporting and storing inventory. These costs are called carrying costs and may include storage rental, utilities, insurance, cost of shrinkage, cost of obsolescence, cost of wages and benefits for labour to move and count stock, and opportunity cost (what could have been gained if the money had been spent on some other investment). It is important that warehouse carrying costs are also calculated. Shrinkage is the cost of loss due to waste, theft, spoilage and other product loss. Shrinkage in retail operations will occur because of theft. Some of the shrinkage can be attributed to spoilage, damage, shipping errors, misplaced product and vendor fraud.

Managing quantities

The correct quantity of inventory is the level at which sufficient product can be produced to meet customer demands. Some safety stock is necessary to prevent manufacturing operations from running out of food. This is valid within retail environments too. For many products, this may mean setting a reorder point. Reorder levels are usually set for items served daily, such as milk and common ingredients used in multiple recipes (for example, sugar, flour, spices). Common measures of inventory efficiency are the number of days of inventory on hand and the turnover rate. The days of inventory on hand and the turnover rate are calculated as follows:

Ending inventory /Average daily food cost = Days of inventory on hand

Number of serving days / Days of inventory on hand = Turnover rate

Food safety

Food safety is a critical consideration in managing the inventory of food products. It is very important to protect food inventories from both unintentional and intentional contamination. It is essential to store food products in appropriate areas to ensure that raw food products do not cross-contaminate other inventories. This is essential for food products that will receive no further cooking, as well as prevent accidental contamination from any chemicals within the vicinity of the storage areas. Products that have not been held at proper temperatures or that have been damaged during transport can be identified using HACCP food safety practices. Food safety practices are important during the transit of food and this may include steps such as recording the names of individuals who handle food as well as locking storage areas and food transport vehicles and limiting access to only certain individuals. Procedures must be in place to track and record specific food product numbers and lot numbers, from the date received to the date served to customers, to maintain traceability. The industry-wide focus on traceability has resulted in a standard method of product identification that is gaining adoption throughout the food industry. The Global Trade Item Number® (GTIN®), along with a lot number, can be used in the event of a food-borne illness, recall, or terrorism threat.

Inventory management requires a systemic or holistic view, looking at the impact each function within the food supply chain has on the management of inventory. Inventory management ensures that quality, cost-effective products are available in the right quantities at the right time.

Procurement

Effective procurement influences inventory control by obtaining the correct items in the correct quantity for the best possible value. A reduction in the number of stock-keeping units (SKUs) will reduce the time required to manage the inventory. An SKU is a discrete item with the same characteristic (for example, a beverage purchased in 3 flavours and in 5 packaging sizes represents 15 separate SKUs). Each SKU will have its own GTIN. For tracking items during a recall, it is helpful to have fewer SKUs of a certain item when trying to account for the status of all recalled product. Reducing SKUs within the manufacturing operation requires the utilization of the same SKU across a number of products, which can be done under bill of material rationalization. Insufficient inventory may sometimes lead to product substitutions, which can lead to a variety of problems, including quality issues, regulatory non-compliance and customer dissatisfaction.

Managing suppliers is also part of inventory management. It is important to identify requirements in bid documents sent to suppliers, to ensure that suppliers also maintain the required levels of food safety. The safety and regulatory requirements should be clearly mentioned in the supplier specifications.

Forecasting and ordering

Forecasting and ordering can greatly affect inventory control. Within the food supply chain, incorrect forecasting creates further problems, as the product will deteriorate over time and it will be essential to sell it. If it cannot be sold quickly, it will spoil or become obsolete, thus losing money. Challenges such as stockouts and emergency buying result from under-ordering. An ordering system should be established to prevent over-ordering. A reorder system establishes a maximum quantity to keep on hand.

Inventory models

- *Economic order quantity.* This model optimizes the cost of ordering inventory and the cost of holding it. The optimization is the quantity to be ordered to keep the total costs low. Total costs are a function of carrying costs and ordering costs. When the inventory level has reached a level called the reorder point, a purchase order is issued for the product. This purchase order will be the optimized quantity, which is called the 'economic order quantity'.

- *The reorder point inventory control system.* In this method, the inventory is continuously monitored and orders are issued when the inventory is depleted to a certain set level, the reorder point (ROP), which triggers a new purchase order.

- *Safety stock.* Safety stock, also known as buffer stock, is the amount of inventory stocked by the system in case some uncertainty arises. The safety stock then shields the system until the inventory is replenished.

- *Delayed product differentiation.* This process does not create finished goods inventory but delays the process until an order is received. The process works on the postponement concept, whereby the process of making the product is postponed until required by the consumer. The system will create modular units which can be assembled together very quickly to create a bespoke product.

- *Just-in-time (JIT)*. The system will hold only the inventory that is required by the consumer. The philosophy is to remove all non-value-adding activities and inventory from the system. JIT follows two concepts:

  - To have less inventory in the system. This will be decided by a Kanban system. If there is a problem in the system, inventory will not hide it and the problem will need to be sorted out immediately.

  - Small lot production. The suppliers will need to deliver inventory in small lots. This means that inventory levels within the company are low and the supplier will need to deliver small batches of inventory every day. In JIT systems, the suppliers are generally located next to the main plant.

CASE EXAMPLE   3D printing of food[7–9]

3D printing[10] or additive manufacturing is a process of making three-dimensional solid objects from a digital file such as a 3D scan or a 3D model created using modelling software. The creation of a 3D printed object is achieved using additive processes whereby an object is created by laying down successive layers of material until the entire object is created. There are different methods of achieving the outcome. The methods differ from the way the material is treated for creating the object. The different methods are:

- selecting laser sintering;

- fused deposition modelling;

- stereolithography.

3D printing has been recently introduced within the food sector. The 'Foodini', a food 3D printer created by Natural Machines, uses edible ingredients squeezed out of stainless steel capsules to print the product, instead of using plastic. It is currently a pilot project and has challenges, as food does not maintain the shape very well. However, this machine has been very successful. The Barcelona-based start-up behind the machine has said that it is the only one of its kind capable of printing a wide range of dishes, from sweet to savoury. The company is now working with food manufacturers to create plastic capsules pre-packed with food (in liquid or semi-solid form). These capsules will be free of preservatives, with a shelf life of five days. These capsules will be loaded onto the machine to create the product.

Like the normal 3D printing process, this one also takes considerable time but is faster than regular 3D printing. It can make complex designs and can be used to make complicated, intricate designs. The Foodini can be useful for creating recipes such as home-made pizza or filled pasta. Currently, the device only prints the food, which must then be cooked as usual. But a future model will also cook the food and produce it ready to eat.

The National Aeronautics and Space Administration (NASA) agency has funded the development of a 3D printer that is able to print food in space.

There are a few companies[7] involved in developing these printers, but high costs make this technology currently prohibitive. As the technology grows, it will become affordable for individuals to purchase it for their homes. The machines have been able to manufacture burgers, complicated cake decorations, sugar confectionery, pasta, ravioli, pasta sauce and so on.

Summary

This chapter has presented a comprehensive discussion regarding food processing. Different types of processing methods have been studied. The methods fall under the following broad processes:

- processing at ambient temperature;
- processing by application of heat;
- processing by removal of heat;
- post-processing.

The chapter also discussed the importance of the processing stage for the food supply chain. To enable the processed foods to reach consumers' forks, effective packaging and logistics are important, along with the appropriate regulations. These topics are discussed later in Chapters 5, 10, 11 and 12.

Notes

1 Fellow, P (2000) *Food Processing Technology: Principles and practice*, 2nd edn, CRC Press, Baton Rouge, FL

2 This is a very comprehensive book on food processing technology: Fellow, P (2009) *Food Processing Technology: Principles and practice*, 3rd edn, Woodhead Publishing, Cambridge

3 Mattsson, B and Sonesson, U (2003) *Environmentally-Friendly Food Processing* (Woodhead Publishing Series in Food Science, Technology and Nutrition), Woodhead Publishing, Cambridge

4 Paine, F A (ed) (1991) *The Packaging User's Handbook*, Blackie, London

5 Paine, F A and Paine, H Y (1992) *Handbook of Food Packaging*, Blackie & Son, Glasgow

6 Boettger, J (2012) *Inventory Management and Tracking Reference Guide*, National Food Service Management Institute, University of Mississippi

7 Kelion, L (accessed 13 February 2015) CES 2014: 3D Food Printers Create Sweets and Chocolates, BBC News [Online] http://www.bbc.co.uk/news/technology-25647918

8 Prisco, J (accessed 13 February 2015) 'Foodini' Machine Lets You Print Edible Burgers, Pizza, Chocolate, CNN [Online] http://edition.cnn.com/2014/11/06/tech/innovation/foodini-machine-print-food/

9 Wong, V (accessed 13 February 2015) A Guide to All the Food That's Fit to 3D Print (so far), Bloomberg Business [Online] http://www.businessweek.com/articles/2014-01-28/all-the-food-thats-fit-to-3d-print-from-chocolates-to-pizza

10 3dPrinting.com (accessed 13 February 2015) Methods and Technologies of 3D Printing [Online] http://3dprinting.com/what-is-3d-printing/#methodsandtechnologies

PART TWO
Operational challenges

Food retailing

04

The retailer is the step in the food value chain before it reaches the consumer. The retailer is an important entity in the chain, as the fulfilment of the supply chain process will depend upon whether the retailer has been successful in selling the product to the consumer, which in turn starts the cash cycle in the supply chain. The retailer creates physical infrastructure, such as a shop, where the products are displayed and the consumer gets an opportunity to purchase them. In our technology-intensive era, the physical space is converted to an online portal which can be used to order the product. The expansion in fulfilment models is being embraced by all major retailers. Some large supermarkets set up specialized services within the main shops to attract consumers from online portals to the physical shop. Some or all of these services will be available at big retailers – for example, in-store bakery (which bakes fresh produce every day), cheese counter, fish counter, meat counter, salad bar and so on. This chapter presents a discussion of the food retailing environment. It considers the different types of food retailers and caterers. The discussion also explains the process of marketing the product to the retail environment. E-tailing or online grocery models are also explained.

The retail environment

The retail environment provides two important processes: it connects the supply chain to the final consumer and it creates value-added products for consumption by the final consumer.

Many entities are involved in the process to produce, manufacture, transport, distribute, market and sell the product. By the time a product is placed on a supermarket or store shelf, it has gathered food miles and has had value added to it by many people. Although supermarkets will carry in excess of 100,000 stock-keeping units in their shops, very few new products that are designed and manufactured in the food supply chain actually reach the final consumer. The food system encompasses many activities, from harvesting to processing, retailing and consuming. This system is known by many names: marketing channel, distribution channel/chain or supply chain. The entities in the chain after the product leaves the manufacturer/processor are as follows:

- Distributors purchase products from a manufacturer and then sell and distribute them to retailers, foodservice companies and other distributors. They will also deal with the physical logistics of the food products.
- Wholesalers buy in bulk from distributors and sell to retailers.
- Traders or brokers act as food manufacturers' representatives or agents and facilitate sales between manufacturers and retailers. They do not take ownership or physical possession of products.
- Large retailers have their own distribution centres and networks. Manufacturers deliver directly to these centres. The retailer then distributes the product to individual retail stores.

Getting the product on the retail shelf

Most food products go through a distribution channel to reach the end consumer in the retail environment. In general, more perishable foods, such as fresh fruits, seafood and so on, will move more quickly through the chain from the producer to the consumer than long-shelf-life foods. Many requirements, such as barcodes, labelling and product packaging, must be satisfied before distributing a product. Some of the factors affecting the product reaching the retail shelf are as follows:

Technology

New technologies and management systems are adopted every year in the food retailing and distribution industries. The goal is to create a more efficient, cost-effective and responsive distribution channel.

Manufacturers need to be aware of the new information and communication technologies (ICT) and management strategies. The management and operational systems within the supply chain should be streamlined (for example: bill of materials, labelling, packaging and so on). The following are a few technologies that have been adopted or are being developed for use in the food distribution industry:

- Electronic data interchange (EDI) is a substitute for paper invoicing, instead using electronic resources such as e-mail and the internet.

- Continuous replenishment uses computer networks shared between retailers and suppliers to view inventory at any time.

- Efficient consumer response (ECR) is a demand-driven replenishment system designed to link all parties in the distribution channel. The data are transparent and replenishment is based on consumer demand and point-of-sale information. Suppliers will replenish shelves based on these data.

- Collaborative planning, forecasting and replenishment (CPFR) is a system to link the supplier and retailer from the supply chain design stage in order to manage the demand effectively.

- Radio-frequency identification (RFID) is an automated radio signal identification used by food distributors and retailers for inventory purposes. RFID allows identification of merchandise while materials are being handled and in transit. It also helps with traceability of the material.

This is discussed in detail in Chapter 10.

Product movement

Most food is distributed by road, using trucks owned by the manufacturer, distributor or a third-party transport company. Large retailers have centrally located distribution centres. It is usually up to the manufacturer to have products delivered to the distribution centre, unless the retailer makes arrangements to receive material at the factory gate. From there, the retailer transports products to individual stores. Efficiency is key in moving products through the food distribution channel, not only for cost reasons, but also for perishability and damage control reasons. The greater the number of times a product is handled, the greater the chance that it will be damaged. Movement of the food products will also be done in a multimodal way (use of two or three different modes of transport) if the distances are long and there is a requirement to cut carbon emissions and generally increase efficiency and lead times. Fresh produce will usually travel by air.

Traceability

Owing to recent food safety scares, such as E. coli outbreaks and salmonella infections, consumers, as well as government agencies, are being more careful in regard to food safety. Traceability systems are used not only for food safety, but also to address issues such as intentional contamination and food fraud. Retailers in the UK have very strict certification requirements for food products and will only accept suppliers who are certified by the British Retail Consortium (BRC). This is discussed in Chapter 11.

Packaging

Retailers use uniform shelving and layouts in all their stores. Manufacturers have to work with them to create packaging that conforms to the space requirements – shelf space, types of trolley and so on. Packaging is also important from the aspect of retaining the integrity of the product. New innovations in packaging will be able to show whether the product has gone off without opening the package.

How does the food reach the consumer?

The following are the food retail formats[1] in which the products will reach the consumer:

- A hypermarket is a very large store which sells both food and non-food items. Hypermarkets are sometimes called 'super stores', a combination of a supermarket and a department store.

- A supermarket is a store with selling space predominantly dedicated to food products.

- Discounters are stores that carry few product lines (predominantly packaged food and non-food products) and sell products at prices lower than those of traditional retail stores. Goods in discount stores are usually own-label or budget brands. Aldi, Lidl, Home Bargains, Poundland and so on are well-known examples of this type of retail outlet.

- Independent grocers do not belong to chain stores, have a small amount of selling space and usually specialize in packaged groceries. Independent grocers sometimes specialize in one type of product, such as meat or vegetables.

- Other independent shops, such as butchers and bakers, will operate on open markets or have free-standing retail sales points or stores.

- Cash and carry: goods are sold from a wholesale warehouse to customers, retailers, professional users, caterers, institutional buyers and so forth, who are usually issued with a commercial invoice.

- Vending machines: sales of packaged food and drinks through machines.

- Kiosks: these are located in streets, parks, tube stations and so on.

- Convenience stores and off-licences sell a wide range of goods and operate extended opening hours. Convenience stores are often located near busy roads, petrol stations and railway stations or in densely populated urban areas to provide quick access.

Catering entities

1 Caterers are foodservice providers and can be grouped into two types:

   - Consumer catering – outlets are open to the public, eg pubs, restaurants, cafés, fast-food places and so forth.

– Contract catering or subsidized catering – catering for the client, eg the supermarket contracts out own-label ready-to-eat meals to a food manufacturer.

As the eating habits of consumers are changing and they seek out more adventurous tastes, both kinds of catering are on the rise. Caterers are among the largest employers in the food sector, with staff ranging from highly skilled chefs to people working in manufacturing units creating chilled meals for supermarket shelves.

2 Fast-food places: these are considered separately from cafés and restaurants because the operational model is different. These places provide one type of meal with many variations of it. The system will use the 'Leagile' concept in order to have standardized operations but provide mass customization to the consumer (eg Subway sandwiches).

3 Hotels (both small and large) will try to provide a catering service for their guests. Depending upon the rating of the hotel, the catering service will vary from having chef-created meals to ready-to-eat microwaveable meals.

4 Airlines: inflight catering is a complicated process and this is provided on most airlines through an intricate supply chain. Long-haul flights have inflight catering as a default (the quality may differ from airline to airline), but short-haul low-price carriers will have chargeable catering on board.

5 Hospitals: in the UK, the National Health Service provides a very large food-catering service in all its hospitals. These meals are provided to all patients who stay in the hospital. Hence, these meals have to be safe, easy on the palate, within budget and conform to stringent medical, nutritional and dietary requirements. This makes the process a very challenging one.

Selling the product to a retail store[2,3]

A new food product can take one of several paths to reach the consumer. One of the first activities is to determine the product's target market. This includes identifying the geographic area, retail markets and consumers that will make up your core market. Distribution options depend on the product, the market, the type of retail establishment and the manufacturer's sales skills. Some manufacturers reach the consumer directly by selling products at farmers' markets. Others use elaborate distribution methods involving several brokers and distributors. Many small food manufacturers do not have the skills or the time to promote and sell their new product. For them, the use of food distributors and brokers is the only way to obtain distribution. The steps involved in introducing the new product to a retail environment are:

Step 1: Know your consumer – do market research.

Step 2: Test consumer preferences. Many new food manufacturers introduce their product at small, local retail markets. This is a great way to test consumer tastes. Many small retailers like to help new local businesses. These retailers are also a valuable resource for advice on pricing, packaging and promotion.

Step 3: Hire a broker or agent. This is not a necessity, but literature suggests that while some new food manufacturers have the skills to sell successfully, most do not. Securing a broker takes time, money and effort.

Step 4. Find a distributor (this step is not required until the business has grown). Distributors purchase, inventory, transport and sell products to retail accounts that the manufacturer has set up. They also assist in gaining new retail accounts. Distributors act as logistics experts for food distribution.

Step 5. Secure the contract. Choosing the right retail account is crucial. All retailers are different and have different requirements. It is important to know the retailers. Market research regarding your competition is advisable as there may be a tussle for shelf space at the retailer.

Step 6: Pricing. Consider the competition's price on the retail shelf. Visit stores and view the competition; note prices and how package size relates to price. Take a life-cycle analysis view to consider the costs. Additional costs include promotions, transportation and slotting fees. A slotting fee is a fee that retailers charge manufacturers to cover the costs of putting a product in their warehouse and on their shelf. This fee and other fees regarding joint marketing plans, or other charges, could be negotiated by the broker.

Supermarkets' own brand

Supermarkets are expanding their own-brand ranges as consumers are moving towards purchasing own-brand products over regular brands. This is due to the price differential between the brands and also because the quality of the own brands is increasing and for some products is at par with the market-leading brand. Supermarkets pay a lot of attention to their own brands as they get a higher margin and are better able to control the supply chain, on account of vertical integration in the supply chain. They are also able to market their products better. Within the retail environment and on the shelves, their own brands will have equal representation with the other brands and in some cases will have a greater representation. Lidl and Aldi are own-label supermarkets and are doing extremely well because they provide good-quality products and very low prices. The strategy for Marks and Spencer was to sell its own label and it stocked only these products in the shop; however, in the past five years Marks and Spencer has changed strategy and is stocking other brands in its shops.

The focus on shelf life and date labelling

Shelf life is the length of time a food can be kept under stated storage conditions while maintaining its optimum safety and quality. Shelf life of a food begins from the time the food is manufactured and is dependent on many factors such as its manufacturing process, type of packaging, storage conditions and ingredients.[4]

The aim of shelf-life labelling is to provide information to consumers so that they can consume foods safely in an informed way. Consumers should follow the manufacturers' instructions regarding storage (temperature) and use after opening the packaging. The dates are valid only if the packaging is not compromised at the time of purchase.[5] European Regulation 1169/2011 states that information such as the date of minimum durability or use-by date should be provided in a conspicuous, legible and indelible format on product packaging.[6] Shelf life is normally indicated on a food label by either a best-before date or a use-by date:

- A *best-before date* reflects the length of time a food can reasonably be expected to retain its best quality, eg flavour. Examples of foods that have best-before dates include canned, dried and frozen foods.

- A *use-by date* is the length of time a food can reasonably be expected to be safe to consume when stored under stated storage conditions. Consequently, these foods may present a risk of food poisoning if consumed after the use-by date. Examples of foods that have use-by dates include chilled dairy products, cooked meats and prepared salads.[7]

In the retail environment, various types of container are used for packaging food products, and these containers also act as a source of information, advertisement and brand-building resource. The appropriate container is required for the specific product, as the first aim of the container is to protect the integrity of the product. These containers are also useful for storing the food product at the consumer's place until it is consumed. Some types of such containers are: metal cans, glass bottles, jars, rigid and semi-rigid plastic tubs, collapsible tubes, paperboard cartons, flexible plastic bags, sachets and overwraps, Tetra Paks and so on.

The shelf life of packaged foods is controlled by the properties of the food (including water activity, pH, susceptibility to enzymic or microbiological deterioration and the requirement for, or sensitivity to, oxygen, light, carbon dioxide and moisture) and the barrier properties of the package.[8] The container or package will not help to protect the product unless proper storage practices are followed within the retail environment. This ensures that foods are kept safe and shelf life is maximized. Foods that are required to be stored in a controlled temperature environment (for example, chilled or frozen) should be monitored on the shelves. The position of the container within the chiller will also have an impact on the actual temperature experienced by the product.[9]

Online grocery retailing

Recent trends that are contributing to increased sales include:

- a focus on mobile technology;
- click and collect business model;
- the introduction of delivery pass schemes.

In order to maximize growth within the channel, retailers need to work closely with suppliers and rely on them to keep up with trends and drive innovation. The products can be bought online from a variety of online formats:[10]

- Price format: online sites specializing in products reaching the end of their lives, or excessive stock being sold at a low price. For example: Poundshops, Home bargains and so on.

- Experiential format: this is the normal format for online shopping. Most retailers will have an online format and they will make their website engaging, with not only the food displayed but also food recipes, articles, loyalty points and so on.

- Community-based format: online purchase is conducted after reading reviews provided by multiple users of the websites.

- Mass customization format: in this format the shopper can go online to the shop and customize the product, which will be delivered as per the specification. For example, this has been done with computers and fashion, but not with food in retail environments. This format is being used by fast-food catering organizations such as Pizza Hut and Domino's, where you can customize the pizza online before ordering.

- Merchandise-oriented format: in this format the online retailer offers a store-in-store experience like Debenhams or John Lewis. Other brands will be able to have a microsite on the retailer's site from which the product can be ordered.

Once the order is placed online, it will reach the warehouse/distribution centre/fulfilment centre of the company where an employee will pick it and send it for packing, after which it will be dispatched. The most challenging leg of this delivery journey is the last mile, which is when the product is delivered to the customer. The formats for this are:

- The delivery is sent to the address on the order. At this juncture, either the recipient collects the order from the delivery person, or the person leaves the package at an alternative location, if agreed initially, or takes it back.

- If the driver takes the package back, the recipient has to reschedule the order (sometime paying extra for this service) or the recipient has to visit the distribution centre of the delivery company to collect the package (this is the collection point).

- With this in mind, and because shoppers were unhappy with this method of receiving their orders, retailers created the 'click and collect' delivery service. In this system the shopper has flexibility and control over receiving the order. Most high-street stores and supermarkets that have branches in major towns and cities set up this service within these regional stores. Shoppers can now choose to collect the order when they have time and are not constrained by having to be at home waiting for the delivery.

- This was a very successful offering, as customers now had flexibility and were not charged for the delivery. With the advent of companies such as 'collect+', many retailers outsourced their delivery service to such organizations. The package is sent to local shops (in partnership) or to a locker situated at a city-centre location (in most cases). Once the package has been dropped into the locker, the customer receives a text message giving them the code to open the locker. If the customer has chosen to collect it from a local shop, a similar text message is sent.

- The changing nature of the click and collect service means that retailers are not restricted to having the service in the shop; however, they may choose to have it in the shop in order to increase the footfall of customers within the shop.

Multi-channel vs omni-channel retailing

Multi-channel and omni-channel are two retail concepts that have influenced how the retailing world needs to operate in the future. Of the two, omni-channel retailing is the future of retail environments and requires a new perspective to engage with the consumer.

Multi-channel retail was about an increased number of channels through which customers could interact with and purchase from retailers. Customers could shop either in a physical store or online, but they could not interact with different channels at the same time. For example, customers were not permitted to purchase online and then return the item to the store.

However, with the advent of sophisticated IT tools and platforms, retailers need to provide a more dynamic shopping experience: in stores, online, mobile, click and collect, and so forth. This provides a seamless retail experience by connecting multiple channels. This type of retailing is known as omni-channel.

For omni-channel retailing, retailers must be ready to deliver to homes and businesses around the world, often with same-day or next-day delivery with multiple options. This requires new operational strategies.[11]

Challenges to the future of food retailing[12]

The UK food and grocery retail environment is struggling. Retail stores are seeing a reduction in footfall and time spent in the store. As more shoppers buy online, retailers are questioning the requirement for hypermarkets and supermarkets in the future. Retailers are experimenting with activities to attract shoppers to the shops and retain them in the shop for a sufficient time. These activities could be free tea/coffee (with a loyalty card) or food-tasting experiences or some other services (for example, within a large out-of-town Tesco store you can find a money exchange counter, photo studio, phone shop, community-centre room, key services and so on). The aim is to attract shoppers into the store. The tussle that store managers face is the utilization of the retail space – food or non-food? However, a recent article[13] discusses how the food retailing environment will change in the future and the challenges faced by the retailers currently. These challenges are as follows:

- Owing to the impact of the 2008/09 recession (which, at the time of writing, is expected to last for several more years), consumers do not have sufficient disposable income to spend on food, or are always trying to find a bargain, which has led to the success of the discounters.

- Shoppers are turning more to online purchasing, for a number of reasons, but an important reason is that most people have to juggle a lot of activities in day-to-day life. Therefore they don't want to spend time planning a weekly trip to the supermarket, when they can access the retailer's online store (which has the same prices and deals) using any mobile device.

- Due to the effect of time, consumers are turning more towards convenience purchasing, which means getting the product when it is convenient for them. This also relates to online shopping, where some supermarkets have created delivery passes or click and collect schemes so that shoppers can use the online platform to order when they feel the need to do so. This also means that shoppers may use local convenience stores more in the future (although the trade-off is between convenience and price).

- The sectoral view is that in the past two years, more people have been eating out rather than cooking at home. This will have an impact on fresh produce, but may increase the market for ready-to-eat meals.

The food and grocery retail environment will require an innovative approach to change the perspective of food purchasing. The focus within the retail environment has been to balance food and non-food and go for a one-stop-shop environment to drive sales in non-food. They have also driven down food prices to get shoppers into the shop, which is detrimental for the supply chain in the long term. The competition will be between the big retailers and the food discounters and the ability to get the business models correct.

Data from IGD[14] demonstrates a positive growth for the UK food and grocery sector in the future. The data state that the UK grocery market is set to be worth £203bn by 2019, increasing by 16 per cent from its current value of £175bn, and will be the largest retail sales format, worth 60 per cent, whereas the discounters, convenience stores and online will be worth 40 per cent. Although this is UK centric data it is still important from a European/US perspective and also for those who are suppliers to this retail chain. The move of customers to discounters currently is not only for the price differential, but also because the customers perceive that the quality of products at discounters has increased. Online provides a higher level of convenience for some and with the advent of new click and collect delivery models this convenience is further enhanced. The future of food retailing is around shopping formats and not so much on price as consumers will wish to organize shopping around their routines and not the other way round.

CASE EXAMPLE   Retailers turning more to 'dark stores'[15–18]

As online food and grocery sales increase, retailers are thinking about better ways to deliver the service and the most efficient way of doing it. Ocado was the first to start an online food and grocery service without having a physical shop. Ocado operates its online service through an automated warehouse from which completed orders are dispatched to the consumers. In the past two years, retailers in the UK and France have turned towards setting up 'dark stores' to fulfil online orders. Tesco has opened six dark stores, and Waitrose and ASDA have also opened dark stores.

A dark store is a dedicated warehouse which is set up exactly like a normal store with shelving and the products on the shelves; however, it is not open to the public and hence 'dark'. The levels of automation will differ between retailers. In the simplest form, when the order is received by the system a person employed by the company will go shopping in the dark store and the retailer will then dispatch this order to the customer. Some dark stores will have high levels of automation (this will again depend upon the levels of investment that the retailer is willing to commit).In the UK, the company will dispatch the order using vans. In France, the store acts as a 'click and collect' pick-up point.

Summary

This chapter has presented a discussion on the retailing operation. It discussed the different types of store format for selling food and groceries. Although it is not retail, the catering business is an important last mile of the food supply chain as it also connects the processor/distributor to the consumer. Hence, a synopsis of the main players within catering is provided. The points to consider for the distribution of the product were discussed, along with a brief on how to approach retailers with a new product for their shelves. Finally, the chapter looked at online retailing and also gave a case example.

Notes

1 International Comparison Program, Outlet Definition, Global Office [Online] http://siteresources.worldbank.org/ICPINT/Resources/270056-1255977254560/6483625-1273849421891/101110_ICP-OM_OutletDefinitions.pdf

2 Beaman, J A and Johnson, A J (2006) *A Guide for New Manufacturers: Food distribution channel overview*, December, Food Innovation Centre, Oregon State University

3 Gaines, M (accessed 20 February 2015) How to Sell Food in a Retail Store [Online] http://smallbusiness.chron.com/sell-food-retail-store-25709.html

4 EUFIC (accessed 20 February 2015) Food Shelf Life and Its Importance for Consumers [Online] http://www.eufic.org/article/en/artid/Food_shelf_life_and_its_importance_for_consumers/

5 European Commission. Fact sheet: What can I do in my daily life to limit food waste?

6 Directive 2000/13/EC of the European Parliament and of the Council of 20 March 2000 on labelling, presentation and advertising of foodstuffs

Regulation 1169/2011/EU of the European Parliament and of the Council of 25 October 2011 on the provision of food information to consumers

7 See note 4.

8 Fellow, P (2000) *Food Processing Technology: Principles and practice*, 2nd edn, CRC Press, Baton Rouge, FL. Also, for technical details of food and packaging, see: Briston, J H (1988) Matching the packaging to the product, in *Food Technology International Europe*, ed A Turner, pp 351–4, Sterling Publications International, London; and Fellows, P J and Axtell, B L (1993) *Appropriate Food Packaging*, pp 49–50, ILO/TOOL Publications, ILO, Geneva.

9 Boettger, J (2012) *Inventory Management and Tracking Reference Guide*, National Food Service Management Institute, University of Mississippi

10 Fernie, J and Sparks, L (2014) *Logistics and Retail Management*, 4th edn, Kogan Page, London

11 CILT (accessed 20 February 2015) What You Need to Know about Multi-channel vs. Omni-channel, 18 September 2014 [Online] http://www.ciltuk.org.uk/News/LatestNews/tabid/235/ctl/NewsItem/mid/589/Id/4157/Default.aspx?returnurl=%2Fdefault.aspx

12 Ruddick, G (2014) The problem food retailing is facing at the moment is as dramatic as the introduction of supermarkets in the 1950s: The Waitrose boss says the weekly shop is finished and customers are buying more locally and online. Supermarkets must adapt, he tells Graham Ruddick, *The Sunday Telegraph*, London, 16 November 2014, p 9

13 See note 11.

14 IGD Media Release (2014) UK Grocery Market to be Worth £203bn by 2019, 30 June

15 Miles, N (accessed 20 February 2015) Shining Light on Dark Stores, 10 December 2013, IGD [online] http://www.igd.com/our-expertise/Retail/retail-outlook/17899/Shining-a-light-on-dark-stores/

16 Watkins, D (accessed 20 February 2015) Tesco Goes into Darkness, Retail Gazette, 6 January 2014 [Online] http://www.retailgazette.co.uk/articles/42030-tesco-goes-into-the-darkness

17 Butler, S (accessed 20 February 2015) Grocers Rush to Open 'Dark Stores' as Online Food Shopping Expands, *The Guardian*, 6 January 2014 [Online] http://www.theguardian.com/business/2014/jan/06/supermarkets-open-dark-stores-online-food-shopping-expands

18 Benedictus, L (accessed 20 February 2015) Inside the Supermarkets' Dark Stores, Blog, *The Guardian*, 7 January 2014 [Online] http://www.theguardian.com/business/shortcuts/2014/jan/07/inside-supermarkets-dark-stores-online-shopping

Food logistics

05

Food logistics is the movement of food through the supply chain until it reaches the consumer's plate. The flow of information from the consumer back into the chain is also an important part of logistics. 'Logistics activities are the operational component of supply chain management, including quantification, procurement, inventory management, transportation and fleet management, and data collection and reporting.'[1] Technological advances in food processing and transportation have allowed industries to move greater quantities of food faster and over longer distances than ever before possible. This chapter presents a discussion of the food logistics environment. It explains the different logistics processes and the movement of food through the supply chain. The influence of technology, requirements for packaging and temperature-controlled logistics is also discussed.

Movement of food

Integration of processes

The modern retail logistics system is heavily dependent on the use of information technology. The importance of movement of information is as profound as the movement of the product through the systems. To distribute the products through the chain, physical infrastructure is required in the form of warehouses, vehicles, packaging boxes, crates, trolleys and so on. However, another form of infrastructure is necessary to control, monitor, track and facilitate this product distribution process. This infrastructure is the ICT hardware which increasingly uses dynamic data to drive logistics environments and organize what gets moved, when it moves and the form in which it is moved and stored. The food supply chain needs to consider warehousing and transport as seamless entities of the same operation and not as discrete operations that someone else does. Logistics is about integration, not only within a company but, increasingly, also externally with suppliers, logistics services providers and customers. Partnerships are a strong component of modern retail logistics, and the ability to work with other individuals and other companies is fundamental to success. The movement of products is also about the movement of products in a safe, tamper-free environment and retaining its quality. This means that packaging and handling systems need to be well thought out as a part of the supply chain design. The food supply chains are increasingly global and logistics of food is no longer the movement of products from a local farm to the shop but includes a host of very complicated procedures to navigate across international boundaries. This will also require a different type of person doing the logistics job, with a different set of skills, and this is currently a challenge within the logistics industry. The people involved in the roles also need to be able to transcend boundaries to be able to partner with their counterparts across the globe to make sure that the consignment reaches the customer as per the specifications. However, as supermarkets compete with each other for the customers' business and try to create product differentiation to suit customers' requirements, some of the logistics are moving from being international to local. As consumer preferences change to trying out local or seasonal produce and reducing food miles, some of the logistics environments will change to local movement to accommodate business models that create product differentiation.

Inherently, logistics is about the movement of product. The success of the system will be measured on the basis of on-time delivery, keeping to the customers' specifications. The focus of development and innovation within logistics is centred around the mechanics and details of product movement and handling, storing and packaging. For example, the retail environment will prescribe the packaging requirements to standardize shelving and movement of the products internally through their systems. Vehicles will be equipped with global positioning satellite (GPS) systems and advanced tachograph and communications equipment, allowing real-time driver and vehicle performance monitoring, including fuel consumption analysis. The delivery to supermarkets and from ports will be held to measurements of windows, facilitating scheduling. In distribution centres, voice-activated or controlled picking has been implemented to maintain accuracy and increase operational efficiency. Taking a cue from the automotive sector and the use of just-in-time (JIT) production management systems, the retail environment has implemented programmes such as vendor-managed inventory and efficient consumer response to maintain inventory levels on the shelves as and when required. This is facilitated by shelf-ready merchandizing of the product, as the product can then go directly onto the shelf without requiring internal processing. The usefulness of technology for all these processes cannot be denied and hence the supply chain needs to gear up with the appropriate technology to achieve the objectives of the system. Such detailed developments remain key elements of supply chain integration. One requirement for the food industry is the management of fresh, chilled and frozen food items. The logistics environment requires temperature-controlled infrastructure. This is not only storage but also temperature-maintained vehicles.

The factors affecting logistics environments

Fifteen years ago, Alan McKinnon[2,3] reviewed and summarized the key components of the transformation of the logistics sector with the UK context. He identified six trends, all of which are closely related and mutually reinforcing. These trends are still very valid and are constantly upgrading, with a big impact on logistics systems:

1 The creation of logistics networks with the mapping of warehouses and distribution centres increased retailers' control over the distribution of the products from the warehouses to their retail environments. The retailers exert a tighter control over the supply chain through the use of information technology (IT), particularly the large, integrated stock replenishment systems that control the movement and storage of an enormous number of separate products.

2 The development of 'composite distribution' (the distribution of mixed-temperature items through the same distribution centre and on the same vehicle) and centralization in specialist

warehouses of slower-moving stock have helped to reduce inventory and increase operational efficiency. In the case of mixed retail businesses, this includes the establishment of 'common stock rooms' (where stock is shared across a number of stores, with demand deciding to which store stock is allocated).

3 There has been an adoption of 'quick response' (QR) approaches with the aim of cutting inventory levels and improving speed of product flow. This has involved reducing order lead time and moving to a more frequent delivery of smaller consignments both internally (between distribution centre (DC) and shop) and across external links with suppliers. This has greatly increased the rate of stock turn and increased cross-docking rather than storage at DCs. This has been possible through the use of technology and electronic point of sale (EPS) data using integration systems such as EDI and ECR.

4 The trend to using JIT and QR also requires control over the inventory in the total supply chain. This led to retailers rationalizing the inventory from the manufacturer to the retail store and not just from the DC. The concept of port-centric logistics (PCL) has helped to cut down on miles and carbon emissions. Coupled with the PCL concept is the move towards multimodal logistics.

5 The advent of integrated supply chain management and efficient consumer response (ECR) has helped to shorten the supply chain from factory to store, with the manufacturer taking more control of the inventory on the shelves. The technology for achieving close integration and sharing of live data is already available. This is also supported by vendor-managed inventory (VMI) systems and collaborative planning forecasting and replenishment (CPFR) systems.

6 Reverse logistics as an important aspect of supply design is an important trend. The costing of products and services will need a life-cycle costing approach, taking into account the costs of the reverse supply chain. This will include return flow of packaged material and handling equipment for recycling/reuse and products returned by the consumer on account of quality. Retailers have become much more heavily involved in this 'reverse logistics' operation.

ICT future trends in agri-food logistics[4]

The proliferation of internet and mobile technology has influenced how logistic services work to deliver the product to the consumer. Tracking of deliveries, using click and collect, modifying delivery times or alternatively booking exact slots for collection and so on are possible through the use of connected networks. Online retailing has changed the rules of the game. When purchasing from Amazon, a consumer will know exactly how many of the item required are in stock and will decide whether it will be bought. This field of study is known as smart logistics, and when applied to the agri sector it is called smart agri-food logistics. The smart agri-food logistic system will utilize tracking and tracing technologies, with access to data being received through the sensors in the system. Some of the characteristics of the smart-agri logistics sector are:

- *Internet of Things (IOT)*: The Internet of Things is a system in which the various types of sensor embedded into the agri-food network communicate with each other and share intelligence. These applications are currently limited in scope and focus on specific subparts of the logistics chain in which the sensors are embedded to capture data such as temperature, humidity and so on. Using communication technologies such as networked radio-frequency identification (RFID), wireless sensor networks and near-field communication, the system can relay important information regarding the status of the shipment to the control system. The technology can work only if the signals are strong.

- *Telematics systems*: Sensors are used in the logistics process to react to changes of ambient parameters (eg temperature, light, ethylene concentration etc) and send this information to the monitoring centre. Further information about location, speed and context coupled with the ambient parameters will help to create effective forecasting. The key challenge of integrating systems across supply chains will need advanced governance models to maintain data integrity and privacy.

- *Tracking and tracing*: To enable greater control over the products in the chain and the chain itself, the level of traceability should focus on the whole supply chain. The system needs to be able to trace across and through the various processes in the chain.

- *Autonomous systems*: Changes are required to enable each entity inside the logistics processes to process information, take decisions autonomously and communicate with other entities. This should capture the intelligence and ensure the integrity of content. 'Mobile software components' to be used in different systems operated by the actors in the food chain need to be certified to ensure data integrity.

- *Business intelligence*: To support strategic and functional decisions, business intelligence systems analyse all relevant electronically accessible data and process models by acquisition, processing and dissemination.

Packaging in logistics

Food will be transported in various types of packaging (not retail packaging with branding) such as containers of boxes, with the aim of holding and protecting the food during distribution and transit. The operational requirements for such containers are that they should:[5]

- hold and protect the products against climate and contamination risks throughout the journey;

- be compatible with the product;

- be easy to fill, seal and handle;

- remain securely closed in transit, but open easily when required (eg customs inspection) and reclose securely;

- carry information for all stages of the supply chain regarding the contents, destination, and how to handle and open the pack (smart containers will also have GPS tracking);
- be readily disposable or reusable.

The material used for some of these containers is:

- corrugated fibreboard cases;
- shrink-wrapped or stretch-wrapped corrugated trays;
- wooden or metal cases, crates, barrels, drums;
- sacks;
- intermediate bulk containers (IBCs) made from metal, plastic or corrugated fibreboard (including combi-bins, large boxes);
- large bags made from woven plastic fabric.

IBCs are reusable industrial containers designed for the transport and storage of liquid and powders with a capacity of around 1,000 litres and having an integral pallet and bottom discharge valve. Many of the food containers are expensive and are returned in the reverse supply chain for reuse. Some containers which are used to handle perishable food with a risk of contamination will be used only once.[6] When transporting perishable food items, there will be a need to use specialized boxes and packing materials, gel packs, thermal blankets, dry ice and other materials.

Temperature-controlled supply chains

Supply chain activities are either managed in-house by food and beverage retailers and manufacturers themselves, or outsourced to third-party logistics providers, such as DHL Supply Chain, Wincanton and Hellman Worldwide Logistics, among others. Logistics activities in the food and beverage sector operate across four temperature bands:[7]

- ambient – eg canned foods, jars of coffee, bags of sugar;
- fresh produce – fruits and vegetables;
- chilled – such as dairy products and ready meals;
- frozen – frozen fresh produce, meals, ice creams, etc.

Temperature monitoring and recording is a legal requirement for the food sector. This also provides more control over the supply chain and can be facilitated by using time–temperature integrators or indicators, which connect to the IT systems, to individually monitor the temperature conditions of food products.[8] A temperature-controlled food supply chain requires products to be maintained in a temperature-controlled environment, rather than exposing them to variable ambient temperatures at the various stages of the supply chain.[9] The complexity of the food distribution will be based on the type of product, the available modes of transport between farm and fork, legal requirements and so on. Retail food supply chains will generally distribute multiple types of product with different temperature requirements within the same journey, and this creates further complexity. If a food supply chain is dedicated to a narrow range of products, the temperature will be set at the level for that product. If a food supply chain is handling a broad range of products, an optimum temperature or a limited number of different temperature settings are used.[10] The temperature zones will differ according to whether the requirement is for frozen(–25°C; ice cream etc), cold chill (0–1°C; fresh meat, poultry, dairy, fruits etc), medium chill (5°C; butter, cheese etc) or exotic chill (10–15°C; (potatoes, eggs, exotic fruit etc).[11] However, when designing the supply chain and food handling it is important to understand that carrying different types of food may cause risk of product interactions; for example, bananas produce ethylene, which accelerates the ripening process of other fruits. Also, food safety within these interactions needs to be considered, as there may be listeria in cheese products, salmonella in chickens and eggs, BSE in cattle, E. coli in vegetables, and so forth.[12]

Temperature-controlled warehouses (multi-temperature composite warehouses) and multi-temperature delivery vehicles are available to meet the strict distribution requirements of the food supply chain, ensuring good on-shelf availability while minimizing wastage. Owing to the availability of multi-temperature vehicles, distribution and vehicle utilization have improved. Another advantage of using multi-temperature warehouses and vehicles is that the goods can come directly into the temperature-controlled zones of the retail store in reusable plastic trays, on 'dollies' or on roll cages.[13]

The logistics of perishables

The logistics of perishable food products and fresh produce is a complex task in which temperature is a very important factor. In the previous section, the discussion was an introduction to the concept of temperature-controlled supply chains. This section will consider the challenges involved in moving perishables in the international supply chain. Perishable products can be transported via air, land or sea. When considering international chains, the default mode of transport that one thinks of is air. The task is to keep the food fresh throughout the journey without losing valuable shelf life. Perishables can be of many forms: flowers, fresh fruit and vegetables, ready-to-eat processed meals, ready-to-eat food such as fresh cream cakes, meat and so on. The mode of transport used will depend upon which product is considered and the required speed of delivery. Innovations in food packaging, fruit and vegetable coatings, controlled ripening techniques, radiation and so on have tried to extend the time taken for the food to deteriorate. This also means that if a product now takes more time to deteriorate, the company may decide to use a transport mode that is cheaper (than air) but takes more time to reach the destination. In some cases, the company will use air cargo services to send the first consignment as 'first harvest of the season' but schedule the subsequent consignments to arrive by sea.[14] Both air and sea cold-chain logistics have their advantages and disadvantages.

The majority of food that is moved globally travels by container freight. This includes almost all dry food and some perishables. Air cargo can be sent via two modes – passenger aircraft and cargo services. Fresh fruit and vegetables from Africa or Asia will use passenger aircraft services to deliver the consignment. However, although the services are less expensive, exporters will need to manage their schedules strictly as per the passenger aircraft timetables. Cargo air services are generally tailor made and could provide a better service (at a higher cost); however, again this will depend upon the location of travel and whether the exporting location has regular flights. As packaging technology improves and innovates, it is possible to ship using refrigerated containers, which provide a better consistency of cold chain than using air. The trade-off is that it will take more time for delivery. For the cold chain to work efficiently and effectively, movement from one cold region to the other should be seamless. With air travel, although the time taken for travel will be less, the length of time that the product spends exposed to the external temperature may be more than is the case when travelling by ship in refrigerated containers. In 2013–14, major shipping lines took a decision to travel slowly (slow steaming) in order to reduce fuel consumption. This has increased the time taken by ships to reach their destinations, leading to some exporters switching from sea to air for transporting their perishables.

There are a number of factors that need to be considered when designing perishable cold chains:

1 Maintaining the seamless cold chain from source to retail – this will also depend upon the type of product being considered.

2 Mode of travel – this should depend upon, among other factors of cost and time, what kind of value the supply chain is seeking to deliver to the consumer.

3 Food safety – the design will need to consider the traceability and regulatory requirements of the importing country and the operational issues of hygiene, using the appropriate containers, employee training and so on.

4 The appropriate packaging technology – to match product characteristics in order to reduce exposure and increase shelf life.

5 Technology for real-time monitoring of temperature, movement, location, humidity levels and so on, and using this data for analysis.

6 Effective on-costs, on-time delivery and understanding of the dynamics of the cold chain.[15–17]

CASE EXAMPLE   The dabbawala[18-21]

The dabbawala or 'tiffin carrier' is a person who carries a lunchbox from the customer's home to the office and back. Simplistically, the person operates a bidirectional delivery system. The same lunchbox comes back to the house to be ready for the next day. The aim of this logistics system may look easy; however, 5,000 men deliver over 200,000 meals a day, picking up the tiffins in the morning from the homes of their customers, typically packed with home-made food. This system operates in the city of Mumbai.

The system of the dabbawalas is managed through strong team working and strict time management. At 9 am every morning, home-made meals are picked up in special boxes, which are loaded onto trolleys and pushed to a railway station. The lunchboxes then travel by train to an unloading station (which is the central hub). The boxes are rearranged so that those going to similar destinations, indicated by a system of coloured lettering, end up on the same trolley. The meals are then delivered – 99.9999 per cent of the time to the correct address, giving this system a six-sigma status. The coding on the lunchbox's outer cover consists of a large bold number in the centre that indicates the neighbourhood where the dabba (lunchbox) is to be delivered; characters on the edge of the lid denoting the office building, floor number and the dabbawala who will make the delivery; and a combination of colour and motif for the railway station of origin. The local journey from the home to the hub is handled by one individual. After the lunchboxes are consolidated at the hub and then deconsolidated as per neighbourhood, they are carried by another person who deals with that route. It may be necessary for someone to carry the lunchboxes from the hub to the neighbourhood, again by train, and then hand over the boxes to another local individual. The dabbawalas operate their system according to the schedules of the Mumbai local railway system, as this is the mode of transport for them to carry the lunchboxes to the hub. The local journey from the hub in both directions is done by bicycle.

The 5,000 dabbawalas of Mumbai are organized into a flat structure of 200 self-managed teams of 25 individuals each, who vary in age from 18 to 65, with the most experienced acting as supervisors in addition to doing their own deliveries. Their motivation is derived from their cultural underpinning that delivering the lunchboxes is like a spiritual act. This system originated in Mumbai about 125 years ago.

CASE EXAMPLE   The journey of green beans from Kenya to UK supermarkets[22]

Fresh and packed green beans available in UK supermarkets travel over 4,000 miles from Kenyan farms. The UK tends to import about 165m packets of beans every year. The beans are sourced from small farms in Kenya. When the beans are ready to be harvested, they are hand-picked using manual labour. The beans have to be perfect in shape and size or supermarkets will reject them, so beans that are curved or not a good shape are thrown away or fed to animals. The beans are picked when the weather is sunny and very hot and have to be stored in chilling rooms as soon as they are picked. However, electrification of villages in Kenya is not a norm, so the farm has to be innovative in order to solve this challenge, as they will lose the day's harvest if the beans are not chilled immediately. The beans ideally have to be maintained at 5°C. The farm has developed a charcoal chilling room that doesn't need electricity. Once harvesting is done for the day, the beans are loaded onto refrigerated trucks and taken to a pack house 20 minutes away. The pack house is temperature-controlled and the packing will be done (in terms of packaging and labelling) as per supermarket requirements. This will give the beans a shelf life of eight days. Once packed, the consignment is sent in a refrigerated vehicle to the international airport and then to the UK in the cargo hold of a passenger aircraft. The beans take 48 hours to get from the farm to the supermarket shelf.

CASE EXAMPLE   The fresh cut-pineapple supply chain from Ghana[23]

One of the regions of the world whence UK supermarkets source pineapple, both as a whole fruit and as fresh cut pieces, is Ghana. Pineapples normally take 18 months to grow before they are ready for harvesting. The harvesting has to be done precisely at the time when he pineapple is the sweetest, as once it is harvested it does not ripen any more but just goes off. The farms use a tool called a refractometer to test the sugar content of the pineapple. If it is found to be the correct amount, the pineapples are harvested. Once picked, they have to be chilled immediately. The harvest is then sent to a processing centre, which prepares the fruit for export. The pineapple is cut into chunks and packaged for dispatch. The centre processes 20 metric tons of pineapple a day. The packaging uses a special film, which has micro pores that let the carbon dioxide out of the pack but do not let oxygen get in from outside. This retains freshness for about six days. The packed consignment is sent to the airport for delivery to the UK.

Summary

This chapter has presented an overview of the food logistics environment. It considered the integration of the logistics environment and the impact it has on the food supply chain. Then a discussion of the trends affecting the logistics environment in general led to a view on smart-agri logistics and the future of internet technology and data systems. A brief overview of the types of material used in packaging food for delivery was given, followed by a discussion of temperature-controlled food supply chains. A lot of fresh produce and perishables is imported into the Western retail environment on a daily basis and the transportation of perishable goods is a complex but interesting task. Hence, a brief discussion on the logistics of perishable products was provided. Finally, the chapter ended with three case examples looking at some of the concepts from the chapter.

Notes

1 Strengthening Pharmaceutical Systems Program (2013) Guide for Malaria Commodities Logistic Management System: Applying the monitoring–training–planning approach for improving performance, submitted to the US Agency for International Development by the Strengthening Pharmaceutical System Program, Management Sciences for Health, Arlington, VA

2 McKinnon, A C (1996) The Development of Retail Logistics in the UK: A position paper, *Technology Foresight: Retail and Distribution Panel*, Heriot-Watt University, Edinburgh

3 Fernie, J and Sparks, L (2014) *Logistics and Retail Management*, 4th edn, Kogan Page, London

4 Verdouw, C N *et al* (2012) Smart Agri-Food Logistics: Requirements for the future internet, 3rd International Conference on Dynamics in Logistics (LDIC 2012), Bremen, Germany, 27 February–1 March 2012

5 Fellow, P (2000) *Food Processing Technology: Principles and practice*, 2nd edn, CRC Press, Baton Rouge, FL

6 See note 5.

7 IGD (accessed 24 February 2015) UK Food & Grocery Retail Logistics Overview, 24 November 2009 [Online] http://www.igd.com/ Research/Supply-chain/Logistics/3457/UK-Food–Grocery-Retail-Logistics-Overview/

8 Giannakourou, M C and Taoukis, P S (2006) Application of a TTI-based distribution management system for quality optimisation of frozen vegetables at the consumer end, *Journal of Food Science*, **68** (1), pp 201–09

9 Smith, D and Sparks, L (2004) Temperature controlled supply chains, in *Food Supply Chain Management*, ed M A Bourlakis and P W H Weightman, Chapter 12, pp 179–98, Wiley-Blackwell, Oxford

10 van der Vorst, J G A J, van Kooten, O and Luning, P A (2011) Towards a diagnostic instrument to identify improvement opportunities for quality controlled logistics in agrifood supply chain networks, *International Journal of Food System Dynamics*, **2** (1), pp 94–105, Available online at www.fooddynamics.org

11 Gustafsson, K *et al* (2009) *Retailing Logistics and Fresh Food Packaging: Managing change in the supply chain*, Kogan Page, London

12 Luning, P A and Marcelis, W J (2006) A techno-managerial approach in food quality management research, *Trends in Food Science and Technology*, **17**, pp 378–85

13 See note 9.

14 Terry, L (accessed 16 February 2015) Perishable Logistics: Cold chain on a plane, Inbound Logistics, January 2014 [Online] http:// www.inboundlogistics.com/cms/article/perishable-logistics-cold-chain-on-a-plane/

15 See note 14.

16 Duggan, B (accessed 16 February 2015) Advances in Cold Chain Tech Make Moving Perishables by Sea Highly Desirable, SupplyChainBrain, 2 May 2014 [Online] http://www.supplychainbrain.com/content/nc/ technology-solutions/global-trade-management/single-article-page/ article/advances-in-cold-chain-tech-make-moving-perishables-by-sea-highly-desirable/

17 Transporting Perishable Food Products . . . Delivering a recipe for success, *The Guardian*, Guardian Small Business Network,

14 November 2013 [Online] http://www.theguardian.com/small-business-network/2013/nov/14/transporting-perishable-food-products

18 Mumbai Dabbawala Association [Online] http://mumbaidabbawala.in/

19 Somaskanda, S and Gahlot, M (accessed 16 February 2015) This Indian Meal Service Is so Efficient It's the Envy of FedEx, Global Post, 14 July 2014 [Online] http://www.globalpost.com/dispatch/news/regions/asia-pacific/india/140630/indian-meal-service-so-efficient-it-s-the-envy-fedex

20 Ganguly, D (accessed 16 February 2015) Food for Thought: What makes Mumbai's dabbawalas successful, *The Economic Times*, 22 August 2014 [Online] http://articles.economictimes.indiatimes.com/2014-08-22/news/53112455_1_mumbai-case-study-stefan-thomke

21 *The Economist* (accessed 16 February 2015) The cult of the dabbawala, 10 July 2008 [Online] http://www.economist.com/node/11707779

22 BBC Documentary, From Crop to Shop – Jimmy's Supermarket Secrets, 3 February 2010

23 See note 18.

Challenges in international food supply chains

06

As markets open up in the developing world and the demand for processed food increases, the agriculture and food-processing sectors are working hard to cope with the new demand challenges. However, the products have to travel across international boundaries before they can be consumed, and this causes even greater challenges of navigating through national regulatory regimes and local politics. Trade in fishery products, exotics, pre-cut products, organic products and off-season fresh fruits and vegetables are in demand owing to the proliferation of the food retail environment. Global market standards are stringent and the products not only have to be safe and of very good quality, but also should have the appropriate packaging and labelling on them. Consumers in developed countries and in urban areas within developing and transition economies demand safe and nutritious food, excellent quality and just-in-time delivery. This presents major challenges to producers and countries that lack state-of-the-art technologies and infrastructure. Particularly for producers in developing countries, collaboration between trade partners has become increasingly important for the success of international trade in the competitive market. A lack of information regarding regulation changes and lack of skills and training in value-adding technologies increase the challenges that exporters in developing countries face on a daily basis. This chapter presents an overview of these challenges and some approaches to overcome them. The chapter also discusses the challenges of international trade from the perspective of politics.

International food supply chains

The advent of fast logistics, organized retail environments and regulatory reforms has provided an opportunity for consumers to access fresh agricultural produce all year round. The debate with regard to using local produce (seasonal varieties) as against food miles will prevail. However, agriculture supply chains across the world are gearing up to get a share of the pie and are trying to coordinate with retailers and importers to fulfil new consumer demands. Since the demand is no longer confined to local, regional supply, systems need to be put in place for fresh produce to be shipped from across the world at lower costs and competitive prices. Advanced information technologies enable traders to respond quickly to changes in consumer demand and facilitate the flow of goods in today's highly complex global marketplace.

The path to international trade is strewn with challenges in the form of regulation, trade barriers and tough retail certification standards. In the developing countries and emerging economies, companies face particular challenges in adapting to these changing requirements as there is poor communication and training opportunities. Producers in developing countries are capitalizing on opportunities by entering into partnerships with multinational businesses active in the global food chain. In the developing world, some local farmers have linked their production activities to the interests of large food companies within vertically controlled operations. These new requirements also put extra focus on new forms of production technologies, labour processes and organizational relations.

Supply chain management

Supply chain management is an important platform to achieve collaboration between trade partners. Collaboration will help producers in developing countries and emerging economies to gain access to markets and the required trade facilitation information. Developing international supply chains is a complex task and requires information and expertise about supply chain design and performance measures.

The advantages of supply chain management are numerous:

- better control of product quality and safety;
- reduction of product losses;
- better demand management;
- reduction of transaction costs;
- technology sharing and access to capital;
- collaborative knowledge exchange among chain partners.

When designing international food supply chains, it is essential to consider sustainability as a variable on which the design will be based. This will ensure that along with the measures of achieving economic stability, the supply chains will help in regional development in the other two sustainability variables – social and environmental. 'For example, it can stimulate the development of local agro-industry, employment generation, local food production, value addition to products, introduction of new technologies, decreasing product losses, increased export earnings, and improved food safety and nutrition by connecting chain partners and their activities.'[1]

Factors affecting the future of international food systems

As the world's population increases and the demand for food simultaneously increases, international food systems are under pressure to fulfil these demands. Although the driving force behind international trade is economic benefit and progress across the world, the environment around us is increasingly becoming unstable and is affecting these food supply chains. A Foresight report from the UK government titled 'The Future of Food and Farming' has discussed the challenges that food supply chains may face in the future. The report also discusses the recommendations to overcome these challenges. Following is a very brief representation regarding the challenges as discussed in the report[2] and in other wider literature.

Global population increases

The population of the world could rise to an excess of nine billion by 2050 and the majority of the rise will be in low- and middle-income countries, which will create further resource challenges as people move from rural areas to cities for employment.

Changes in the size and nature of per capita demand

There are patterns depicting a change of dietary preferences across the world as diets move from grain to meat consumption. This also affects agricultural output, as it creates competition for grain consumption between humans and animals (for meat). Dietary changes will also affect the fishing industry and will require an expansion of aquaculture.

Future governance of the food system at both national and international levels

Many aspects of governance have a significant impact on the workings of the food system:

- The emergence and continued growth of new food superpowers, Russia, Brazil, China and India.

- The trend for consolidation in the private sector, with the emergence of a limited number of very large transnational companies in agribusiness, in the fisheries sector and in the food-processing, distribution and retail sectors.

- Production subsidies, trade restrictions, other market interventions and the extent to which governments will act to face future challenges, collectively or individually.

- The control of increasing areas of land for food production (such as in Africa) will be influenced by both past and future land-purchase and leasing agreements – involving both sovereign wealth funds and business.

Climate change

Rising global temperatures and changing patterns of precipitation will affect crop growth and livestock performance, the availability of water, fisheries and aquaculture yields and the functioning of ecosystem services in all regions. This will increase volatility in production and prices along with challenges in logistics. There will also be pressure to reduce greenhouse gas emissions.

Competition for key resources

Several critical resources on which food production relies will come under more pressure in the future. These resources are:

- land available for food production;
- energy availability, as the demand is increasing;
- water availability, for agriculture, industry and domestic use.

Perception of consumers

Consumer perceptions regarding the food they consume will have an impact on future food security, governance of the system and policy making: for example, perceptions regarding genetic modification, nanotechnology, cloning of livestock, organic food, animal welfare and so on.

Managing challenges in international food supply chains

As shown by Figure 6.1, there are four key interrelated factors which should be kept in mind when managing the challenges of an international food supply chain.

Trust

A high degree of trust between the partners in a buyer–supplier relationship is favourable for coordinated behaviour, whereas low trust

FIGURE 6.1 Factors to manage international supply chains

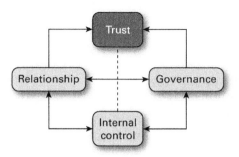

leads to competitive behaviour. Long-term relationships and trust encourage effective communication, information sharing and joint pay-offs. Within a food supply chain, trust is very important when traceability and transparency are difficult to achieve. Trust built up through long-term relationships also requires a mutual agreement to meet international certification standards and other auditing requirements. Alternatively, certification programmes, shared values and reciprocity in benefits can help in developing trust and long-term relationships. Chapter 7 discusses this concept further.

Governance

As food supply chains become global and complex, it is getting extremely difficult for individual companies in the supply chain to monitor the supply chains themselves. ISO 22000 standardizes global food safety standards and emphasizes interactive communication and traceability right through the supply chain. The Sanitary and Phytosanitary Measures Agreement, or SPS, is an international agreement on food safety and animal and plant health standards that sets out the basic rules. However, it allows individual countries to set their own food safety standards. Member countries are encouraged to use international standards, guidelines and recommendations where they exist. If an exporting country can demonstrate that the measures it applies to its exports achieve the same level of health protection as in the importing country, the importing country is expected to accept the exporting country's standards and methods. International exporters will need to acquaint themselves with the relevant legislation and certification requirements within the retail environment. This is discussed further in Chapter 11.

Relationship

Supply chain relationships have been seen to be an important aspect of managing supply chains. It is important to focus on the actual dynamics of the supply chain and the role of each entity at the inter-organizational boundary. The emphasis upon managing the supply chain as a source of competitive advantage has led many organizations to reassess the role of their suppliers to achieve or sustain competitiveness and customer service. Within the food supply chain, better relationships could help to reduce opportunistic behaviour and facilitate better implementation of food safety, thus reducing the proliferation of the food risk through the global supply chain.

Internal controls

Some of the internal controls which an organization within the food supply chain can utilize are shown in Table 6.1.

TABLE 6.1 Internal controls to manage risks in international food supply chains

IT disaster recovery plans	Identification of mission-critical assets and activities
Recall procedures	Scenario planning
Crisis management team/Incident management team	Relocation readiness
Risk registers	Continuity planning with suppliers and customers
Risk analysis and categorization (likelihood/impact)	Supplier compliance audits and risk diagnosis

International politics and food

The relationship between food security, conflict and food availability needs to be discussed. The objective of achieving food security has a major influence on national politics. Overseas conflicts or challenges affecting individual countries will sometimes escalate to endanger domestic interests and lead to countries taking protectionist decisions which in turn will have an impact on trade and the economy. The fallout from the event will affect food availability, cause displacement of people and incur the expense of post-event reconstruction. Food price inflation is about not only the relationship between supply and demand but also the likelihood of governments panicking and subsequently taking decisions to hoard food or limit exports. For example, following a severe drought and wildfires in 2010, Russia announced that it would be banning all grain exports to prevent a rise in domestic food prices.[3] This raised global wheat prices to a two-year high, and prices of other crops, including barley, rice and corn, also rose sharply. This action affected the costs of food processors using wheat as a raw material (for example, bread manufacturers).

The Final Act of the Uruguay Round of Multilateral Trade Negotiations was conducted and signed in Marrakesh on 15 April 1994. This Agreement on Agriculture and other agreements contained in the Final Act, along with the General Agreement on Tariffs and Trade as amended (GATT 1994), are part of the treaty which established the World Trade Organization (WTO) in 1994. The WTO superseded the GATT as the umbrella organization for international trade. The Technical Barriers to Trade (TBT), 1979 was superseded by the WTO TBT, 1994. The Agreement on Agriculture also formed the application of the Sanitary and Phytosanitary Measures. The three agreements that have an impact on food trade and regulation are:[4]

1 SPS;
2 TBT 1994;
3 GATT 1994.

The SPS Agreement covers the following measures:

- to protect human or animal life from risks arising from additives, contaminants, toxins or disease-causing organisms in their food;

- to protect human life from plant- or animal-carried diseases;
- to protect animal or plant life from pests, diseases or disease-causing organisms;
- to prevent or limit other damage to a country from the entry, establishment or spread of pests.

Measures for environmental protection (other than as defined above), to protect consumer interests or for the welfare of animals are not covered by the SPS Agreement, but are addressed by the TBT Agreement or Article XX of GATT 1994.

National food safety and animal and plant health measures which affected trade were subject to GATT rules (when it is not relevant under SPS). Article I of GATT 1994, the most-favoured nation clause, required non-discriminatory treatment of imported products from different foreign suppliers, and Article III required that such products be treated no less favourably than domestically produced goods with respect to any laws or requirements affecting their sale. These rules are applied, for example, to pesticide residue and food additive limits, as well as to restrictions for animal or plant health purposes. The rules provided an exception (Article XX:b) in which, where necessary, for purposes of protecting human, animal or plant health, governments could impose more stringent requirements on imported products than they required of domestic goods.

The TBT Agreement covered technical requirements resulting from food safety and animal and plant health measures, including pesticide residue limits, inspection requirements and labelling. It was agreed that governments would use relevant international standards (for example, codex). In terms of food labelling requirements, nutrition claims and concerns, quality and packaging regulations are generally not considered to be sanitary or phytosanitary measures and hence are normally subject to the TBT Agreement.

Supply chain development

International food supply chains play a very important role in economic development in both importing and exporting countries. The movement of goods and cash stimulates employment and social regeneration. Supply chains that are governed well will also protect the environment and create ethical behaviour not only between the transacting partners but hopefully across the network. However, developing the supply chain and the relationships requires effort and commitment from partners and help and support from governments. Public-sector support plays an important role in the development of supply chains to create an enabling environment for private-sector infrastructure development. Developing countries and emerging economies have a lack of government support for communication and transport infrastructure (eg roads and ports), agricultural research and extension services, and financial institutions. This stifles trade and growth, thus affecting supply chains. Some countries are realizing the potential of international food supply chains in creating long-term value and development, and their governments are increasingly moving towards creating policies conducive to the development of the food sector. Within the international political arena, agricultural trade is integrated into the WTO commitments. The discussion around how countries should evolve their agricultural policies and open markets will hamper developmental programmes domestically. Coupled with these scenarios, SPS measures, export subsidies and tariffs, quotas and strict safety and quality regulations imposed by importing countries will create barriers for developing countries.

Governments can improve the environment for agri-chain development by:

- creating information and skills training platforms for people in the food sector to upskill;
- investing in logistics infrastructure;
- creating incentives for sustainable use of resources;
- developing financial instruments for the agriculture sector – to promote growth;
- establishing and enforcing judicial processes for land and property rights, and for resolving contract disputes;
- ensuring the availability of market information and statistics to facilitate market activity and to monitor market progress;
- creating joint R&D between the public sector, the private sector and universities.

CASE EXAMPLE The growth of the Brazilian agriculture industry[5-9]

At the beginning of 2014, Brazil's Ministry of Agriculture, Livestock and Food Supply anticipated a record year for the agriculture and agribusiness sector. The ministry forecast an output of 90 million tons of soybeans (making it the world's largest soybean producer) and 193 million tons of harvested grain, moving Brazil closer to becoming one of the world's top food producers. When Russia banned imports of certain key food items from Europe as a retaliation for Europe's ban on companies working with Russian banks and the energy sector, Russia had to turn to Brazil for its supply of chicken and beef. Brazil is the world's largest meat exporter. Brazilian food exporters could take the opportunity to build supply chain relationships with Russian importers to replace European competitors when Russia lifts the ban.

In a report on the Brazilian agriculture industry in 2010, *The Economist* explained how Brazil in the previous 30 years had turned from being a food importer into one of the world's top food producers and exporters. Companies such as BrasilAgro are using a combination of farming methods and new technology to make the projects successful. BrasilAgro buys neglected farms and modernizes them, uses radio transmitters to monitor weather patterns, uses SAP software to create efficiencies and provides employment to the local population, along with infrastructure development of the road network, which facilitates the harvest's journey to Brazil's ports thousands of kilometres away. Brazil currently uses only about 15 per cent of its arable land and it has an abundance of renewable water, hence as a country it does not have the challenges faced by some other countries with regard to land and water scarcity. However, the challenge in Brazil was the unskilled approach to farming. The Brazilian Agriculture Research Corporation, set up in 1973, modified the farming approach to farming using a scientific approach and created a robust method of agriculture. Instead of cutting down the Amazon jungles, it used land within the savannah (1,000 kilometres away from the forests) for agriculture. The land was not arable and so it created arable land using scientific methods. For cattle feed, it crossbred a species of grass from Africa to create a high-yield grass cattle feed and it also crossbred soybeans to make a variety that would grow in Brazil's climatic conditions. Farming moved from one crop per year to two crops per year, doubling the yield. The organization worked on creating a forest, agriculture and livestock integration farming system where the same land is used for farming and livestock feeding alternately. Also, it pioneered a new farming technique known as 'no-till' in which, during harvest, it leaves the stalk quite high and lets it rot into the soil as natural green manure. The ground is not tilled for the next crop; instead, the seeds are sown directly over the green manure.

The biggest challenge for Brazil's agribusiness sector is logistics infrastructure. The movement of harvest is mainly done using roads and lorries, which takes a lot of time as the major port is far from the farms. China, however, has interests in Brazilian commodities and will be taking the opportunity to invest in railroads to reduce transportation time and costs. Initially, China had a strategy of investing in farmland, mines and so on. However, since this was viewed with suspicion by the government, it has changed strategy to invest in processing plants rather than farms. This puts China very strategically into the agri-chain and hence it will have access to the produce directly.

Univar Brasil is a diversified company with interests in sectors including food, cosmetics, polyurethane and industrial paints. Its food business distributes additives and ingredients from well-known manufacturers to clients in markets such as bakery, meat and dairy products, sauces, soups, condiments, beverages, pet food and sweets. The company was formed when the parent company Univar made the move into the Brazilian market two years ago. The company has seen a very high growth within the processed food sector too, and as a supplier of food ingredients and sweeteners it has had the opportunity to innovate as the capability of the agribusiness sector increases and export markets open up. The company believes that the Brazilian agribusiness sector will need government support to develop infrastructure but that the industry also needs to concentrate on the global supply chain with a drive to innovate and create strategic partnerships.

CASE EXAMPLE The impact of the Fukushima disaster on Japanese food exports[10–15]

On Friday 11 March 2011, a very powerful earthquake of magnitude 9.0 struck northeast Japan, 80 miles east of the city of Sendai, in Miyagi prefecture, in the Pacific Ocean. The earthquake generated a massive tsunami that struck the coasts of Iwate prefecture, just north of Miyagi prefecture, and Fukushima, Ibaraki and Chiba, the prefectures extending along the Pacific coast south of Miyagi. The tsunami disabled the power supply and cooling of three Fukushima Daiichi reactors, causing a nuclear accident on 11 March 2011. All three cores largely melted in the first three days. This caused a radiation leak over a 29 km zone. Officials in Japan issued warnings against the consumption of local food and water. The Japanese government halted shipments of local produce and advised against eating leafy vegetables from the region. The World Health Organization, Food and Agricultural Organization and the International Atomic Energy Agency were monitoring radioactivity within food levels. Singapore stopped imports of milk, meat, vegetables and grain. As a precaution, the United States, Australia, New Zealand and Russia banned food imports from the regions of Fukushima, Gunma, Ibaraki and Tochigi. Stores across Asia withdrew Japanese food from the shelves, restaurants and hotels dropped Japanese food from their menus and major airlines stopped ordering Japanese food. In September, South Korea banned all fish imports from Japan's northeastern coast owing to the suspicion of radioactive water leaking into the Pacific Ocean. This ban was for all fish caught around the 692 km coastline and did not restrict it to the affected region only.

In March 2013, two years after the incident, 44 countries and regions were still restricting imports from Japan. Canada and Mexico decided to lift the restriction; however, China and South Korea continued with restrictions on mushrooms, fish and spinach. The Japanese government and the Japan External Trade Organization have been working on restoring consumer confidence and trying to reconnect Japanese food to the international food network.

In August 2014, Fukushima exported the first batch of rice (300 kg of the Koshihikari brand) to Singapore. The nuclear fallout affected the Japanese food export sector and it will take a considerable amount of time for the food supply chains to resume as normal.

CASE EXAMPLE   The cucumber fallout between Germany and Spain[16-19]

An outbreak of E. coli occurred in Germany in May 2011. As the outbreak spread and people were infected with the bacteria, German health officials announced on 26 May that cucumbers imported from Spain were the sources of the E. coli outbreak. Spanish authorities went on the defensive as the outbreak spread to 10 countries, killing 16 people and affecting in excess of 1,500 people. The outbreak also spread to Sweden, Denmark, The Netherlands, Norway, Switzerland, Poland, France and Britain. However, no one in Spain was affected.

The origin of the outbreak was blamed on organic cucumbers grown in the Andalusia region of southern Spain. After Germany's announcement, European countries recalled the cucumbers and took them off the shelves. Belgium blocked the import of cucumbers, whereas Austria and Russia banned cucumbers and tomatoes from Spain. After tests were conducted on the cucumbers from the Andalusian region and on water and soil samples, it was found that the contamination did not originate in Spain. However, by the time Germany's agricultural minister Robert Kloos had publicly cleared Spanish cucumbers, it had affected international trade in fresh vegetables across Europe as most farmers growing cucumbers had to throw away their produce, which amounted to hundreds of tonnes per day.

Summary

This chapter has presented a discussion of international food supply chains and the external factors that influence them. The benefits of supply chain management have been discussed in brief. International food supply chains are influenced by environmental changes, over which they have no control. The chapter discussed some of the factors that currently, and will in the future, influence how these chains operate. Managing the challenges within these chains is difficult, hence there are recommendations to use four factors to alleviate some of the challenges. These factors are: trust, relationships, governance and internal controls. Since food supply chains cross international boundaries, they are affected by national politics and it is important to get a perspective on this. Finally, the chapter ended with a few case examples that depict the points discussed within the chapter.

Notes

1 Roekel, J V, Willems, S and Boselie, D M (2002) Agri-Supply Chain Management: To stimulate cross-border trade in developing countries and emerging economies, World Bank, Washington, DC

2 Government Office for Science (2011) Foresight. The Future of Food and Farming: Final Project Report, Government Office for Science, London

3 Cha, A E and Zacharia, J (2010) Russia bans grain exports because of fire and drought, sending prices soaring, Washington Post Foreign Service, 6 August

4 WTO (accessed 20 February 2015) Understanding the WTO Agreement on Sanitary and Phytosanitary Measures, May 1998 [Online] http://www.wto.org/english/tratop_e/sps_e/spsund_e.htm

5 Rudrakanchana, N (accessed 20 February 2015) Brazil's Record Harvest: Grains, soybeans and cattle to see interesting 2014, IBTimes, 11 February 2014 [Online] http://www.ibtimes.com/brazils-record-harvest-grains-soybeans-cattle-see-interesting-2014-1554721

6 Rapoza, K (accessed 20 February 2015) Putin's European Food Ban, Bad for Russia Good for Brazil, *Forbes*, 8 October 2014 [Online] http://www.forbes.com/sites/kenrapoza/2014/08/10/putins-european-food-ban-bad-for-russia-good-for-brazil/

7 Cremaq, P (accessed 20 February 2015) Brazilian Agriculture: The miracle of the cerrado, *The Economist*, 26 August 2010 [Online] http://www.economist.com/node/16886442

8 Trevisani, P and Jelmayer, R (accessed 20 February 2015) China Looking to Play Larger Role in Funding Brazil's Infrastructure, *The Wall Street Journal*, 13 July 2014 [Online] http://www.wsj.com/articles/china-looking-to-play-larger-role-in-funding-brazils-infrastructure-1405288036

9 Ingredients Insight (accessed 20 February 2015) Brazil: A cornerstone of the ingredients supply chain, 1 November 2013 [Online] http://www.ingredients-insight.com/features/featurebrazil-a-cornerstone-of-the-ingredients-supply-chain/

10 BBC News (accessed 20 February 2015) Japanese Imported Vegetables in Singapore 'Radioactive', 24 March 2011 [Online] http://www.bbc.co.uk/news/business-12834153

11 World Nuclear Association (accessed 24 February 2015) Fukushima Accident (updated 2015) [Online] http://www.world-nuclear.org/info/Safety-and-Security/Safety-of-Plants/Fukushima-Accident/

12 http://www.cbsnews.com/news/south-korea-bans-fish-imports-from-japan-coast-affected-by-leaking-fukushima-nuclear-plant/

13 CBS News (accessed 24 February 2015) South Korea Bans Fish Imports from Japan Coast Affected by Leaking Fukushima Nuclear Plant, 6 September 2013 [Online] http://www.japantimes.co.jp/news/2013/03/09/national/japanese-food-still-banned-in-44-states/#.VMAnd0esVqU

14 Bloomberg Business (accessed 24 February 2015) Asian Stores, Eateries Drop Japan Food on Radiation Fears, 21 March 2011 [Online] http://www.bloomberg.com/news/2011-03-21/asian-hotels-stores-restrict-japanese-food-imports-after-radiation-found.html

15 Hongo, J (accessed 24 February 2015) Fukushima Rice Exports to Resume: First batch to Singapore, Wall Street Journal Japan, 19 August 2014 [Online] http://blogs.wsj.com/japanrealtime/2014/08/19/fukushima-rice-exports-to-resume-first-batch-headed-to-singapore/

16 Govan, F (2011) Killer cucumbers row between Spain and Germany, *Daily Telegraph*, 30 May

17 Neild, B (2001) How serious is Germany's E Coli outbreak? CNN, 3 June

18 Magnusson, N (2011) Hamburg bistros suffer salad-shunning after E Coli outbreak, Bloomberg, *Businessweek*, 9 June

19 DW (accessed 24 February 2015) Blame Game Begins over German E. coli Outbreak, 1 June 2011 [Online] http://www.dw.de/blame-game-begins-over-german-e-coli-outbreak/a-15118081

Collaboration and relationships

07

Supply chain relationships are of vital importance within food supply chains. In recent times, when instances of food fraud and crime have surfaced across international food supply chains, the debate and discussion around relationships and trust is vociferous. Food supply chains are dynamic not only because of the characteristics of the product they carry but also the fact that they are vitally important to the final consumer and the health of a nation. The topic presented in this chapter regarding supply chain relationships is multidisciplinary, as it covers an array of influencing subject areas from psychology, human resources, innovation, sustainability, power, finance and economics, to name a few. Hence, the area is dynamic and relationship analysis can take various forms based on the influencing variables. The chapter presents various perspectives and theories on buyer–supplier relationships and applies them within the food supply chain.

Trends in supply chain relationships

The actual dynamics of the supply chain and the role of each entity at the inter-organizational boundary are very important. Supply chain relationships across different sectors have been studied in the context of changing business trends:

- increasing incidence of vertical integration and disintegration;
- implementation of supplier-base programmes;
- focusing on operations;

- outsourcing;

- just-in-time (JIT);

- increasing popularity of partnerships and partnership sourcing.

The emphasis upon managing the supply chain as a source of competitive advantage has led many organizations to reassess the role of the supplier within their strategic plan to achieve or sustain competitiveness and customer service. This has led to the development of supplier partnership programmes and vendor development as a strategic function. However, not every relationship provides a mutual benefit, and in the food sector power in the chain has become a concern where the upstream feel squeezed. Generally, the most powerful entity controls the chain and dictates the operation of the chain. Relationship management is thus also a function of the power structure of the chain. Most research focuses on improving relationships, but the solutions are more tailored to meet the requirements of the most powerful entity in the chain. It is thus important to understand the tenets of these relationship scenarios and the theoretical underpinnings before applying them to the food sector. The following pages discuss various theories within supplier relationship management.

Transaction cost economics (TCE)

TCE focuses on the costs involved in making transactions rather than the costs of producing a product. Williamson put forth the theory of TCE to explain how buyer–supplier relationships are constructed and managed. The governance mechanisms under these relationships are influenced by three assumptions:

- Individuals in any economic system have a bounded rationality. It means that while people intend to be rational, in reality their cognitive capabilities are limited.

- At least some individuals are inclined to be opportunistic or to act in self-interest or guile.

- Information is asymmetrically distributed. Thus, parties in many transactions have access to only incomplete, imperfect or imbalanced information.[1,2]

In the TCE framework, the costs of any transaction comprise the costs of planning, adopting and monitoring operations. In the case of a high level of collaboration, the buyer–supplier relationship will be close to the vertical mode of governance, whereas in cases of lower levels of collaboration, the relationship will be close to the spot-market mode of governance. Transaction-specific investments in the form of physical or human assets (dedicated solely to the relationship) are critical and could transform the nature of the exchange between the partners. These dedicated investments could also be effective in limiting opportunistic behaviour within the relationship.

Relational contracting

Macneil[3] developed a typology of business relationships as discrete versus relational exchanges. A discrete exchange is under the assumption that individual transactions are independent of past or future relations between the contracting parties and constitute nothing more than the transfer of ownership of a product or service. This resembles the spot-market transaction. In a relational exchange, historical and social contexts in which recurrent transactions have taken place influence the relationship. Relational exchange views the enforcement of obligations due to the mutuality of interests between a set of parties.

The creation of a relational exchange also suggests that the relationship is recurrent and hence requires a more strategic view than a one-off transaction. However, the original approach to purchasing was to 'get the right component at the right price', and was based on one-off transactions between buyers and sellers, namely two individuals within two separate organizations. The transactions would generally tend to be the active buyer dictating terms and conditions to a passive supplier. Hence, most of the focus in the purchasing literature and in the industrial environment tended to favour the buyer, the customer being the most important entity in the relationship. Even though terms such as 'collaboration' or 'partnership' have expanded the approach taken by purchasing to supplier management and supplier development activities, the dominant role played in these relationships is generally by the buyer or customer. Supplier development also has connotations of a process where the active buyer will help to improve its suppliers either through skills or through a financial resource approach.

Collaboration

Collaboration is a process to create integration between supply chain members for mutual benefit, resource sharing and to achieve common objectives. Collaboration will promote exchange of information and resources (including human skills). Close collaboration can help in reducing business uncertainty and risks. It also increases opportunities with access to technology and innovation.

Vertical collaboration involves collaboration with customers and suppliers and within the organization's internal supply chain. Horizontal collaboration involves internal collaboration within the organization and its entities, but also external collaboration with competitors and other organizations. Internal collaboration refers to an organization's collaborative culture (for example, existence of elements of trust and commitment). External downstream collaboration involves customer relationship management, while external upstream collaboration involves supplier management. Within a supply network there will be different levels of relationship. There will be a few relationships that are strategic with close collaboration, whereas others will be transactional. Collaboration can be discussed under three forms:

- Transaction collaboration: this involves simple communication and partners exchanging data.
- Cooperative collaboration: this involves partners sharing data and processes and setting common supply chain objectives.
- Cognitive collaboration: this requires higher levels of involvement, as partners work together in joint planning and decision making and develop a relationship of mutual trust and interdependence.

Partnerships

A partnership is a relationship between individuals or organizations which is based on mutual interdependence and the agreement to cooperate towards achieving common goals and objectives. This is derived to some extent from cognitive collaboration. Partnering increases the ability of the organization to coordinate communication between the supply chain entities and utilize resources efficiently. In a partnership, failure to perform by either party severely impacts the performance of the other. The human element within supply chain partnerships is extremely important in order to make the partnership work, and hence changes to organizational culture and behaviour are necessary when forming supply chain partnerships. The transition from adversarial supply chain relationships to cooperative relationships is difficult for many managers, and supply chain entities should spend time and effort in training the individuals involved in partnering relationships and work towards a cultural change within the organization.

Power influences within supply chain relationships

Power is defined as the ability of one actor to affect the behaviour of another. Having or acquiring power is an attractive option for a business in a supply network, because it increases its ability to gain maximum advantage for itself. However, the situation is complex in that, although a business may have power as a supplier to one firm, it may not have power with another supplier and may also be subject to the power of a buyer. All firms attempt to frame their relationships with outside bodies to their own advantage. This advantage is designed to maximize their own revenue and keep competitors out. Having and wielding power does not necessarily have negative connotations for the others in the relationship that are less powerful. All companies will be in a variety of relationships, some where they do have power and many where they do not. The important decision for companies when getting involved in supply chains is about how they will control and manage the primary supply chain. They face decisions about where they should position themselves in the chain. At one end, they can decide to integrate the whole chain vertically, from raw material to end customer, or, at the other end, can decide to own only one or two of the resources that exist in the chain. The suppliers will have counter-strategies to gain power. The routes the suppliers will try to take will be to increase value appropriation from their relationships with buyers.

Some companies will see it as their role to control, or try to control, the network. Generally, the roles that each entity in the network perceives for itself as a member of the network will decide the power structure of the network. A firm may try to increase its power over activities and resources. The series of dyadic relationships between entities will eventually lead to a pattern of power in the network and, as many proponents of network theory have said, a supply network rarely has a single powerful entity; the network has firms exerting power at different positions depending upon the relative dyadic relationships around the position.

The issue of power is usually accepted as a circumstance of collaboration and many companies accept the rules and conditions applied by their often larger and more powerful collaborator. The situation becomes more serious if there is a problem to be negotiated where one of the partners stands to lose a considerable amount if it does not at least achieve some compensation. In a problem situation when a consignment of goods has been received but is now not wanted, the more powerful member may attempt to maximize its own position, perhaps at the expense of the other, less dominant partner. Hence power has value in that it enables a business to optimize its relationship strategically in favour of its preferred strategy, but can also be used inappropriately or in a manner that causes damage to a relationship. The application of power applied appropriately to define rules of partnership or inappropriately to gain advantage in a problem situation is not always the same as opportunistic behaviour.

Opportunistic behaviour

Opportunism extends the conventional assumption that economic agents are guided by considerations of self-interest to make allowances for strategic behaviour. This can lead to opportunistic behaviour, which includes actions such as lying, cheating and stealing, dishonouring an implicit contract and failing to fulfil promises or obligations, the implication being that the party that is opportunistic is not trustworthy. Opportunistic behaviour involves one partner either having access to information that the other partner does not have or taking advantage of the information asymmetry to gain business advantage. Within a scenario of asymmetric information and uncertainty about the future, there will be incentives for opportunistic behaviour by both parties. A variety of behaviours can occur between partners; some may involve opportunistic gaming to acquire more power for one organization or the use of power to get some desirable end result for one partner. Opportunism may involve misrepresentations, not responding to the transaction within the stipulated time or making unreasonable demands on account of power asymmetry.

As a buyer and supplier become increasingly suspicious of each other, there is a decreasing motivation to make the exchange successful through coordination efforts, common investments and information sharing. If any of the parties are suspicious of opportunistic behaviour, the information sharing stops and exchange deteriorates. If the agents in the transaction have established trust over a prolonged period of time, this tends to limit the opportunistic behaviour and encourage more open communication. Similarly, if they have bilateral and shared investments in the outcome of the collaboration and they have shared goals about outcomes, this limits the opportunistic behaviour.

Unethical behaviour

Unethical activities identified in buyer–supplier relationships are:

- over-committing resources or production schedules;
- increasing prices when there is a shortage of supply of the purchased material or product;
- allowing the supplier to become dependent on the purchasing organization for most of its business;
- cancelling purchase orders in progress and trying to avoid cancellation charges;
- overestimating demand to gain volume discounts;
- concocting a second source of supply to gain advantage over suppliers;
- allowing the personalities of the supplier to affect decisions.

Considering the activities depicted as unethical, it will seem as if these activities are normal and that a company may have to follow any or all of them in order to make profit and stay afloat. But these are deemed unethical[4] as they hurt the other party and create a regressive relationship. Purchasing managers can have a significant influence over a firm's reputation. Because these individuals interact frequently with suppliers and other upstream channel members, their behaviour can and does affect how the firm is viewed by suppliers and other outside organizations. The human factor has thus a very important part to play in keeping the perceptions right and thus maintaining the relationship. The discussion in this section is regarding how organizations engage in unethical behaviour within the relationship. This section does not deal with the unethical behaviour depicted by suppliers (for example, employing child labour in manufacturing activity, dispensing toxic effluents within the local water streams, and so on), as this will be discussed under the aspects of sustainability. However, if a supplier is engaging in this activity as a breach of trust within the relationship, it will be unethical behaviour within the relationship or collaboration.

Trust

The need for trust between partners has been identified as an essential element of buyer–supplier relationships. Trust is an important lubricant of relationships and binds parties into a common objective. Trust guides behaviour in business settings, and when trust is operative the risk of opportunism and market instability is reduced. Long-term relationships and trust encourage effective communication, information sharing and joint pay-offs. Trust therefore leads to an expectation that the collaborative party will not engage in opportunistic behaviours, but instead will create opportunities that are beneficial to both the organizations involved in the relationship. Trust takes time to build, and is the result of a succession of positive experiences. Trust has been discussed with the intention of making the reader aware that it plays a major factor in the relationship even after the transaction between the collaborating partners has ended. The result or pay-off of the transaction will decide whether trust is building up or deteriorating. Hence, simplistically, whenever collaborating supply chain entities conduct any transaction, all that they need to ask is whether this transaction will help in increasing trust or reducing it.

Current relationship models within the food sector

The retail environment has been instrumental in influencing relationship models within the food supply chain. These models are common across the retail sector; however, the complexity of the food supply chain and the product characteristics present additional challenges. Some of the most popular models are as follows.

Just-in-time (JIT)

JIT is an inventory management methodology in which inventory is ordered and stored as required by the process. The methodology was adopted from the automotive sector and works on the philosophy of 'pull'. Inventory is 'pulled in' only when there is a demand for it. This can be as raw material in the manufacturing supply chain or finished goods in the retail chain. The objective is to have only demand-led inventory in the chain, thus reducing costs by reducing excess inventory. The chain relies less on forecasts and tries to create a smooth flow by responding to demand quickly. Partnerships and close working with the suppliers are important for JIT systems to work efficiently. Clear communication of demand, objectives and timelines is essential for suppliers to deliver the products or raw material effectively. However, since the demand flows upstream to ensure a smooth flow downstream, it also leads to a flow of power upstream, as the suppliers have to buy into the requirement to deliver non-standard inventory numbers at short notice. As uncertainty creeps in, JIT can be modified to 'just-in-case', leading to excess inventory. However, in cases of uncertainty and risk it has been noticed within the food sector that JIT is not tenable and causes more challenges than advantages.[5] The ideal situation would be to have continuous replenishment of inventory managed by the supplier. This has led to the development of a new methodology, 'vendor-managed inventory'.

Vendor-managed inventory (VMI)

VMI is one of the most widely discussed partnering initiatives in recent times for improving supply chain efficiency. It is also known as continuous replenishment or supplier-managed inventory and was introduced by Walmart and Procter & Gamble. In a VMI partnership, the supplier is in charge of the main inventory replenishment decisions for the downstream organization. The vendor monitors the buyer's inventory levels (physically or via electronic messaging) and makes periodic decisions regarding order quantities, shipping and timing. Since this is a close working partnership, it is in the interests of the buyer to provide the necessary information to the supplier to enable quick and timely decision making. Successful implementation of VMI often depends on computer platforms, communications technology, product identification and tracking systems. Barcoding for product identification or RFID technology is also helpful at distribution centres in order to have dynamic visibility of the inventory. With VMI, the frequency of replenishment is usually decided by the supplier to suit their production/transfer schedule and to maintain a much smoother demand signal at the factory. This reduces costs through efficient resource and reduces the need for large buffer stocks. The vendor can make replenishment decisions according to operating needs with a greater awareness of demand trends and volatility. The buyer benefits from low stocks, which helps the buyer's performance. From a food retailer's perspective, product availability is essential to provide excellent customer service levels. Ensuring product availability on the shelf to guarantee a sale in normal circumstances and, more importantly, in scenarios of product promotion is essential. Hence, a dependable supplier is a necessity. Short-shelf-life food products such as ready-made meals, salads, yoghurts, desserts and so forth require regular replenishment (ideally on a daily basis), whereas long-life items such as canned foods could be replenished based on inventory models such as ROP (reorder point) or Kanban, among others. The retailers will need to share EPOS (electronic point of sales) or shelf inventory data with the suppliers to ensure timely delivery of the required inventory.

Efficient consumer response (ECR)

In the early 1990s, the US grocery sector and subsequently the European sector laid the foundation for the launch of the 'efficient consumer response' process. JIT and VMI had focused the upstream supply chain to work on the basis of pull philosophy coupled with access to downstream inventory information and the ability to take replenishment decisions. To enable the food sector to work using a collaborative partnership approach, the ECR initiative provided the platform for cooperation and coordination facilitated by the exchange of information. The basis of ECR is to have a holistic view of the complete chain and for firms to work together to create value-adding processes that work efficiently at appropriate levels of cost. Value addition is done by identifying consumer needs and choices. The process can work effectively and efficiently only if there is a seamless flow of information upstream through the chain. Although the process was used for commodity items, fresh fruit, vegetables and fresh meat, it was more popular for 'own-label' retailer products. This required retailers to have complete control over their supply chains and the ECR methodology provided this effectively.

Collaborative planning, forecasting and replenishment (CPFR)

CPFR is a tool used to enhance the supply chain performance to lower inventories and logistic costs and to create efficiency in the whole supply chain for all participants. CPFR works through sharing key information about the supply chain between suppliers and retailers (sellers and buyers) who work together to satisfy the needs of the end customer. CPFR uses cooperation and information sharing continuously in all phases, from strategy and planning to the execution phase. The stages within CPFR are as follows:

1 In the *collaboration arrangement* phase, the buyer and seller set up the scope of the framework and define common goals

and responsibilities. After the arrangement process is finished, both parties should form a joint business plan, where significant events affecting supply and demand are identified.

2 In the *forecasting* phase, consumer demand is forecast through the sales forecasting task. This is used to build an order-planning/forecasting schedule by mapping out the inventory lead-times, current inventory stocks and logistic restrictions.

3 In the *execution* phase, order generation is used to transform forecasts to firm up the demand profile.

4 In the *order fulfilment* phase, the goods are produced, shipped and stocked for further processing.

5 In the *analysis phase*, exception management and performance assessment are used to monitor constantly any sudden changes in quality. The phase provides key metrics to evaluate the success of the business goals and to monitor the trends in the industry that can help to change the strategy more quickly if necessary.

The benefits of the CPFR process include better store-shelf stock rates, lower inventory levels, higher sales and lower logistics costs. Store-shelf stock rates refer to the rate at which products are replenished on the store shelf after purchase. Joint sales forecasting drives production scheduling, distribution planning and store activity planning. If there are any changes to the forecast demand beyond an agreed-upon threshold, an exceptions report helps in generating collaborative actions by both parties to rectify the variance.

Other trends within supply chain collaboration

There are some other trends emerging within supply chain collaboration which are not covered by the collaborative platforms. These trends are discussed under the following activities:

- *Managing demand.* Some of the other trends for managing demand at the customer's end are managing stocks and products using merchandizing and category management principles and the effective and efficient utilization of retail and warehouse space. On the manufacturer's side, trends in collaborative product design and new product introductions are creating collaborative provisions.

- *The fulfilment process.* Transportation carriers, freight forwarders and public warehouse operators are currently not involved in the collaborative mechanism. For dynamic management of supply chains and stocks, these entities are required to be part of the collaborative platform.

- *Optimization.* This involves utilizing collaborative relationships and data systems to optimize operations across the entire supply chains.

- *Real-time collaboration.* This requires managing uncertainties and risks both on the supply and on the demand side, using real-time collaboration platforms.

CASE EXAMPLE   Starbucks and collaborative relationship with suppliers[6]

Starbucks prides itself on its commitment to buy and serve high-quality coffee that is sourced ethically and grown sustainably. Starbucks focuses on a holistic approach to map its coffee supply chain and work with suppliers and their network of farmers to implement responsible purchasing practices. It has developed an approach known as the Coffee and Farmer Equity Practice (C.A.F.E.) in collaboration with Conservation International. The C.A.F.E. process is a set of measurable standards focusing on:

- product quality;
- economic accountability;
- social responsibility;
- environmental leadership.

The standards are utilized to measure the performance of the individual farms. However, they also make sure that the suppliers are treating the farmers fairly and providing the correct price for the consignments.

To maintain long-term sustainability of the coffee plantations and farms, Starbucks invests in the farmer network through farmer support centres, loan programmes and forest conservation efforts. The company helps farmers by training them in farm management techniques and also supports coffee plantations through coffee replanting and tracking climate-change impacts.

Summary

This chapter has presented the current thinking and activities around creating collaboration within food supply chains. Multidisciplinary theories were presented, which dealt with collaboration and relationships. These are:

- TCE;
- relational contracting;
- collaboration;
- partnerships;
- power;
- opportunistic behaviour;
- unethical behaviour;
- trust.

The chapter also discussed four collaboration models currently used in the food sector. These are: JIT, VMI, ECR and CPFR. The challenge in the food supply chain is to utilize the appropriate collaborative tool to balance supply-side inventory to consumer demand. This will ensure that the products flowing downstream to the consumers fulfil the consumer requirements in terms of product choice, quality and safety.

Notes

1 Williamson, O (1979) Transaction cost economics: the governance of contractual relations, *Journal of Law and Economics*, **22**, pp 233–61

2 Williamson, O (1985) *The Economic Institutions of Capitalism*, Free Press, New York

3 Macneil, I R (1980) *The New Social Contract: An inquiry into modern contractual relations*, Yale University Press, New Haven, CT

4 Dubinsky, A J and Gwin, J M (1981) Business ethics: Buyers and sellers, *Journal of Purchasing and Materials Management*, **17** (4), pp 9–16

Felch, R I (1985) Standards of conduct: The key to supplier relations, *Journal of Purchasing and Materials Management*, **21** (3), pp 16–18

Husted, B W, Dozier, J B, McMahon, J T and Kattan, M W (1996) The impact of cross-national carriers of business ethics on attitudes about questionable practices and form of moral reasoning, *Journal of International Business Studies*, **27** (2), pp 391–411

Van den Hengel, J (1995) Purchasing ethics: Strain or strategy?, *Purchasing and Supply Management, September*, pp 50–52

Trevisan, R E (1986) Developing a statement of ethics: A case study, *Journal of Purchasing and Materials Management*, **22** (3), pp 8–14

Rudelius, W and Buchholz, R A (1979) What industrial purchasers see as key ethical dilemmas, *Journal of Purchasing and Materials Management*, **15**(4), 2–10

5 Peck, H (2006) Resilience in the Food Chain: A Study of Business Continuity Management in the Food and Drink Industry, Final Report to the Department for Environment, Food and Rural Affairs, London

6 Starbucks (accessed 17 February 2015) Coffee [Online] http://www.starbucks.com/responsibility/sourcing/coffee

Food sourcing and procurement   08

Sourcing of raw material has been an important activity in all types of organization. Raw material takes various forms – material for further processing, material for secondary use (for example, stationery) and material for selling to the final consumer (retailers). Sourcing in this case is identifying the appropriate source of the material and evaluating it for conformance. However, after identifying the source, it is important to manage the process of ordering the material and receiving it. Broadly this is the 'purchasing' process. The process that manages the sourcing and purchasing process is broadly referred to as 'procurement'. These terms are used synonymously in the literature and in industry. However, this is not so much of a problem as the nomenclature within industry is dependent upon the size of the company and the organizational structure. Within an SME (small or medium-sized enterprise), the three roles may be conducted by a single person, whereas in a large company there will be individuals in procurement, sourcing, purchasing and supply chain roles. Hence, it is important to understand these processes and how they influence the food supply chain. Trade liberalization has opened up national boundaries and increased international trade. The opening of markets has increased retail environments across the globe to cater to increased market demand in emerging markets. However, within the food sector a number of factors have increased the complexity of food sourcing. Some of these challenges are: sustainability practices and the influence on public policy, price volatility in food commodities, food availability, climatic impact, traceability and food safety. This chapter presents the concepts of sourcing and strategic sourcing, and also discusses sourcing challenges within the food sector and the guidelines for sustainable procurement.

Sourcing

Sourcing is the activity of securing raw materials or services needed by an organization for further value addition or for direct selling to the customer. Organizations employ different kinds of sourcing strategies depending on the sector and business model. A source is a place to acquire the raw material or the inputs to produce goods or services. Companies purchase resources from different locations, based on the scope of their activities or services. Some companies may source only locally, whereas others may source internationally with an objective to achieve the lowest costs. There will be different strategies and reasons for sourcing across different categories of product. Some categories will be more important than others and hence will need a greater strategic focus when sourcing. Sourcing strategy is defined as the approach developed by the company to procure supplies, for which four elements are required in the process: 'the buying policy, the number of sources, the type of source and the nature of the company supplier relationship'.[1] Global sourcing does have many benefits, lower costs being the primary one. Some other benefits include:

- access to new technology;
- access to market information;
- access to resources not available locally;
- development of alternative vendors.

However, there are certain risks associated with global sourcing. The risks will be shaped according to the country or region from where the products are being sourced. Some of the major drawbacks with global sourcing are: increased transportation costs due to fuel price volatility, increased possibilities of supply disruption due to natural disasters or political problems, hidden costs connected with cultural differences and time zones, financial risks due to changing economies, increased risk of intellectual property loss, and increased monitoring costs in comparison to domestic supply.[2]

Sourcing models

Low-cost sourcing

In this model, the company sources materials from different countries and locations with lower labour and production costs, with the aim of lowering operational costs. The principle is to achieve sourcing efficiency by identifying and utilizing cost differences between locations. The other variables also included in the sourcing decision will be quality and lead time.

Outsourcing and insourcing

Outsourcing is the act of purchasing goods or services from an external source. The strategy is usually functional, based on a decision to shift from an internal source to an external one. A company will decide to focus on its core competencies and prefer to outsource activities or products that are non-core. There are various advantages in outsourcing, such as cost reduction resulting from economies of scale and access to specialized investments and expertise. On the negative side, control over the operations will be reduced, leading to reduced flexibility to react to unpredictable changes in requirements. The problems with outsourcing depend on the type of outsourced items or services and their importance within the supply chain. Some challenges will arise due to quality and lead time non-conformance. There is also a threat from new competitors to emulate the business models and products if the sourcing is not conducted properly. Within the food industry, supermarkets will outsource the manufacturing of their own-label food products. Beverage companies will prefer to outsource bottling across international market sectors instead of setting up their own plants.

Internal sourcing, or insourcing, mainly aims at internal production or purchasing from a subsidiary of the organization, or bringing outsourced activities back into the company. Some companies will both outsource and insource critical raw material/products if they cannot rely completely on the supplier.

Single sourcing or multiple sourcing

There are different models of choosing the number of suppliers from which to source. This will depend upon the material or service being sourced, the availability of supply and the strategic importance to the sourcing company. If there is only one supplier in the world for the material and it is a monopolistic situation, the sourcing will be a *solo* sourcing approach. However, in a situation where there are a number of suppliers and the company decides to source from only one supplier, with the intention of creating a close collaborative relationship, the approach is termed *single* sourcing. At other times the company will prefer to have flexibility for responding to strategic consequences of source failure or for having more negotiating power in the relationship, and will utilize the approach of *multiple* sourcing. Some companies will use the multiple sourcing approach but restrict it to only two suppliers, in order to have close relationships and also create a safety net against supply disruption. This approach is termed *dual* sourcing.

In some cases, to maintain traceability and food safety it can be preferable to have a single source of supply, whereas within commodity-buying scenarios multiple sourcing can be advantageous. However, both have their disadvantages. Single sourcing creates the risk of disruption, whereas multiple sources may create quality and control issues.

Partnerships

Many professionals believe that managing sourcing relationships as partnerships, whether upstream or downstream, can lead to a considerable competitive advantage for the partners involved. In partnership sourcing, the supplier provides the customer with extensive access to its operations and management systems. The scenario is not limited to relationships that focus on single sourcing or cost reduction. For partnerships to work, collaboration between the supplier and customer is very important. This should be enabled by effective communication and mutual dependence on each other. Within close partnerships, as discussed in Chapter 7, customers will share data with the supplier to enable joint planning and demand management.

Purchasing models

Managing suppliers is an essential strategic issue for companies. As increasing numbers of products are purchased from external companies, the need for efficient and suitable purchasing strategies is vital. It is also important to consider not just the profitability or transactional aspect of the buyer–supplier relationship, but also the supplier's perspective and the interdependencies between the transacting entities. There are different approaches discussed in the purchasing literature with regard to the most effective methods for managing suppliers. One of the approaches is to create a purchasing portfolio for differentiated purchasing strategies across the supplier portfolio base. Other approaches focus on segmenting suppliers and/or supplier development. These approaches will also work in conjunction with the relationship strategy of the transacting entities, as discussed in Chapter 7.

Kraljic matrix

There are a number of portfolio approaches presented within the academic literature. However, one of the approaches that has been regularly followed both in industry and in academia is the Kraljic matrix, put forth by Peter Kraljic.[3] An example of the Kraljic matrix can be seen in Figure 8.1. The matrix introduced a model to classify the company's products in a two-dimensional matrix: profit impact and supply risk. The purpose of the Kraljic matrix is for companies to analyse their purchasing portfolio. With the pressure on purchasing professionals to consider sustainability parameters within their decision making, this model has come under some criticism for being overtly simple. However, it is still a very robust model for creating the initial purchasing strategy. The model is utilized in a four-stage approach: classification, market analysis, strategic positioning and action plans.

Classification

In the classification stage, the company has to classify all its purchased items. This is conducted by considering two different dimensions:

FIGURE 8.1 Kraljic matrix to classify purchasing

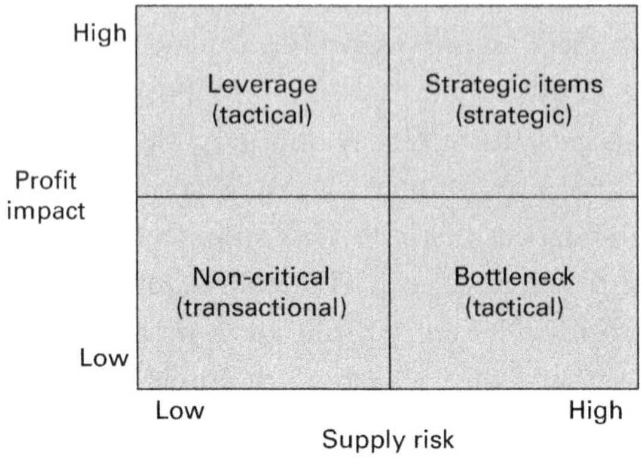

SOURCE: adapted from Kraljic, 1983

importance of purchasing and *complexity of the supply market.* The variable 'importance of purchasing' measures the importance of the purchased material to the company's operations, for example the percentage of raw material in total costs or the value added by the product line. The other variable, 'complexity of supply market', considers elements such as the availability of supply, the entry barriers to sourcing, the logistic cost and so on. The matrix classifies the type of purchased items into four types based on two variables: level of profits and the risk to supply. The four classifications are:

- *Strategic items (high profit impact, high supply risk)*
  These items are of high importance to the company. The focus should be on ensuring that there is no disruption to supply. The company should aim to develop long-term supply relationships, analysing and managing risks regularly and planning for contingencies.

- *Leverage items (high profit impact, low supply risk)*
  These items are important as they have an impact on profit. The company should have an approach of negotiating for low costs and using multiple sourcing with economies of scale.

- *Bottleneck items (low profit impact, high supply risk)*
  These items have a low influence on profit but can cause

problems through non-availability. It is necessary to make sure that these items are always available. Suitable approaches would be to have safety stock in the system, identify alternate suppliers and have more control over existing suppliers.

- *Non-critical items (low profit impact, low supply risk).* These items are not critical to the operations; however, they still need to be managed before they turn out to be critical or a bottleneck. The approach should be to use standard products available in the market and optimize order quantities.

Market analysis

In this stage, the company analyses its bargaining power in relation to the supplier. This involves an analysis of the market positioning of the two transacting companies, the relative utility to each other and the alternative sources of supply in the market.

Strategic positioning

The identification of the power position will determine the purchasing and negotiating strategy of the company. The company will determine its position in the relationship.[4] Power was discussed in Chapter 7.

Action plans

Depending upon the relative positioning of the company with its supplier and the status of interdependency, a purchasing strategy that includes volume, price, inventory policy and supplier selection should be considered. The plan can be based on three strategies:

- *Exploit:* the customer will use high buying power to secure good prices and long-term contracts to reduce the supply. This is a more aggressive stance.

- *Balance:* work towards close relationships on a level of interdependence mutually beneficial for both parties.

- *Diversify:* if the supplier is in a powerful position, reduce the supply risks by seeking alternative suppliers or alternative products.

Supplier segmentation

A normal buyer will have a relationship with a number of suppliers at any given time. The more complex the product, the greater will be the number of suppliers involved in the relationship. As discussed in Chapter 7, the relationship between the buyer and supplier will work at different levels of engagement depending on how close the relationship is. Levels of dependence on each other and the importance of the supply to the buyer company will influence how the relationship is nurtured.[5] One of the approaches to managing multiple suppliers across multiple product categories is to segment the supply base into categories, with a different strategy to manage each one. These categories can be organized depending on levels of risk, lead time and inventory policies, costs and so on. One of the segmentation approaches will be based on the levels of dependency and level of risk. This was discussed from the aspect of the product within the Kraljic matrix. In this section the discussion is around the relationship with the supplier. Suppliers can be segmented in three ways:[6]

1 *Strategic supplier*
  Within the portfolio of the supply base, a small number of suppliers will be in a very close working relationship with the buyer. These suppliers will be involved in new product development, will have shared assets and intellectual property and the supply will be very important for the buyer. The levels of risk will be high and the supplier will work with the buyer in a proactive approach to mitigate risks. The relationship will be based on transparency, joint communication and sharing of operational information. The relationship is based on interdependence and the supplier also has sufficient power in the relationship.

2 *Tactical supplier*
  These suppliers are vital to the day-to-day operations of the supply chain. They work with the buyer to maintain costs, lead times and quality standards, and in general they work to achieve the contractual terms. The relationship will largely be based on dependence, with the buyer setting out the terms of

the relationship. These suppliers are, however, still important to the company from a risk perspective and it is in the interests of the buyer to maintain close working relationships from a governance perspective.

3 *Transactional supplier*
These form the bulk of the suppliers in the portfolio, providing products on a transactional basis. The models used will be spot-buying or short-term sourcing. The relationship is buyer dominated, with a large number of suppliers to choose from, and decisions are based on lowest cost and best quality. The ability of the supplier to deliver the specific transaction is important. Long-term joint working plans do not feature in this relationship.

Supplier development

For strategic suppliers and supply situations that involve high risk, it is in the interests of the buyer to develop the capability of the strategic suppliers. The focus is to improve performance, invest in capabilities and work jointly to achieve common objectives. This approach is necessary to protect the supply base and develop it for competitive advantage. The buyer and supplier work together to improve performance by sharing operational data and working together on solutions. The buyer can help the supplier in lean implementation, work together on joint six-sigma projects or work with each other as regulatory environments change. The development process is both cost and time intensive and hence the buyer must choose the appropriate suppliers to develop. The process could be a formal supplier development programme or informal meeting of personnel or joint conferences or workshops. A formal supplier evaluation will be performed by the purchasing company in order to assess its suppliers. This evaluation process can help to identify where supplier development activities should be focused and will provide guidelines to review the outcomes derived from supplier development strategies.

Strategic sourcing

Strategic sourcing is an important activity in purchasing and supply management. It is a commercial process requiring extensive knowledge of the supply base and the strategic requirements of the company. It can be defined as 'satisfying business needs from markets via the proactive and planned analysis of supply markets and the selection of suppliers with the objective of delivering solutions to meet predetermined and agreed business needs'.[7] Developing the strategic sourcing strategy is a fundamental part of the purchasing and supply management process. Strategic sourcing provides: 1) improved ability of the organization to achieve strategic goals by aligning the purchasing function with strategic planning, and 2) improved return on investment (ROI) due to a better-focused purchasing approach.

Some of the approaches to enable strategic sourcing are:[8]

1 *Total cost procurement models*: These include all costs in the supply chain when comparing sources and source chains. Consider the total landed or life-cycle cost when purchasing, instead of just the transactional lower cost.

2 *Supplier relationships*: As seen in the previous section, segmenting suppliers as per relationship status will be essential to understand the strategic suppliers within the portfolio. One of the ways to create the segmentation is 'ABC analysis', also known as 'Pareto analysis'. Using this analysis, it can be ascertained that 20% of the suppliers will be accountable for 80% of the purchasing expenditure and will be classed as 'strategic' or 'A'. Roughly, 30% of the suppliers will account for 10% of the expenditure and will be classed as 'B' and the remaining 50% will account for the final 10% of the expenditure and will be classed as 'C'.

3 *Value-added services*: A value-mapping of the supply chain will help in understanding those activities or suppliers that add the maximum value to the product. Similarly, the analysis will disclose the non-value-adding activities. The strategic sourcing process will focus on the value-adding activities and work to optimize these further.

Sustainable procurement

The United Nations World Commission on Environment and Development defines sustainability as 'ensuring that we meet our needs without compromising the ability of future generations to meet their own needs'. This also means that as companies strive to increase their profitability, they should consider the impact of their operations on the environment and social system. The supply chains connecting companies across the world have a greater responsibility to create an equitable environment for all. Within the food industry, sustainability has a very important place as the raw material is derived from the planet. This part of the chapter will highlight specific processes to achieve sustainability within the sourcing of food. Sustainability within food supply chains is discussed in Chapter 13.

Sustainable food

The UK government's new food strategy, *Food 2030*,[9] sets out a vision for what it wants to achieve by 2030. These aims are:

- Consumers are informed, and can choose, and afford, healthy, sustainable food. This demand is met by profitable, competitive, highly skilled and resilient farming, fishing and food businesses, supported by first-class research and development.
- Food is produced, processed and distributed to feed a growing global population in ways that:
  - use global natural resources sustainably;
  - enable the continuing provision of the benefits and services given to us by a healthy natural environment;
  - promote high standards of animal health and welfare;
  - protect food safety;
  - make a significant contribution to rural communities; and
  - allow us to show global leadership on food sustainability.

- Our food security is ensured through strong UK agriculture and food sectors, and international trade links with EU and global partners which support developing economies.

- The UK has a low-carbon food system which is efficient in using resources – any waste is reused, recycled or used for energy generation.

The Scottish Government's National policy on Food and Drink[10] defines sustainable food as 'food that, through its production, processing, distribution, sale and consumption, provides a wide range of associated benefits, such as good-quality food, food which promotes good health and education, protects the environment, avoids unnecessary use of natural resources, and contributes towards economic development'.

One of the approaches taken by procurement professionals is to ascribe to certification programmes such as 'Fairtrade'. Fairtrade works for fairer conditions that help disadvantaged producers to tackle poverty and invest in a better, more stable future.

Requirements for sustainable procurement

Most large multinational food companies now follow a supplier code of conduct on the principles of the UN Global Compact.[11] The Code sets out a desire to do business with suppliers that follow responsible social and environmental practices. The UN Global Compact's ten principles focus on areas of human rights, labour, the environment and anti-corruption. The principles are derived from the following Acts:

- The Universal Declaration of Human Rights;
- The International Labour Organization's Declaration on Fundamental Principles and Rights at Work;
- The Rio Declaration on Environment and Development;
- The United Nations Convention Against Corruption.

A European project under the seventh framework identified the following key actions that public-sector organizations should implement for sustainable procurement:[12]

1 *Good governance*: Sustainable development goals should be linked to corporate objectives and must be represented in the procurement strategy.

2 *Identify sustainable food as a priority*: When procuring food, sustainable food should be the priority. The purchasing procedure should account for this priority in choice.

3 *Sustainable menus can deliver multiple dividends*: Within public-sector organizations such as the National Health Service, which procures and uses food on a regular basis, the menus and recipes should be prioritized for health, carbon reduction, seasonality and for a capacity to promote biodiversity, animal welfare, sustainable fisheries, good employment practices and training opportunities.

4 *Account for sustainability*: Create a methodology for evaluating supplier contracts that applies a whole life-cycle costing approach. This should account for social, environmental and economic benefits which accrue through sustainable food procurement and should also include an assessment of regional impacts.

5 *Help create the market for sustainable food*: Procurement organizations should actively work with foodservice contractors and suppliers to source sustainable food. Measures should be in place to include participation from small businesses (SMEs). This will help to develop a sustainable and more competitive supply base.

6 *Ensure contracts strengthen competition*: Priority should be given to include SMEs alongside larger businesses whether for food purchased through its own contracts or through a foodservice contractor on behalf of the organization. This will allow a range of businesses to participate.

7 *Stimulate demand for sustainable food*: Local and regional governments should inculcate policies to stimulate demand for sustainable food. This includes the support and infrastructure for food production and carbon reduction, food safety and quality accreditations, etc.

8 *Work with suppliers*: Work with suppliers, especially SMEs, to build ability and capability for supplying sustainable food.

9 *Skill and training*: Employees within the purchasing and catering functions should be skilled and trained to source and use sustainable food.

10 *Origin of sourced food*: All food procurement contracts should record the place of origin of food. This should be monitored by the public buying agency.

11 *Monitor food waste*: Create transparency and mechanisms to monitor food waste and report progress on minimizing food waste and on recycling.

The sustainable procurement process

'Sustainable procurement is a process whereby organizations meet their needs for goods, services, works and utilities in a way that achieves value for money on a whole life basis in terms of generating benefits not only to the organization, but also to society and the economy, whilst minimizing damage to the environment.'[13] This means that the procurement process in organizations focuses on sustainability variables equally when evaluating potential suppliers. The purchasing process will consider environmental and social factors as much as economic ones. Procurement professionals will consider variables such as carbon emissions, energy consumption, water consumption, child labour, living wage, effluent treatment, packaging waste and so on when considering supply contracts. The *Forum for the Future*[14] has suggested steps for public-sector organizations to integrate sustainability into the procurement process. These steps cover the following activities:

- Prioritizing contracts: This should be done on the basis of sustainability parameters.

- Demand analysis: Ensure the correct levels of ordering required. This will reduce wastage in the system.

- Identifying sustainability impact: Implement processes to improve the sustainability impact of the contract.

- A whole life-cycle costing approach to selecting suppliers: This will ensure that the costing process compares operating and disposal costs of sustainable alternatives.

In 2010, the British Standards Institute (BSI) published the world's first standard on sustainable procurement. This is the British Standard BS8903: Principles and framework for procuring sustainably. This builds upon the flexible framework[2] and gives practical guidance in areas such as policy and strategy, risk management, leadership and measurement as well as the procurement process itself. The standard is generic and is applicable to any organization or industry.

CASE EXAMPLE Mondeléz International[15,16]

Mondeléz International created the 'cocoa life', a cocoa sustainability programme. The programme proposes to invest $400 million over the next 10 years to fund sustainable cocoa production in the Asia Pacific region and around the world. The programme aims to reach more than 200,000 farmers across six countries and to source cocoa sustainably, with third-party verification, in turn benefiting more than a million people.

The approach of the programme is to work with partners in four key ways:

- *Farming*: helping farmers improve their yields and livelihoods to earn larger incomes.

- *Community*: empowering cocoa-farming families to create sustainable communities.

- *Youth*: working towards eliminating child labour by helping communities tackle its root causes, and making cocoa farming a more attractive profession.

- *Environment*: protecting landscapes to maintain ecosystems and provide viable environments and farming land for future generations.

The programme currently works with third-party experts such as the United Nations Development Programme, the World Wildlife Fund and Anti-Slavery International. The programme aims to collaborate with governments, civil society and suppliers, with a mission to transform the cocoa supply chain.

CASE EXAMPLE PepsiCo – responsible and sustainable sourcing[17]

PepsiCo's responsible sourcing strategy works in four main areas: supplier social capability management, environmental supplier outreach, sustainable packaging and sustainable agriculture.

Within the supply chain PepsiCo works globally with thousands of independent farmers, market intermediaries and some company-owned farms. The sourcing team works closely with the suppliers on a number of fronts:

- Supplier standards: The PepsiCo Global Procurement Supplier Social Capability Management Program helps suppliers to adhere to the PepsiCo's Supplier Code of Conduct, which comprises four elements: accountability, engagement, risk assessment and mitigation.

  The supplier code of conduct states the expectations from suppliers in the areas of labour practices, health and safety, environmental management and business integrity.

- Supplier diversity: PepsiCo views supplier diversity as an essential approach within supplier development and sourcing. Supplier diversity is considered an advantage as it helps to create a supplier base that mirrors the company's customer base and helps to develop innovations and develop minority communities economically.

- Environmental supplier outreach: PepsiCo works with suppliers to educate them to improve social responsibility performance across the supply chain. The company works with strategic suppliers on specific initiatives, including resource conservation programmes, setting quantifiable goals for energy, greenhouse gas, water, agriculture and forestry resource conservation within the extended supply chain.

- Rural development: The company works with farmers in rural areas who have small land holdings or low incomes. In India, PepsiCo India contracts directly with 24,000 potato farmers. In Colombia, it uses a direct purchasing model with small farmers, eliminating intermediaries.

Summary

This chapter has focused on the aspects of sourcing and procurement. The chapter discussed sourcing and purchasing. It discussed sourcing models and provided an insight into where these models can be applied. Purchasing was discussed within the aspects of portfolio analysis, supplier segmentation and supplier development approaches. An important development in the supply chain sector is the consideration of sustainable approaches and their impact on the procurement process. Governments in the EU are working towards creating an approach for sustainable procurement and would like supply chains to follow this. However, since this is a new paradigm, there are barriers to implementation on account of leadership, support and training. To help organizations, they are leading by example and have created sustainable procurement policies for public-sector organizations, especially in the UK. This chapter has touched upon sustainability, which will be discussed in detail in the context of food systems in Chapters 13 and 15.

Notes

1 Nicosia, N and Moore, N Y (2006) *Implementing Purchasing and Supply Chain Management: Best practices in market research*, RAND Corporation, Santa Monica, CA

2 Tsay, R and Pullman, G (2008) Unraveling the food supply chain: strategic insights from China and the 2007 pet food recalls, *Journal of Supply Chain Management*, **44** (1), pp 22–39

3 Kraljic, P (1983) Purchasing must become supply management, *Harvard Business Review*, **61** (5), pp 109–17

4 Buyer supplier power models – see work by Andrew Cox, Hunt and Levin, Porter's five forces.

5 Cox, A *et al* (2002) *Supply Chains, Markets and Power: Mapping buyer and supplier power regimes*, Routledge, London

6 Giguere, M and Goldbach, G (2012) Segment your suppliers to reduce risk, *Supply Chain Quarterly*, Quarter 3

7 CIPS (nd) Developing and Implementing a strategic Sourcing strategy, CIPS Knowledge Works, Knowledge Summary [Online] http://

www.cips.org/Documents/Resources/Knowledge%20Summary/
Strategic%20Sourcing%20Strategy.pdf

8 Kauffman, R G and Crimi, T A (2000) Procurement to Strategic
Sourcing: How to make the transition, ISM, 85th Annual International
Conference Proceedings [Online] http://www.ism.ws/pubs/proceedings/
confproceedingsdetail.cfm?ItemNumber=11534

9 Department for Environment, Food and Rural Affairs (2010) *Food
2030*, DEFRA, London, January

10 The Scottish Government (accessed 24 February 2015) National Food
and Drink Policy: 'Walking the Talk – Getting Government Right' –
The Procurement of Food by Public Sector Organizations [Online]
http://www.scotland.gov.uk/Publications/2009/11/12111724/1

11 United Nations Global Compact (accessed 24 February 2015) The Ten
Principles [Online] https://www.unglobalcompact.org/aboutthegc/
thetenprinciples/

12 Foodlinks (accessed 24 February 2015) Revaluing Public Sector Food
Procurement in Europe: An action plan for sustainability [Online]
http://www.foodlinkscommunity.net/fileadmin/documents_
organicresearch/foodlinks/publications/Foodlinks_report_low.pdf

13 Department for Environment, Food and Rural Affairs (2006) Procuring
the Future, DEFRA, London

14 Forum for the Future (2007) Buying a Better World: Sustainable public
procurement, Forum for the Future, London

15 Food and Drink Federation (accessed 24 February 2015) FDF Awards
2014 – Environmental Leadership: Mondeléz International – Cocoa
Life [Online] http://www.fdf.org.uk/2014-fdf-award-winners-
environmental-leadership.aspx

16 Mondeléz International – Cocoa Life (accessed 24 February 2015)
Home page [Online] http://www.cocoalife.org/

17 PepsiCo (accessed 24 February 2015) Responsible & Sustainable
Sourcing [Online] http://www.pepsico.com/purpose/Environmental-
Sustainability/Responsible-Sourcing

Risk management

09

The food sector has witnessed a number of high-profile food safety and contamination events in the recent past. These have not been focused in one country or one region, but spread across the world. Some of these have been due to negligence, but some have been intentional fraud. The global nature of food supply chains presents major challenges, as any contamination means that a number of supply networks across the globe may be affected, causing further problems. As global supply chains strive to deliver these products to the supermarket shelves, organizations start losing control over them. The exact supply chain path for a particular food product depends on the product characteristics, size and market power of the supply chain members.[1] The food supply cycle spans different organization types, continents, cultural systems, regulations and so forth. As entities within the supply chain increase, complexity increases due to issues related to trust, traceability and transparency. International food supply chains have challenges of *complexity and visibility*. In cases of food safety, it is not only important to understand the speed at which the contamination spreads globally, but also the responsibility and accountability for limiting the contamination.[2] As in any industry sector, the food sector and its extended supply chain is subject to many other sources of risk. It is important to understand the sources of these risks and the different ways to manage them. This chapter presents a discussion regarding risks encountered within food supply chains. It discusses risk sources, impacts and mitigation strategies.

Risk management and uncertainty

In his influential work *Risk, Uncertainty, and Profit*, Frank Knight[3] established the distinction between risk and uncertainty. According to Knight, a phenomenon which is unmeasurable is 'Uncertainty', whereas one that is measurable is 'Risk':

- Uncertainty cannot be assigned such a (well-grounded) probability (for example, when the SARS epidemic or the Avian flu happened the first time) when the event has never happened before and hence is an unknown event.

- Risk is defined as uncertainty based on a well-grounded (quantitative) probability (for example, hurricanes, machine breakdown, logistic delays, etc.). Events which may or may not happen; however, there will still be a probability that they can happen. So these events can be considered as a risk that may be encountered sometime in the future.

    Risk = (the probability that some event will occur) × (the consequences if it does occur).

According to the Royal Society,[4] 'risk is the chance, in quantitative terms, of a defined hazard occurring'. It is essential to understand that managing uncertainties is clearly a different process from managing a risk; however, it is also true that once an uncertainty has manifested the first time, it can be assigned a quantitative probability, making it a risk for future planning. The assignment of the probability is a perception of the humans in the supply chain, and hence it also depends upon the risk behaviour of the human element in the chain. The assignment of probability will be affected by the 'risk-taking' or 'risk-averse' behaviour of the humans in the supply chain. A manager's perspective of risk is associated with the notion of economic loss.[5] However, some managers may consider risk as an opportunity to create solutions or even create growth. In the literature, risk is generally associated with a negative outcome.

Risks in the supply chain

In today's business context, a global supply chain works hard to provide the customer with the product at the lowest costs and highest quality. These global supply chains are exposed to challenges and uncertainties that can create chaos and disruption. Local political upheavals, rapidly changing weather conditions, terrorism, counterfeiting, pandemics (for example, Ebola) and a host of other such issues create external risks in the supply chain. The supply chain is equally subjected to risks internally. These include a supplier failing to supply the goods on time and in the correct quality specification, strikes, production problems, logistics issues and so on, and lead to internal operational risks, which need a different level of mitigation.

Sources of supply chain risk

A number of researchers have tried to categorize supply chain risks. These categories provide an indication of various sources of risk. One methodology considers the source of risk as the position in the chain:[6]

- internal to the firm: process, control;
- external to the firm but internal to the supply network: demand, supply;
- external to the network: environmental.

Another methodology[7] considers the sources and drivers of supply chain risk as operating at several different levels. These are intricately linked as elements of a system, and are described within four discrete levels of analysis:

1 Level 1 – value stream/product or process;
2 Level 2 – assets and infrastructure dependencies;
3 Level 3 – organizations and inter-organizational networks;
4 Level 4 – the environment.

The source of supply chain risks can also be identified by focusing on the operational process within the supply chain:[8]

1 physical movement of goods;

2 flow of information;

3 flow of money;

4 security of the firm's internal information systems;

5 relationship between supply chain partners;

6 corporate social responsibility and the effect on a firm's reputation.

Not all risks (hazards or threats) can be avoided, controlled or eliminated. So supply chains need to be prepared to manage risks and get back to a state of normality once the risk has ended. The Oxford dictionary describes this feature of having 'the capacity to recover quickly from difficulties' as 'resilience'. Supply chain resilience is an important term within the risk management literature.

Risks in the food supply chain

Food supply chain risks can be classified on the basis of those risks occurring due to variance in matching supply and demand and those arising from supply disruptions. The risks arise from a wide range of causes, which may be intentional or unintentional. Robust and flexible systems need to be built to handle contamination incidents effectively and increase the risk management capability of the firm in the wake of an event.[9] This also means that the manager's focus on internal safety measures needs to expand to include safety awareness and building a proactive safety culture, increasing supply chain resilience.[10] The peculiarities of the food supply chain stem predominantly from the perishable nature of the products and the high levels of risk associated with food. Despite extensive food safety legislation, in recent times there have been frequent instances of food safety and security scares, recalls and disruptions. Food supply chains are fragile owing to the geographic, economic and legislative spread of participating entities, and this leads to a rapid propagation of the risk through the chain.

Impact of supply chain risks

The varied approaches to risk management can be broadly classified as *proactive*, referring to taking precautionary measures to tackle risks, and *reactive*, referring to reacting once the risk materializes. Although it advisable to invest in proactive risk management systems, being prepared for a reactive scenario is equally important. The increase in food safety incidents and environmental uncertainty shows the challenges in creating reliable proactive methods and that business reliance measures are currently not adequate in the food industry.[11] It is also important to plan effective reactive strategies.

According to a survey conducted within the UK food supply chain by the author in 2009,[12] the following three factors were considered to be the greatest risks:

1 loss of reputation (due to food contamination);

2 loss of power (electrical, oil etc);

3 loss of IT.

Table 9.1 presents a selection of major risks that have been identified through literature. The risks are not mutually exclusive and often one risk leads to another, for example a natural disaster will affect power lines and subsequently affect the premises. Another example is the loss of IT functions, leading to faulty products and ultimately causing

TABLE 9.1 Types of food supply chain risks

Product contamination	Loss of power	Loss of IT
Product recall other than contamination (packaging problems)	Loss/disruption in logistics	Unexpected economic challenges
New food safety regulations	Loss of water	Increased labour costs
Unavailability of raw material	Loss of premises	Strikes
Pandemics	Loss of supplier	Natural disasters
Rise in fuel price	Loss of asset	Terrorism

FIGURE 9.1   Impact of supply chain risks

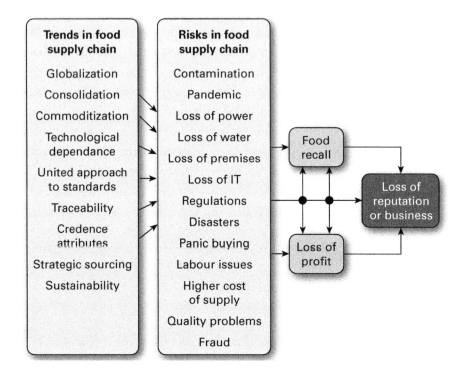

a product recall. Hence it makes more sense to analyse the risks with respect to their final impact, if the risk is not managed correctly. Figure 9.1 demonstrates how the impact could lead to either recall of product or loss of revenue, or a mix of both, finally resulting in a greater impact of 'loss of reputation' and in some extreme cases 'loss of business' (as in the case of the Peanut Corporation of America).

The three major trends affecting the food industry are:[13]

- Globalization refers to the global nature of food supply chains and encompasses global sourcing of raw material, food processing, packaging and transportation.

- Consolidation refers to the trend among food supply chain members to combine as many food categories as possible, as well as levels of the supply chain, in pursuit of higher margins. This has led to an increase in both vertical and horizontal integration within food chains.

- Commoditization refers to food products being traded and sourced as commodities. Commodities are traded as undifferentiated goods competing mostly on price, for example grains, for which traceability back to the farmer becomes particularly difficult.

Figure 9.2 demonstrates the reasons for contamination as revealed by recent cases. The need for companies to stay competitive on the basis of costs increases their propensity to create global supply chains and consolidate suppliers to get economies of scale. With the push towards consolidation, a major factor in the relationship is to empower suppliers to deliver at the required quality on the basis of trust. However, in the recent past, various cases have brought forth complexity in the supply chain and the difficulty in understanding the reasons behind the tainting. As the figure demonstrates, the two ends of the spectrum are intentional causes and unintentional causes. Under intentional causes, terrorism is at the farthest end of this spectrum. As seen in several recent cases, including the British horsemeat scandal and the Chinese milk scare, the intention of the contamination was to commit fraud for monetary gain. This occurred in the supplier network, with the customer being oblivious to the fraudulent processes behind the scenes. This case also demonstrated that the customer was blind to the process beyond the first tier. At the other end of the spectrum are unintentional causes, the first being negligence, which is a cause in most food supply chain recalls and issues. This is evident from the Cadbury case study, PCA (although later the

FIGURE 9.2   Reasons for contamination

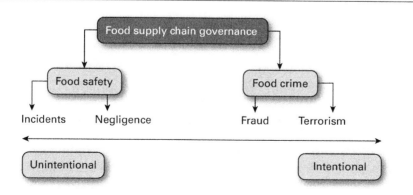

verdict turned to fraud as the investigation found out that the directors of the company were aware of the problem but did not take the necessary steps to curb it) and Sudan 1 case examples. The other end of the unintentional cause spectrum is an occurrence of incidents that the company has no control over and has to deal with using reactionary measures.

Managing supply chain risks

Efficient risk management provides value to various stakeholders of a firm. Compliance with appropriate procedures and corporate governance policies can help to reduce or avoid crisis situations and manage risks. The risk management process strives to maintain operational performance by identifying operational risks and developing mitigation procedures. The generic risk management process comprises the following steps:

1 Identify different types of risk.

2 Estimate the likelihood of each type of major disruption occurring.

3 Assess potential loss due to a major disruption.

4 Identify strategies to reduce risk.

Risks can be managed in a number of ways:[14]

- carrying buffer stock and improving inventory management;
- using alternative sources of supply;
- use of contracts to manage price fluctuations; and
- quality initiatives.

Risks associated with poor selection of suppliers are supply disruption, poor quality and recalls. These risks can be reduced by developing quality certification programmes and auditing the suppliers to ensure they meet required standards. Risk management processes have also focused on minimizing inventory and considering the optimal number of suppliers to minimize disruption. Researchers have put forth enablers for better supply chain risk management and to create visibility, transparency and effective control. These are lean, six sigma, agile philosophies, event management software and radio-frequency identification (RFID). The stages of the risk management process can vary from risk identification/analysis (or estimation) via risk assessment (or evaluation) to different ways of risk management.

Proactive supply chain risk management

Supply chain risk management strategies can be reactive or proactive. Being reactive is a default position when a risk materializes suddenly and the supply chain goes into a crisis management mode. This works as a strategy when a supply chain operates without worrying about risks on a day-to-day basis but reacts to alleviate the situation. In a proactive strategy, potential risks are identified at the supply chain design stage and their probability and impact are assessed. This will lead to risk management plans and a need to develop and implement contingency plans to minimize the impact if and when the risk occurs. This process sounds like the most logical thing for supply chain managers to do, but it needs resources upfront in terms of investment and people.

The process of managing risks proactively has not been thoroughly examined in the literature. The proactive risk management process for controlling the uncertainty in product development[15] uses the following variables to identify a proactive risk management strategy:

- the probability of risk occurring;
- risk event drivers;
- risk events;
- the probability of the impact.

Organizational training and a risk management culture are important for providing resources and motivation to employees to develop risk contingency plans. The process will have challenges if:[16]

- employees feel that no steps are taken towards managing risks identified and reported, but more done after the impact;

- employees feel that top management would look upon them negatively if they are involved in proactively identifying risks;
- exposing risks to shareholders may have an adverse effect on the value of the firm.

Reactive risk management

Risk management can take different forms and most companies in some form or another rely on risk management practices to control the effects of risk. If a risk never materializes, it becomes very difficult to justify the time spent on risk assessment, contingency plans and risk management.[17] This also leads to evaluating the total cost of an undesirable event occurring against the benefits realized from having strategies in place that significantly reduce the chance and/or effects of detrimental events with supply. Also, it is not always possible to obtain reliable estimates of the probability of the occurrence of any particular disruption and accurate measures of the potential impact of each disaster. Crisis is defined as 'a low probability, high impact event that threatens the viability of the organization and is characterized by ambiguity of cause, effect and means of resolution, as well as by a belief that decisions must be made quickly'.[18] Reactive risk management is very important when there is a crisis. There are a number of risk management strategies which take into account various entities within the supply chain.

Managing risks in food supply chains

As discussed throughout this chapter, risks can be managed through various mechanisms. The risk management process is broken down into two main processes: hard processes, focused around technology, traceability and testing, and so on; and soft processes: trust, relationships, contracts and so on. Over the years, the focus has been on creating more trust and collaboration across supply networks to minimize testing and keep costs down. The advent of lean systems and Japanese-style supply chains meant that the focus was more on soft processes than hard ones (barring those products that need to have traceability). However, recent cases have brought forth the need to have technology and testing to minimize occurrence of contamination across the supply chain. Both processes are equally important and a link should be created between the hard and soft processes in order to have a more cohesive and holistic process to manage upstream visibility. Proactive risk management involves predicting risks, and hence the use of technology and data analytics is key to identifying and assessing them. Food supply chains will, on a regular basis, work very successfully in proactively reducing instances of risk before they materialize. However, there are instances where the risk manifests (food safety) and it is essential to react quickly to curb the spread of contamination. The reaction to these risks will depend upon whether the risk affects food safety. If food safety is a concern, the reaction has to be fast and in most cases management will be led by the national regulatory agencies. If the risks in the food supply chain do not affect food safety but affect supply, reactive risk management will require good communication, multi-partner collaboration and standard risk management procedures.[19]

Risk mitigation strategies

These strategies utilize a range of activities, from avoiding the risk to taking complete control of the risk and managing it. Some of these activities are:[20]

1 Risk avoidance: In this process the risk is identified, assessed and the decision made to avoid the risk. This decision will be made in context of the trade-offs involved in conducting the business. Avoiding the risk is likely to include many different activities, for instance not entering a market owing to demand uncertainty or not procuring from a certain part of the world.

2 Postponement: This is a delay in the final formulation of the product or service until the customer has requested it. Although postponement is an opportunity to create mass customized products, it is also an important activity in managing demand uncertainty. Postponement can take various

forms – postponing manufacturing, assembly, packaging, labelling and logistics. This requires a certain level of product modularity and flexibility (for example, Subway has a fixed number of choices of ingredient – bread (6 types), meat and cheese (6–8 types), salad (8–10 types), sauce (5 types). The operation does not create the sandwich in advance but maintains the stock of ingredients and when a customer orders a sandwich using the ingredients available, the operation will make a fresh sandwich. The process is postponing the sandwich until there is a demand.

3 Speculation: Although this process can in itself create more risk, the basic premise is to manage demand uncertainty by anticipating demand, either by robust forecasting or by using predictive analytics.

4 Hedging: This is the process of ensuring that no major risks can affect the supply chain financially. Simply, this can take the form of buying an insurance product (see Zurich Insurance – supply chain risk insurance) to hedge against the risk or hedge against uncertain supply by having a portfolio of suppliers. This risk management process creates alternatives in case a risk manifests. For example, to avoid natural disasters, the portfolio of suppliers and customers may be globally dispersed, dual or multiple sourcing may help to hedge against quality problems, supply disruption, price fluctuations and so on.

5 Control: In this process, the focal company utilizes a host of controlling mechanisms (vertical integration, flexible contracting, cost control) to manage risks associated with opportunism and buyer–supplier power balance.

6 Transferring or sharing: Transferring or sharing of risks can be achieved through outsourcing, offshoring, vendor-managed inventories, offering discounts for advance purchases or competitive pricing for just-in-time inventory management. These activities are conducted so that the focal company does not experience financial risks by carrying excess inventory or excessive costs due to inefficiencies and capacity constraints.

7 Security initiatives: These are specific initiatives to control and manage risks. The use of technology, sensors, scanning and biochemical processes can help in identifying at-risk shipments or products. Initiatives such as CTPAT (Customs Trade Partnership Against Terrorism) in the United States are introduced to manage risks within logistics environments without affecting efficiency.

CASE EXAMPLE   China milk scare[21-26]

In November 2008, the milk scare arose after milk and milk powder manufactured by Sanlu in China was found to be contaminated with melamine. Kidney dysfunction caused by the melamine led to 240,000 infants being affected, with 50,000 hospitalized and 6 deaths confirmed. Although this was a case of deliberate contamination, the global dimension of the problem was only apparent when the contamination was confirmed in New Zealand. Despite warning signs and tests confirming contamination, the issue became public and production at Sanlu stopped only when Fonterra, a group based in New Zealand which owns a 43 per cent stake in Sanlu, confirmed the contamination and informed the New Zealand government, which in turn notified the Chinese government and the World Health Organization. This led to a trade recall of products containing Chinese milk derivatives and at least 11 countries stopping all imports of Chinese dairy products. The contamination spread across a wide range of products using the tainted milk powder and across 11 countries. The contamination had been intentionally conducted by two people in the upstream supply chain from the supplier to Sanlu. Sanlu had to file for bankruptcy. The two people who committed the intentional contamination were sentenced to death in China and sentences were handed out to 19 others, including Sanlu executives and milk producers and traders.

News articles suggest that this was not an isolated case and that melamine had been used previously by poor farmers, milk collectors and milk dealers as 'protein powder' to enrich test results for milk produced by weak or malnourished cows. Also, the literature suggests that melamine can enter the food chain through the use of pesticides such as Cyromazine. Testing at lower levels of the supply chains, for example farmers and marketers, is difficult as it can be expensive and time consuming.

CASE EXAMPLE Sudan 1[27–29]

In 2005, a case of food contamination which affected the UK was the detection of Sudan 1 dye in Worcestershire sauce produced by Premier Foods, a UK-based food manufacturer. Sudan 1 dye was identified as a contaminant in chilli powder and is associated with increased risk of cancer. Sudan 1 was first identified in a consignment of Worcestershire sauce exported to Italy. This led to a recall of over 580 products, mostly ready meals, snacks, sauces and drinks. Although inspection requirements had been in place to test for Sudan 1 in all chilli powder being imported into the UK since 2003, the contaminated consignment identified in 2005 was reported to have originated before 2003. The risk for humans was low level; however, the case depicted a greater operational risk. A review of the incident was commissioned, to be carried out by an independent panel. The report identified major failures in communications and coordination between agency, industry and the local enforcement authorities.

CASE EXAMPLE Salmonella Typhimurium in peanut butter[30,31]

One of the biggest cases of food product recall in US history is the most recent case (2008) of outbreak of illness caused by Salmonella Typhimurium. The Food and Drug Administration (FDA) and Centre for Disease Control and Prevention (CDC) identified the source as peanut butter and peanut butter paste in the processing plant of Peanut Corporation of America (PCA) at Blakely, Georgia. This contamination was directly linked to at least 486 cases of Salmonella-related illness and eight deaths. The contaminations lead to PCA filing for Chapter 7 bankruptcy on 13 February 2009. As the case investigation by the FDA unfolded, the lack of preparedness was highlighted by the fact that what began as voluntary recall of specific lots gradually expanded into a recall of all products, including dry- and oil-roasted peanuts, and stopping production. The contamination spread through various products and product categories across a number of supply networks that used PCA's products as an ingredient in their manufacturing process. The recall date was also changed through the course of the investigation and finally was dated to any peanut-related product from PCA dating back to 1 January 2007. The contamination was identified at another PCA manufacturing facility at Plainview, Texas, on 21 January 2009. The company executives knew as far back as 2006 that the peanut butter was contaminated, but they delivered it to the supply chain. The manufacturing plant was found to be poorly maintained and the premises unclean. There was a criminal investigation against the executives and they were convicted in September 2014 of conspiracy, fraud and other federal charges.

CASE EXAMPLE   UK horsemeat scandal[32-34]

In 2013, the British horsemeat scandal brought to light the complexity of food supply chains and the propensity to commit fraud. Products containing horsemeat were supplied by Comigel to Tesco, Findus and Aldi – Figure 9.3 shows a visual representation of the complexities of the meat's movement.

Comigel is a company based in northeast France. However, on investigating the issue, the buyers of these products found that the supply chain of these products was extremely complex and criss-crossed through Europe. Comigel subcontracted to Taviola in Luxembourg, which placed an order with Spanghero in the south of France. Spanghero in turn subcontracted the order to a trader in Cyprus, who placed an order with a Dutch supplier. The Dutch company in turn subcontracted

FIGURE 9.3   Map of horsemeat scandal

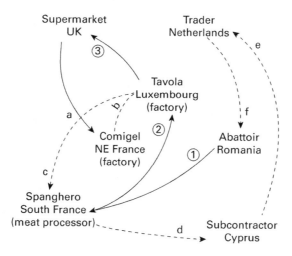

①–②–③   Movement of meat
a–b–c–d–e–f Order/subcontract process

the order to abattoirs in Romania, which sent the supply of meat directly to Spanghero. It was also discovered that the Romanian company claimed to have labelled the meat properly (as they knew that the meat supplied by them had horsemeat added to it) and they alleged that the mislabelling had occurred somewhere else in the chain. The fallout from the issue has affected meat supply chains, meat-based product manufacturers and retail stores. Supermarkets had to recall products, create a new regime of testing and change their purchasing policies rapidly. Although the issue was not about contamination involving harm to humans consuming these products, it was a clear case of mislabelling and fraud that affected the relevant supply chains.

CASE EXAMPLE   Cadbury salmonella contamination, 2006[35–38]

In June 2006, Cadbury withdrew a million chocolate bars which were contaminated by a rare strain of salmonella (Montevideo). The withdrawal happened when Cadbury was approached by the Food Standards Agency and Health Protection Agency when they were investigating a Montevideo infection in over 50 children over a period of 4 months leading up to June. The health officials traced a sample of the bacteria to a sample sent a few weeks earlier by the Cadbury factory in Marlbrook, Hertfordshire. When the officials approached the company, they were told that Cadbury had detected salmonella in its chocolate crumb (being manufactured in Marlbrook but then sent to Birmingham for making chocolate bars and Easter eggs) in January but they had not taken any action on it as they felt that the levels of bacteria were too low to cause a risk. The source of the contamination was a pipe from a cleaning machine which had dripped water on a conveyor belt in the manufacturing process. The company had also detected that the salmonella was the rare strain as early as February. A total of 42 people fell ill and 3 had to be hospitalized.

Birmingham City Council prosecuted the company for health and safety violation at its Bourneville plant and the Hertfordshire Council prosecuted the company over the state of its Marlbrook factory.

In the verdict, negligence by Cadbury was proved and Cadbury pleaded guilty. Cadbury was fined a total of £1 million on all counts and had to pay £152,000 towards costs. The company also spent around £30 million changing procedures to prevent future lapses.

Summary

This chapter presented a discussion on supply chain risks in general and then discussed food supply chain risks in detail. The chapter lists the sources of risk, the impact caused by the risk and the suggested risk mitigation plans. A number of high-profile cases have been discussed which demonstrate how the risk was propagated and the resulting impact on account of the risk. The chapter discusses both proactive risk management and reactive and crisis management. It considers the aspect of intentional and unintentional contamination in food. The challenges with regard to intentional contamination or food fraud are also covered in Chapter 11.

Notes

1 Maloni, M J and Brown, M E (2006) Corporate social responsibility in the supply chain: an application in the food industry, *Journal of Business Ethics*, 68 (1), pp 35–52

2 Dani, S and Deep, A (2010) Fragile food supply chains: reacting to risks, *International Journal of Logistics Research and Applications*, 13 (5), pp 395–410

3 Knight, F (1965) *Risk, Uncertainty and Profit*, Harper & Row, New York (first published 1921)

4 Royal Society (1992) *Risk Analysis, Perception and Management*, Royal Society, London

5 Chiles, T H and McMackin, J F (1996) Integrating variable risk preferences, trust, and transaction cost economics, *Academy of Management Review*, 21 (1), pp 73–99

6 Christopher, M and Peck, H (2003) Building the resilient chain, *The International Journal of Logistics Management*, 15 (2), pp 1–14

7 Peck, H (2006) Reconciling supply chain vulnerability, risk and supply chain management, *International Journal of Logistics: Research and Applications*, 9 (2), pp 127–42; Peck, H (2005) Drivers of supply chain vulnerability: an integrated framework, *International Journal of Physical Distribution and Logistics Management*, 35, pp 210–32

8 Spekman, R E and Davis, E W (2004) Risky business: expanding the discussion on risk and the extended enterprise, *International Journal of Physical Distribution & Logistics Management*, 34 (5), pp 414–33

9 Sheffi, Y (2005) *The Resilient Enterprise*, MIT Press, Cambridge, MA

10 Sheffi, Y and Rice, J B, Jr (2005) Building the resilient enterprise, *MIT Sloan Management Review*, **47** (1), 41–48

11 Peck, H (2006) Resilience in the Food Chain: A Study of Business Continuity Management in the Food and Drink Industry, DEFRA, London

12 Dani, S and Deep, A (2009) Investigating risk management capability within UK food supply chain, EUROMA Conference 2009, Gothenburg, Sweden, 14–17 June

13 Roth, A V *et al* (2008) Unravelling the food supply chain: strategic insights from China and the 2007 recalls, *Journal of Supply Chain Management*, **44** (1), pp 22–39

14 Zsidisin, G A (2003) Managerial perceptions of supply risk, *Journal of Supply Chain Management*, **39** (1), pp 14–26

15 Smith, P G and Merritt, G M (2002) *Proactive Risk Management*, Productivity Press, New York

16 Smeltzer, L R and Siferd, S P (1998) Proactive supply management: the management of risk, *International Journal of Purchasing and Materials Management*, **34** (1), pp 38–45

17 Zsidisin, G, Panelli, A and Upton, R (2000) Purchasing organization involvement in risk assessments, contingency plans, and risk management: an exploratory study, *Supply Chain Management: An International Journal*, **5** (4), pp 187–97

18 Pearson, C M and Clair, J A (1998) Reframing crisis management, *Academy of Management Review*, **23** (1), pp 59–76

19 See note 2.

20 Manuj, I and Mentzer, J T (2008) Global supply chain risk management, *Journal of Business Logistics*, **29** (1), p 133

21 WHO (2008) Toxicological and Health Aspects of Melamine and Cyanuric Acid: Report of a WHO Expert Meeting, WHO, Geneva

22 England, V (2008) Why China's Milk Industry Went Sour, BBC, 29 September

23 Reuters (2008) Melamine Use Rampant in China Feed Business, Reuters, 25 September

24 Fairclough, G (2008) Tainting of milk is open secret in China, *The Wall Street Journal*, 3 November

25 Coghlan, A A R (2008) Melamine 'widespread' in China's food chain, *New Scientist*, 23 September

26 BBC News (accessed 24 February 2015) Timeline: China milk scandal, 25 January 2010 [Online] http://news.bbc.co.uk/1/hi/7720404.stm

27 FSA (2005) Sudan Dyes, 3 April 2005 – last update [Online] http://www.food.gov.uk/safereating/chemsafe/sudani/

28 BBC News (accessed 24 February 2015) Food Recalled in Cancer Dye Scare, 18 February 2005 [Online] http://news.bbc.co.uk/1/hi/health/4277677.stm

29 FSA (accessed 24 February 2015) Report of the Sudan 1 Review panel, 23 July 2007 – last update [Online] http://www.food.gov.uk/multimedia/pdfs/sudanreview.pdf

30 FDA (accessed 24 February 2015) FDA Investigation: Peanut product recalls, 2009 [Online] http://www.fda.gov/oc/opacom/hottopics/salmonellatyph.html

31 Basu, M (accessed 24 February 2015) Unprecedented Verdict: Peanut executive guilty in deadly salmonella outbreak, CNN, 20 September 2014 [Online] http://edition.cnn.com/2014/09/19/us/peanut-butter-salmonella-trial/index.html?hpt=hp_t2

32 Addy, R (accessed 24 February 2015) Supermarkets Took Supply Chain 'on Trust' – horsemeat, 10 January 2014 [Online] http://www.foodmanufacture.co.uk/Food-Safety/Supermarkets-took-supply-chain-on-trust-horsemeat

33 Lawrence, F (2013) Horsemeat scandal: where did the 29% horse in your Tesco burger come from?, *The Guardian*, 22 October

34 Press Association (2013) Horsemeat scandal has highlighted complex supply chain of cheap UK food, *The Huffington Post*, 13 February

35 BBC News (accessed 24 February 2015) Cadbury Salmonella Scare Probed, 24 June 2006 [Online] http://news.bbc.co.uk/1/hi/uk/5112470.stm

36 Derbyshire, D (2007) Cadbury Prosecuted over Salmonella Scare, *Daily Telegraph*, 23 April 2007 [Online] http://www.telegraph.co.uk/news/uknews/1549474/Cadbury-prosecuted-over-salmonella-scare.html

37 FSA (accessed 24 February 2015) Cadbury Recall Update 1 August 2006 [Online] http://webarchive.nationalarchives.gov.uk/20120206100416/http://food.gov.uk/news/newsarchive/2006/aug/cadbury

38 BBC News (accessed 24 February 2015) Cadbury Fined £1m over Salmonella, 16 July 2007 [Online] http://news.bbc.co.uk/1/hi/england/6900467.stm

Technology trends in food supply chains

10

As the demand for food in the world increases, the process of supplying it is ever more stretched. To add to the challenges of sufficiency, food safety and quality are of the utmost importance as these attributes affect the health and well-being of the final consumer. Hence, the challenges are paramount within the food supply chain. How do we ensure that there is sufficient quantity of food produced? How do we ensure that the quantity produced reaches the consumer in the right amount, in time and safely? With the proliferation of global food supply chains and the availability of food sources around the world, governments as well as food companies can plan their food supply strategies. However, one of the biggest challenges is post-harvest food losses. In the developing world, around 40 per cent of the food produced is lost post-harvest.[1] It is also important that food is not wasted because of improper processes or the inability to understand the needs of the market as the food travels in various forms of production through the supply chain. One of the solutions to ensure that food reaches our plates in the right quantity, right quality and when we need it is the relevant use of technology. It is therefore necessary to understand the current uses of technology in the various stages of the food supply chain with only one aim: to provide sufficient and safe food to meet the demands of the consumer. There are two sides of this aim: one from the aspect of food security and the need to match the demands of the growing world population, the other from the perspective of the food companies which are in business to sell food to the consumer and make sufficient money to keep their companies and the livelihoods of their employees intact.

The basic tenets of this chapter are to understand the use of technology within the various stages of the food supply chain. Traceability of food along the supply chain is a major concern and the chapter provides a robust discussion of this topic. The chapter also considers technology within the supply chain by focusing on four stages: food production, food processing, food packaging and food logistics. The recent proliferation of e-shopping models that have transformed food shopping are technology intensive but are discussed in Chapter 4.

Traceability and use of technology

Traceability of food has been increasingly mentioned in the news in recent years owing to multiple scandals involving international food supply chains. These events have affected both developing and developed countries, as the supply chains – although crossing international boundaries – still operate as single channels for food to reach consumers (wherever they are). The erosion of trust within these chains has led to an increase in the demand for traceability and testing. This is from both a company perspective and a governmental one (a recent government-independent report on the horsemeat scandal[2] and the subsequent issues of food fraud). The past few decades have seen a tremendous increase in both availability and adoption of technology in the food sector. In fact, food supply chains have inspired the introduction and popularity of many leading technologies in today's world, ranging from barcoding to radio-frequency identification (RFID) tagging, which will be discussed later in this chapter. Technology has been embraced as an essential tool in eliminating food risks, and also as a tool to maintain traceability in times of recall.

Traceability

The Codex Alimentarius Commission defines traceability as 'the ability to follow the movement of a food through specified stage(s) of production, processing and distribution'.[3] It refers to the identity of the product but can also relate to its origin, processing history, distribution and location. The prerequisites for effective traceability in food systems are:[4]

- depth of traceability (how far upstream and downstream the food components can be traced);
- breadth of traceability (the number of variables or attributes of the food that are tracked);
- precision in measuring these attributes.

Traceability is beneficial in many ways, and can lead to a number of advantages, including:

- increased transparency;
- reduced risk of liability claims;
- more effective recalls;
- enhanced logistics;
- improved control of livestock epidemics;
- possible positive effects on trade;
- easier product licensing;
- possible price premiums.

Effective traceability is perceived to lead to increased consumer trust and confidence in the product, as well as trust between producers and suppliers. However, the process of creating traceability requires appropriate data. To obtain these data, the food supply chain needs to invest in technology, enabling the gathering, storing and sharing of data. A balance is needed between the costs of traceability and the benefits achieved from it. Traceability is strongly advocated by all compliance guidelines, including Hazard Analysis and Critical Control Points (HACCP) and those issued by the International Standards Organization (ISO), and can be categorized into mandatory traceability and voluntary traceability.

Mandatory traceability

Within Europe, the framework provided by the General Food Law (GFL) Regulation (EC) No. 178/2002 has been set up to ensure mandatory traceability of food and food ingredients with effect from 1 January 2005. The regulatory requirements require all food and feed business operators to be able to identify the source of all food and ingredients, and to provide the basis for further monitoring throughout the supply chains. The operators must know from whom they obtain ingredients and products (one step back) and register to whom they sell their ingredients or products (one step forward). The focus of both regulatory and compliance standards is on the availability of these data rather than how the data are gathered; the organizations can choose a suitable method from available protocols. The regulation requires food operators to keep records of the names and addresses of the supplier and customer in each case, as well as information regarding the product and date of delivery. Operators are also encouraged to keep information on the quantity of a product, the batch number (if there is one) and a more detailed description of the product and also information such as whether it is a raw or processed product. In addition to the general requirements, sector-specific legislation applies to certain categories of food product (fruit and vegetables, beef, fish, honey, olive oil), special traceability rules for genetically modified organisms (GMOs) and 'tagging' for animal products.

Voluntary traceability

In addition to mandatory traceability, it is possible, in the EU, to outline a second traceability level, which is voluntary and provides a higher degree of information associated with a single product. This voluntary traceability system is regulated by a number of European organizations accredited to deliver food safety standards, such as AFNOR (Association Française de Normalization) in France, BSI (British Standards Institute) in the UK and UNI (National Standards Organization) in Italy. The framework of ISO 22000:2005 contains a specific voluntary traceability standard.

The GS1 Global Traceability Standard[5] provides a process standard describing the traceability process independent of the choice of enabling technologies. The standards also provide implementation procedures to help companies create the appropriate traceability and recall procedures.

Radio-frequency identification

Radio-frequency identification (RFID) is a technology that uses radio waves to transfer data from an electronic tag, called an RFID tag or label, attached to an object, through a reader for the purpose of identifying and tracking the object. Some RFID tags can be read from several metres away and beyond the line of sight of the reader. The benefits include greater speed and efficiency in stock operations, better tracking throughout the chain and enhanced forecasting. RFIDs are considered invaluable in ensuring traceability, as advances in technology and the decrease in costs for these devices allow various types of information to be recorded with minimal human intervention.

Retailers can use RFID to:

- track products within the logistics system;
- manage inventory efficiently by always having the right goods available at the right time in the right place;
- manage the security of the inventory;
- manage consumer demand through better control of inventory and replenishment.

Food companies and services can not only utilize RFID for the above-mentioned reasons but also to track returnable assets, including kegs, trolleys and pallets, and track ingredients used within the food.

RFID tags can be classified as Active and Passive. In some instances semi-passive tags are also available. Active tags have an integral battery which keeps the tag on all the time and hence they can be tracked over long distances. Passive tags do not have a battery and use power from the RFID reader to transmit the signal. Semi-passive tags have a battery to keep the circuit on, but they do not transmit data until powered by a reader. Each has its own use. Passive tags are inexpensive and can be used on food packaging for traceability, in which case the data are not transmitted until the tag is read. However, if the food needs to be tracked across long distances, a pallet can be tagged using an active RFID tag which will be GPS tracked. The tags can be further divided as read only and read-write.

Barcoding

A barcode is a code made up of numbers and letters that can be processed by a computerized system. Generally the code is represented physically on the product using black parallel lines of varying widths and spacing. The data within this representation can be read using scanners. These scanned data are then analysed by the appropriate software to identify the information regarding the product. This information may be the type of product or service, physical locations at any point in the supply chain, price, number of inventory items and so on.

Barcodes are useful in:

- capturing sales data, which helps with forecasting and also replenishment, especially when the inventory is being managed by the vendor;
- managing the pricing of products, as it removes the need to apply pricing labels;
- traceability of ingredients;
- matching the elements of the process (eg matching ingredients to the recipe, employee to the process, and so on).

GS1 DataBar[6] is a new barcode that is being introduced by GS1 for use in the retail sector. It is smaller and can encode more information, such as expiry dates, batch numbers, prices, weights and more.

The food manufacturing and services sector use barcodes to:

- improve food safety by keeping track of ingredients and inventory;
- increase efficiency by having the correct information regarding the supply and storage of food ingredients and processing assets;
- improve supplier transactions.

Printing barcodes

Barcodes and RFID provide accuracy, but only if the printers and label material provide the quality and durability needed for food storage and supply chain operations. Inkjet printing may create challenges with printing on packaging, especially if it is absorbent. Thermal printers are a good option to print labels for food, and these can be used to create automated print-and-apply systems that have the speed, barcode support, print quality and variable data processing capabilities required for successful case coding.[7] In cases of a recall, the appropriate labels, barcodes and product identification particulars, matched appropriately with customer orders and shipping information, provide an effective system.

The barcode technology is developing rapidly and can now permit on-demand printing with thermal transfer or thermal printers, for example on product trays or opened packages. Laser marking can also be used to place a barcode directly on the skin of fruit and vegetables.[8] Barcode systems are termed 'closed loop' or 'open loop'. Closed-loop systems are not required to adhere to GS1 or Universal Product Code (UPC) standards as they are used internally. Open-loop barcode systems, which are used externally, must meet GS1 and UPC guidelines.[9]

The Foodservice GS1 US Standards have the following information on the barcode:

- Location identification: every entity in the supply chain should have a Global Location Number (GLN).
- Product identification: the Global Trade Item Number® (GTIN®) for each product.
- Product attributes: standardized product information for exchanging data easily and efficiently.

GS1 has built an open platform, the Global Data Synchronization Network®, an environment for secure and continuous synchronization of accurate data.[10] SMEs and international suppliers find it difficult to keep abreast of barcoding standards, which presents an obstacle to uniform labelling.

DNA barcoding[11]

DNA barcoding is a molecular-based system of identifying species of plants and animals by comparing short genetic markers within the

DNA. For this process to be effective and the comparison accurate, there must be sufficient molecular variability between the species being investigated, and an available repository of DNA reference sequences. The DNA barcoding process can be useful for the identification and traceability of mammals, birds, seafood and plants. The applicability is relevant within unprocessed food. During processing, the DNA structure of many ingredients (for example, seeds, fruits, plants and animal parts) can be transformed as a result of physical processing (heating, boiling, UV radiation) or chemical treatments (addition of food preservatives, artificial sweeteners). This may lead to the process being ineffective. However, certain exceptions may occur depending on the level of processing (such as elements of fruits within commercial teas, yoghurt, chocolates, cookies and so on).

The International Barcode of Life project[12] is a large-scale global project focused on constructing a detailed DNA barcode library of eukaryote organisms (organisms whose cells have a nucleus). A DNA barcode is a specific DNA sequence of the species that helps in identifying the species. The work of finding the DNA barcodes is being conducted by hundreds of researchers across 25 nations. In 2003, Paul Hebert, a researcher at the University of Guelph in Ontario, Canada, proposed 'DNA barcoding' as a way to identify species.[13] Barcoding uses a very short genetic sequence from a standard part of the genome. The Barcode of Life (barcodeoflife.org) and DNAbarcoding101 (dnabarcoding101.org) databases record the DNA barcodes.

Food production

The food production environment has seen a massive growth in technology in terms of both increasing productivity and yield and creating disease-resistant crops. As companies strive to create GMO crops, which are not accepted in many countries, organic farming is also on the rise, creating three sets of consumers – those who are happy with GMO crops, those who will not use GMO but also will not pay for expensive organic products, and a third group who will buy only organic produce. Organic production (if done as per the appropriate organic farming standards) is also supportive of 'green farming'. Technological trends in farming will focus on better seeds, less toxic pesticides, good fertilizers, efficient harvesting equipment and, most importantly, the appropriate infrastructure (warehouse, transport, and so on) that will reduce post-harvest food losses.

Agencies such as CABI run the *Plantwise*[14] programme, which helps farmers in developing countries to understand crops and their diseases so that farmers can choose techniques that will produce the correct yield. The use of ICT within the agriculture sector has also provided the benefit of information to farmers. Testing and tracking technologies are important as post-harvest tools to reduce instances of fraud and to make sure that the product flowing downstream is of the appropriate quality.

The important technological trends within food production are influenced by:[15]

- *Informatics*: This is the collection and application of insight gathered from the study of large integrated datasets. Agriculture informatics will bring together data across genetics, economics, agronomy, hydrology and soil science to create insight into innovations and processes required to feed the ever-increasing population of the world, which is set to reach 9 billion by 2050. These approaches can be used to identify gene sequences to identify favourable traits in crops, such as disease resistance and an ability to adapt to climate change.

- *Big Data*: The availability of a huge amount of data from laboratories, farms, retailers and social media has the potential to work with informatics to generate and drive innovation within food production. For example, at the individual farm level, more precise data will increasingly be used to provide evidence of compliance with regulatory and quality assurance and traceability requirements. Benchmarking information, through data analysis, provides farmers a mechanism to compare their own performance with local, regional and national averages. The ability to integrate farming data with information on consumer preferences and trends and climate-change data can benefit businesses and consumers in the long run. This analysis, along with the appropriate metrics, will also help in supporting the sustainable agenda within the food sector.

- *Technology and mechanization*: Increasing yield and reducing post-harvest loss require help from advanced mechanization within the agriculture sector. Precision agriculture, remote sensing technologies and robotic applications help in increasing efficiency, productivity and, more precisely, the safety of the produce from climatic changes and diseases.

- *Skills development*: As technology changes and improves, the workforce needs to be trained and developed to utilize the technology advancements to their benefit. There is also a need for businesses in the supply chain to exchange knowledge for the benefit of the complete supply chain.

- *Regulatory frameworks*: With the advent of new technologies and innovations within the food sector, regulatory frameworks need to be made 'smarter' rather than pedantic to keep pace with the changing landscape within the industry. Regulations should be in place to safeguard the interests of the environment, livestock and end consumers; however, these should respond to changing market conditions and advancements without stifling innovation. Hence, the debate over GMO or the use of harmful pesticides and fertilizers is valid, as this originates from the market. However, non-uniformity between MRLs (minimum residue levels) of pesticides within agri-products across different parts of the world creates an additional challenge for food supply chains. SMEs and small producers across the international food value chains do not have the expertise or access to understand changing regulatory requirements. Hence the use of ICT to educate them (for example, about the MRLs within the crops they produce and the ban on certain pesticides) and keep them informed is essential.

Food processing in a technological context

Foods must frequently be processed to ensure safety and increase shelf life, quality and nutritional properties, all while making them more convenient. Processing techniques are employed at various stages to transform raw food into value-added food products. Transformation of food through processing provides an opportunity for food innovation but, more importantly, increases the life of the food, albeit in a different format (for example, apples converted to jams or chutneys). A current technological approach to reduce the environmental footprint in food processing is the use of enzymes.[16] As biological catalysts, enzymes speed up reaction rates and, in so doing, offer savings in terms of time, energy and cost. In addition to environmental benefits, the action of enzymes in foods may result in products with extended shelf life, improved texture, appearance, flavour, functionality and yield, enabling a variety of food products to be fabricated from harvested produce.[17] Enzyme engineering is a process of developing enzymes with superior activities which can be used in food processing under mild conditions. Another priority concern in food processing is food safety. Thermal treatments such as pasteurization, sterilization, aseptic processing, refrigeration and chemical preservatives have been traditionally used to decrease microbial growth in foods and to enhance safety and shelf life. Methods for microbial control in food processing include: microwave and radio-frequency heating (MW/RF), pulsed electric fields (PEF), high pressure processing (HPP), ionizing radiation, ohmic heating (OH), treatment with ultraviolet light, and ozonization.[18]

Food packaging in a technological context

Technology trends within food packaging are focused around two main objectives: (1) to keep food fit for purpose (until it reaches the fork); and (2) to indicate when food has gone off. The first objective has been partially fulfilled with advances in packaging to keep food fresh and matching the correct quality specifications. These advances have been in packaging for fresh fruit and vegetables, Tetra Paks for drinks and other liquids, canning technology, and packaging for frozen foods. One of the common examples is the packaging of freshly cut pineapple chunks using a specially designed film with micropores. The film covering the pineapple container has small pores in it that do not permit air/oxygen to enter the container, but permit carbon dioxide created within the container to escape, increasing the life of the pineapple chunks until they reach the consumer.

To combat counterfeit products, anti-counterfeiting technologies are used on the packaging for high-value products. These comprise:[19]

- Overt or visible features: these help consumers to verify the authenticity of the product (based on the packaging), as the fact that the packaging is tamper-free will be evident. Some of the examples of these features are: holograms, optically variable devices, colour-shifting security inks and films, and sequential product numbering.

- Covert features: covert features are created for the brand owner (not the end consumer) to identify counterfeit products. This is important from a supply chain perspective. Some examples of this are: invisible printing, embedded images and digital watermarks.

- Forensic markers: these are features that require laboratory testing or field kits to prove authenticity. Examples of this technology are: chemical markers, biological markers, and DNA markers.

Some packaging trends for the future are:

- edible packaging;
- use of nanotechnology in packaging to prevent decomposition of food;
- smart packaging that will change colour if the food is contaminated or spoilt;
- self-cooling/self-heating packaging.

Food logistics

Food products in food supply chain networks (FSCNs) are required to be maintained in a temperature-controlled environment, rather than being exposed to whatever ambient temperatures prevail at various stages of the supply chain.[20,21] Fresh foods need controlled temperatures to maintain product attributes. The increasing consumer demand for ready-to-eat products (such as ready meals and prepared salads) imposes additional stress on the food logistics environment to maintain the quality and safety of food products. Temperature-controlled logistics is required to maintain the short-shelf-life requirements of fresh food. This needs to focus on the speed and reliability of logistics systems, and hence requires special transportation and storage equipment. However, with increasing trends towards JIT logistics and keeping inventories low, most logistics systems now have to carry small quantities of several varieties of product, putting pressure on the transportation system to maintain different temperature zones to accommodate these products. This also increases complexity, as different products may produce different by-products within the temperature zone, thereby accelerating the need to create better technologies for food logistics. For example, bananas produce ethylene, which accelerates the ripening process of other fruits. This was discussed in Chapter 5.

Food logistics environments utilize ICT trends such as smart containers, GPS tracking, RFID and mobile phone apps to keep track of the products in the logistics system and also to maintain the quality, inventory and safety of the products. The latest trend, buying food via online shopping, saves costs, time and physical effort, and provides 24-hour product information. The logistics environment needs the ability to store the necessary inventory at the appropriate levels of safety and also deliver to the consumer when the orders come in.

Some of the aspects of this service are:[22]

- Cold-chain logistics: a constantly secure and monitored cold chain. Chilled items as well as ambient ones must be delivered at customer-preferred times with a minimum of packaging, ready to be stored away.

- Pick-up and delivery: automated pick-up and delivery solutions to enable cold-chain services.

- Packaging innovation: smart, reusable and recyclable packaging to enable the efficient handling of food products, reduce customer effort in handling, storing and disposing of packages, and support environmental protection.

New IT platforms and communication networks have helped to integrate supply chain partners downstream into the retail environment. Processes and platforms such as VMI and CPFR create better visibility and customer fulfilment. This also helps with keeping abreast of consumer choices and managing inventory 'smartly', reducing excessive waste.

Summary

This chapter has presented an overview of some of the technologies currently being used in food supply chains and some that are being developed and are at an experimental stage. Technology is used at all stages of the supply chain. Each process, from food production to final delivery to the consumer, requires technology to ensure that the food moves from the 'farm to the fork' safely, at the best quality, and in quantities to manage demand sustainably. The chapter also presents a comprehensive discussion regarding traceability and the various technology trends, from RFID and barcodes to DNA barcodes and DNA markers. The chapter also explains technology trends in packaging and how this helps to keep food safe and fresh. This chapter works in conjunction with Chapter 11 on food regulation and Chapter 12 on food innovation.

Notes

1 Chauhan, C (accessed 24 February 2015) India wastes more farm food than China: UN, *Hindustan Times*, 11 September 2013 [Online] http://www.hindustantimes.com/newdelhi/india-wastes-more-farm-food-than-china-un/article1-1120755.aspx

2 HM Government (2014) Elliott Review into the Integrity and Assurance of Food Supply Networks – Final Report, A National Food Crime Prevention Framework, July, London

3 CAC/GL 60-2006 Principles for Traceability / Product Tracing as a Tool Within a Food Inspection and Certification System, CCFICS, 2006

4 Souza-Monteiro, D M and Caswell, J A (2010) The economics of voluntary traceability in multi-ingredient food chains, *Agribusiness*, 26 (1), pp 122–42

5 GS1 (accessed 25 February 2015) Traceability in Retail [Online] http://www.gs1.org/traceability-retail

6 GS1 (accessed 24 February 2015) GS1 Barcodes [Online] http://www.gs1.org/barcodes/technical/bar_code_types

7 Zebra Technologies (accessed 25 February 2015) Bar Coding and RFID Enable Food Supply Chain Traceability and Safety, A Zebra Technologies White Paper, 2011 [Online] https://www.zebra.com/content/dam/zebra/white-papers/en-us/food-traceability-en-us.pdf

8 Verified Inc (accessed 24 February 2015) Barcodes in the Food Service Industry [Online] http://www.verifiedlabel.com/knowledgecenter/know_barcodes_foodservice.aspx

9 See note 7.

10 GS1 (accessed 24 February 2015) Global Data Synchronisation Network (GDSN) [Online] http://www.gs1.org/gdsn

11 Food Executive.com (accessed 24 February 2015) DNA Barcoding: A new tool for food traceability, 8 October 2013 [Online] http://www.foodexecutive.it/en/food-safety/item/338-dna-barcoding-a-new-tool-for-food-traceability.html

12 International Barcode of Life (accessed 24 February 2015) How DNA Barcoding Works and What it Will Do [Online] http://ibol.org/about-us/

13 Barcode of Life (accessed 24 February 2015) What Is DNA Barcoding? [Online] http://www.barcodeoflife.org/content/about/what-dna-barcoding

14 Plantwise (accessed 24 February 2015) Home page [Online] http://www.plantwise.org/

15 HM Government (2013) *A UK Strategy for Agricultural Technologies*, London

16 Boyce, J I and Arcand, Y (2013) Current trends in green technologies in food production and processing, *Food Engineering Review*, 5 (1), pp 1–17

17 Simpson, B K, Rui, X and XiuJie, J (2012) Enzyme-assisted food processing, in *Green Technologies in Food Production and Processing*, ed J I Boyce and Y Arcand, Springer, New York

18 Ngadi, M O, Latheef, M B and Kassama, L (2012) Emerging technologies for microbial control in food processing, in *Green Technologies in Food Production and Processing*, ed J I Boyce and Y Arcand, Springer, New York

19 Power, G (2008) Anti-Counterfeit Technologies for the Protection of Medicines, World Health Organization, Geneva

20 van der Vorst, J G A J *et al* (2007) Quality controlled logistics in food supply chain networks: integrated decision-making on quality and logistics to meet advanced customer demands, 14th Annual EUROMA Conference, 17–20 June, Turkey

21 Smith, D and Sparks, L (2004) Temperature controlled supply chains, in *Food Supply Chain Management*, ed M A Bourlakis and P W H Weightman, Chapter 12, pp 179–98, Wiley-Blackwell, Oxford

22 DHL (accessed 18 February 2015) Logistics Trend Radar 2014 – Delivering insight today. Creating value tomorrow! [Online] http://www.dhl.com/en/about_us/logistics_insights/dhl_trend_research/trendradar.html

PART THREE
Sustainability and future challenges

Food regulation, safety and quality

11

Supply chains work towards their goal of delivering products or services to end consumers. Food supply chains work towards this objective in very dynamic conditions, and are set apart from other sectoral supply chains owing to the unique nature of their design. The food supply chain has unique attributes which are created to achieve a safe product fit for consumption. Unsafe food has fatal outcomes, and as seen in the cases of Sanlu and Peanut Corporation of America discussed in Chapter 9, this can have a negative impact not only on the company but also on the sector. This chapter presents a discussion of the various regulatory systems and standards that have to be followed by food supply chains, with the aim of providing safe and quality food to consumers. The chapter provides an overview of the laws and regulations in Europe and the certification standards followed by retailers.

Attributes to consider when designing food supply chains

Perishability

The fundamental feature of food that governs the design of its supply chain is that it is perishable. Depending upon the nature of the food product, whether it is ready to eat or used as a raw material for further processing or cooking, the life of a product could vary between a single day and a couple of years. However, the reality is that food will perish and will become unsafe to eat. Fresh food, which can range from fruits and vegetables to ready-to-eat meals, has a short shelf life and hence the supply chain is tasked with closer, regular quality inspections and the concept of display-until/use-by dates on the food product. As the entire farm to fork cycle is being squeezed to provide short lead times and efficiency, supply chain designs have to rely heavily upon logistics and warehousing functions that provide temperature-conditioned transport and storage, and increased use of advanced information and communication technologies. Recent research[1] states that in perishable-product supply chain design, a trade-off should be made between transportation costs, shortage costs, inventory costs, product waste and expected shelf-life losses and quality decay.

Seasonality in production

Inherently, food production is seasonal and unpredictable. Where the food is grown has a major influence on what is grown and how seasonal it is. People in most developing countries will utilize food products in their diet according to local availability. However, owing to new food retail business models in most developed economies, consumers are used to the availability of seasonal fruits and vegetables all year round. Seasonal cycles vary north and south of the equator, which in turn provides an opportunity for supermarkets and food processors to extend their supply chain, thus ensuring all-year-round availability. The seasonality of the product, along with weather conditions, leads to supply variation. To guarantee the planned delivery of supply, companies will often integrate vertically across the chain. Unpredictable climatic conditions affect the quality and quantity of produce, and consequently the unpredictable nature of supply makes operational planning extremely difficult. Hence, the formulation of purchasing contracts will take into account the seasonal nature of the sourced products.

Heterogeneity of the product

Food products are heterogeneous in nature. There is a significant variation in product features such as taste, smell, appearance, colour, size and image. Even the same type of product may have different features. The heterogeneous nature of food is both advantageous and complex to control. It is advantageous because it fulfils individual consumer demand, as different people have different requirements in relation to taste, appearance, smell and so on. Thus, supermarkets stock different varieties of the same food category, for example types of apple, tomato, onion, potato, yoghurt and cheese. The flow of the product in the supply chain, whether as a raw material or as a consumer item, will determine how it is bought and sold. When the product enters the supply chain as a raw material, it is more of a commodity and customers are purchasing it on the basis of costs and available quantity (for example, coffee beans, cocoa beans, orange juice). Food products aimed at end consumers have seen a trend of moving away from the commodity perspective towards a more value-added system. Consumers are increasingly basing their buying decisions on credence, content or process attributes, which are difficult to detect during or after food consumption. Examples of these attributes include the country of origin, whether the product is organic or produced under fairtrade conditions, health factors such as added calcium, and so forth.

Edible nature of product

Since the ultimate purpose of food is consumption, this characteristic has an important influence on supply chain design as well as inspection and certification requirements. Food supply chains are highly regulated and any breakdown can have catastrophic effects. In the past decade, the most-discussed topic within the food supply chain has been food safety and regulation, followed closely by traceability. Product safety and quality form the basis for food logistics and supply chain design. As soon as the item of food (from the farm) enters the food supply chain, it starts to deteriorate, and hence speed is vital in ensuring that the food is edible by the time it reaches the fork.

Information asymmetry

Information asymmetry is a scenario in which one party has more or better information than the other transacting party, creating an imbalance of power in the relationship. This feature has a unique role within the food supply chain and has an impact on the operation and design of the chain. Within a supply chain this feature may manifest as information asymmetry in quality, where the buyer cannot identify a good product but the seller knows the history and condition of the product. This was evident in the recent horsemeat scandal that affected retailers in the UK. If the product is manufactured or grown by the seller and the seller keeps selling a bad product over a period of time, buyers will leave the market. However, owing to information asymmetry, there is an element of trust on the part of the buyer that defects will not occur downstream. While there are institutions and regulations to protect against opportunism and cheating, the geographical extent of food supply chains means that the importance of trust cannot be underestimated.

Increasing pressure for price reduction from the markets and the power of the retailers will also have an adverse effect on the food being supplied. Producers and processors will find substitutions for raw materials or modify recipes or packaging volume in order to maintain margins. Although this will not always lead to unsafe food (due to contamination), it will influence the characteristics of the final product and sometimes have an adverse effect post-consumption (for example, the use of trans-fats in confectionery and snack foods to reduce costs and increase shelf life affects human health).

Food regulation and its effect on safety

All aspects of the food supply chain (production, processing and retail) are subjected to regulation and standards to ensure that the food is fit for human consumption. (This also is true with regard to animal feed, but this is outside the scope of this book.) Food regulation is a highly debated and researched area of the food supply chain literature. Food quality has an influence on market competition and hence it is important to understand and keep abreast of the latest regulations and standards. Academics have studied a number of different topics in relation to food regulation and safety, focusing on:

- the impacts of regulation on the supply chain;
- traceability and transparency;
- auditing procedures;
- private standards;
- quality assurance;
- risk assessment.

The debate around this topic stems from two fundamental points: (1) consumers' increasing awareness of food safety, which is intensified by the number of food safety incidents reported in the media; and (2) despite the prevalence of a number of standards, there still exists significant confusion around the scope and depth of these standards, especially in small to medium-sized suppliers and developing countries which struggle with these standards when exporting. The task of maintaining safety and quality in the food supply chain can be facilitated using the following resources.

Minimum quality standards

The minimum quality standards required are the product specifications. These relate to the inherent characteristics of the product and are specific to each product. Each process in the supply chain will have quality conformance standards which must be met before food travels down the chain.

Regulation and standards

Regulation and standards can be classified into four major categories:

- food laws and regulation;
- reference standards;
- compatibility standards;
- private standards.

The basic standards from a UK/European perspective are discussed below. Every country has its own laws and regulations with regard to food safety. Even within the UK, each individual process within the food supply chain will have a regulatory requirement and this will also be focused around the food category.

Food laws and regulation

With the context of the UK and Europe, food supply chains are governed by both national and European laws. In the UK, the Food Standards Agency (FSA) has a statutory objective to protect public health and consumers' other interests in relation to food and drink. The FSA was established through the introduction of the Food Standards Act 1999 in the House of Commons.

The main food laws that apply to these policy areas in the UK[2]

- The Food Safety Act 1990 (as amended) provides the framework for all food legislation in Great Britain – similar legislation applies in Northern Ireland.

- The General Food Law Regulation (EC) 178/2002 is EC legislation on general food safety.

- The General Food Regulations 2004 (as amended) provide for the enforcement of certain provisions of Regulation (EC) 178/2002 (including imposing penalties) and amends the Food Safety Act 1990 to bring it in line with Regulation (EC) 178/2002. Similar legislation applies in Northern Ireland.

- The EC Standing Committee on the Food Chain and Animal Health was established following the adoption of Regulation (EC) 178/2002, which set out the general principles and requirements of food law in the EU.

- Council Regulation (EC) No. 834/2007: principles, aims and rules of organic production and labelling of organic products.

- EU Regulation No. 2073/2005 on microbiological criteria for foods (as amended by EU Regulation No. 1441/2007) complements the food hygiene legislation and applies to all food businesses involved in the production and handling of food.

- New EU Regulation 1169/2011 on the provision of food information to consumers consolidates and updates two areas of labelling legislation – general food and nutrition labelling. The information has a focus on nutrition, allergens and country of origin as well as being in larger print and increased clarity. The new rules apply from 13 December 2014. The obligation to provide nutrition information will apply from 13 December 2016 for manufacturers that have yet to introduce nutrition labelling on their products, whereas manufacturers that already provide nutrition information must comply with the new rules by December 2014.

Reference standards

Codex Alimentarius[3]

The Codex Alimentarius Commission (CAC) was formed in 1963 by the Food and Agriculture Organization (FAO) and the World Health Organization (WHO) to develop food standards, guidelines and related texts such as codes of practice under the joint WHO/FAO food standards programme. It also sets out guidelines for food hygiene and promotes the control of hygiene at the production and processing stage using the Hazard Analysis and Critical Control Points (HACCP) system, which will be described later in this chapter. New considerations such as risk analysis and determination of equivalence in different food control systems have an impact on the new approach to international food hygiene regulations. The main aim of HACCP is protecting the health of consumers, ensuring fairtrade practices in the food trade, and promoting coordination of all food standards work undertaken by international and government and non-government organizations (NGOs). It has two elements: (1) a set of guidelines for all food-related companies, and (2) guidelines for specific food products, such as the codices for the fruit chain, meat chain and so on. The general principles lay out specific ways in which member countries may adhere to the Codex standards. These ways are clearly specified, but the general forms of acceptance are full acceptance, acceptance with minor deviations, and free distribution.

Sanitary and Phytosanitary Agreement (SPS)[4]

The SPS Agreement was created to ensure that regulations are not used for protectionist purposes and for creating unnecessary barriers to entry into international trade but at the same time to safeguard the food supply chain. It allows different governments to maintain the sovereign right to provide the level of heath protection it deems appropriate. It promotes the Codex Alimentarius as a minimum level of regulation and, if a WTO member considers that a higher level of sanitary protection than the Codex is necessary, it will have to provide scientific evidence based on valid risk assessment techniques to support its claim. The SPS Agreement covers all laws, decrees, regulations, testing, inspection, certification and approval procedures, as well as packaging and labelling requirements directly related to food safety.[5] In doing so, it addresses the objective of reducing unjustified barriers to trade that take the form of health and safety measures. Facilitating trade, not improving food safety standards, forms the chief objective of SPS.[6]

The SPS Agreement is based on 14 articles and its key principles, which members of the WTO have to follow, are:

1 National sovereignty: Member countries are allowed to use risk standards that are different from the international standards. They must, however, inform the WTO secretariat, which then circulates the notification to other WTO members.

2 Harmonization: This is aimed at common measurement according to officially recognized international standards, which include the Codex Alimentatrius Commission, International Office of Epizootics and International Plant Protection Convention. This means that if a specific regulation follows the relevant Codex structure, it cannot be challenged by an exporting nation as a non-technical barrier.

3 Equivalence: Members must accept that the SPS measures of another country are equivalent if they result in the same level of public health protection, even if the measures themselves differ.

4 Science-based measures: Regulations cannot impose requirements that do not have a scientific basis for reducing risk.

5 Regionalization: The concept of pest- or disease-free areas within an exporting country is recognized. Exports from such areas can be allowed, even if other areas of the country still have pests and diseases.

6 Transparency: Nations have to publish their regulations and provide an enquiry point for answering questions from trade partners about the country's SPS measures.

7 Dispute resolution: International standards are often higher than the national requirements of many countries.

Although SPS measures aspire to provide benefits in promoting trade, they presently apply only to governments. The growing power of retailers is noticeable as they apply private standards that may not be legally binding by government legislation but are equally important for the small food processors to follow. Another growing trend worth mentioning is the growing importance of credence factors such as country of origin, fair trade, ethical practices and so on, which are driven by moral standards rather than a utilitarian basis. These have a deep consequence in terms of creating trade barriers, but are very difficult to address through legislation or regulation.

Compatibility standards

These are a category of standards which are aimed at international standards of compliance. ISO, HACCP and other QA schemes are included in this category. Within food legislation, the most common standard is the HACCP standards.

Hazard Analysis and Critical Control Point (HACCP)

HACCP is widely recognized as the most important standard for safety and suitability of foodstuffs. It can be applied to any organization involved in any of the following activities: preparation,

processing, manufacturing, packaging, storage, transportation, distribution, handling, sales and supply. The EU Directive 93/43/EEC on
food hygiene requires all operators in the food business to implement
HACCP (REP).

HACCP as a process was developed with the collaboration of the
Pillsbury Corporation and the US National Aeronautics and Space
Administration (NASA) for the production of safe food for the US
space programme.[7] The requirement from NASA was the guarantee
of safe foods consumed by astronauts in space. The HACCP system
focused on the manufacturing process rather than end-product
inspection. HACCP was built around giving operators more control
over the manufacturing process, as far upstream as possible, by continuously monitoring critical control points. The process was publicly
announced by Pillsbury in 1971 and was adopted by major food
companies in the 1980s. The process was supported by the Food and
Agriculture Organization, the United Nations and the World Health
Organization.

The Codex Alimentarius described earlier lays down the steps and
guidelines involved in implementing the HACCP system. HACCP has
a significant overlap with the ISO systems within the area of food
manufacturing. If an organization has implemented the HACCP
system successfully, generally the majority of the requirements for
ISO 9000 are fulfilled. The HACCP system is also the foundation for
some other standards worldwide (for example, see EU, 1992, 1993
for Europe; FDA, 1972, 1989, NAS, 1985, Taylor, 1993 and the US
Federal Register, 1994, 1995 for the United States; Agriculture
Canada, 1993 for Canada; or ANZFA, 1995, 1996 for Australia and
New Zealand).

The system is a science-based and systematic process of identifying
the critical control points within any process. Critical control points
are steps in the process where hazards or contamination can enter,
and HACCP aims at controlling this through prevention rather than
inspection. In this respect, HACCP can be applied throughout the
supply chain, from production to consumption. HACCP does not
have a manual or a list of prescriptive actions but is based on 7 principles and 12 guidelines.

Henson *et al*[8] list the advantages and disadvantages of HACCP:

Advantages:

1 Reduced product *wastage*;
2 Increased product *shelf life*;
3 Reduced product *microbial counts*;
4 Increased product *prices*;
5 Increased product *sales*;
6 Reduced production *costs*;
7 Increased *motivation of production staff*;
8 Increased *motivation of supervisory/managerial staff*;
9 Increased ability to attract *new customers*;
10 Increased ability to access *new overseas markets*.

Disadvantages:[9]

1 Increased *production and supervisory costs staff*;
2 Need to *retrain supervisory/managerial staff*;
3 Need to *retrain production staff*;
4 Attitude/motivation of *production staff*;
5 Attitude/motivation of *supervisory/managerial staff*;
6 *Reduced staff time* available for other tasks;
7 Recouping *costs of implementing* HACCP;
8 Reduced flexibility to *production process*;
9 Reduced flexibility of *production staff*;
10 Reduced flexibility to introduce *new products*.

International Standards Organization (ISO 9000 and ISO 22000:2005)

The ISO standards are voluntary technical standards which are globally recognized. They lay down specific standards for particular products, material or processes. However, the ISO 9000 is a generic standard and is not aimed specifically at the food sector. ISO 22000:2005 is a standard dealing with food safety and is a general derivative of ISO 9000.

ISO 9000 is a uniform standard for quality management. It provides recognition within the marketplace of quality assurance. Implementing the standard helps the organization to optimize its processes and create appropriate governance structures for them. The standard helps the company to formalize its management system of quality assurance, which also provides traceability of root causes of quality problems. However, it is a lengthy process and requires major resources to achieve certification. Small and medium-sized organizations find it difficult to implement ISO 9000 on account of resource requirements.

ISO 22000[10]

The ISO 22000 is a quality management system approach applied to food safety by incorporating the widely used and proven HACCP principles into the quality management system. The standard provides an opportunity to minimize system and audit variations on account of location, types of products and so on. It also reduces barriers to trade across borders and the supply chain.

Food Safety System Certification 22000 (FSSC 22000)

The FSSC 22000 combines the ISO 22000:2005 Food Safety Management standard with the Publicly Available Specification (PAS) 220:2008 and other additional requirements. The FSSC 22000 is recognized by the Global Food Safety Initiative and the Food and Drink Federation.

Threat Analysis and Critical Control Point (TACCP)

PAS 96:2014 is the guide to protecting and defending food and drink from a deliberate attack. PAS 96 describes the TACCP, a risk management methodology, which aligns with HACCP; however, it has a focus on identifying threat (an action that can cause loss or harm arising from someone's ill-intent). This requires a wider systems view of the operation from the position of an attacker. Diverse people within the organization, such as HR, procurement and/or security, can help in anticipating the threats to the food supply chain (from an attacker's perspective), outlining steps for early detection of an attack and devising protection to deter the attack.

Private food standards

Private standards are standards set by commercial and non-commercial organizations, for example private companies, industry associations and non-government organizations. These standards, although not legally binding, are the gateway to the supply chain for most suppliers. As the large chains and processing firms compete among themselves in national and regional markets and attempt to differentiate their products to protect and gain market share, they find, firstly, that the public standards needed for that differentiation do not exist, or the ones that exist are currently inadequate. Also, there isn't a satisfactory capacity to monitor their enforcement, leaving a gap for private standards. Secondly, private standards enable increased profit through promoting product differentiation. Private standards and certification provide assurance to the customer of product reliability and therefore increased sales. Thirdly, private standards help reduce costs and risks in their supply chains. The main cost reduction comes from using the standards as guidelines for standardizing processes and systems. Some of the examples of private standards are as follows.

Individual company standards

These standards are set by individual companies within the supply chain, predominantly buyers and large food retailers, and are adopted across their supply chains. Examples include Tesco's Nature's Choice and Marks and Spencer's Field to Fork assurance standards.

Collective national standards

These standards are set by national organizations, including industry associations and NGOs. These organizations represent the interests of commercial entities (for example, food retailers, processors or producers). In some cases the standards have been successful in reaching out through international supply chains. Examples include the British Retail Consortium (BRC) retail standards and the Ethical Standards Initiative.

Collective international standards

These standards are set by international collective organizations. They are designed to be adopted and implemented internationally. Examples include the Marine Stewardship Council, the Forest Stewardship Council and GlobalGAP.

BRC Food Safety Standard[11]

The BRC Food Safety Standard is a quality and safety certification standard developed by the British Retail Consortium. This is used for standardizing quality, safety and operational criteria to establish good manufacturing practices and fulfil legal obligations for creating safe food products that meet customer requirements. It can be used by any food-processing operation where open food is handled, processed or packed. The BRC food standard is followed by most major food retailers and hence suppliers must be BRC certified. The standard is divided into seven sections:

1 *Senior Management Commitment and Continual Improvement*: For any food safety system to be effective, it's essential that the senior management team is fully committed to its application and continued development.

2 *The Food Safety Plan (HACCP)*: The basis for the Food Safety System is an effective HACCP programme based on the requirements of the internationally recognized Codex Alimentarius system.

3 *Food Safety and Quality Management System*: This sets out requirements for the management of food safety and quality, building upon the principles of ISO 9000. This includes requirements for product specifications, supplier approval, traceability, and the management of incidents and product recalls.

4 *Site Standard*: This sets out expectations for the production environment, including the layout and maintenance of the buildings and equipment, cleaning, pest control, waste management and foreign body controls.

5 *Product Control*: This includes the requirements for product design and development stage, including allergen management, product and ingredient provenance, product packaging and product inspection and testing.

6 *Process Control*: This includes the establishment and maintenance of safe process controls, weight/volume control and equipment calibration, and ensures the documented HACCP plan is put into practice.

7 *Personnel*: This sets out the standards needed for staff training, protective clothing and personal hygiene.

Other initiatives within the food supply chains

Global Food Safety Initiative (GFSI)[12]

During the 1990s, retail and food manufacturers operated individual in-house standards within their supply chains without having an overview of the requirements of the food sector. Owing to the non-convergence and inconsistency of these standards, suppliers spent resources and effort trying to meet the requirements of multiple retailers. This, however, did not stop the food safety crises within Europe during the 1990s. Hence, the CEOs of major food retailers came together in 2000 to set up the Global Food Safety Initiative, a non-profit foundation, to share knowledge and create a harmonized and benchmarked approach to managing food safety across the industry. In the late 1990s, The British Retail Consortium set up its first BRC food safety and quality certification standard. The German and French retailers had the International Food Standard (IFS) and the trade association for North American retailers developed the Safe Quality Food Standard. The GFSI chose the benchmarking approach to create harmony between these standards with a message 'once certified, accepted everywhere'. This means that once the supplier is certified against one standard (as recognized by the GFSI), the supplier should be in a position to supply to the membership of the organization. The BRC standard is the most accepted and difficult standard to adopt. However, once adopted and certified, the BRC standard provides acceptance across the world.

The work of the GFSI is advanced through collaboration between the world's leading food safety experts from retail, manufacturing and foodservice companies, as well as international organizations, governments, academia and service providers to the global food industry. They meet together at Technical Working Group and Stakeholder meetings, conferences and regional events. GFSI is managed by the Consumer Goods Forum (CGF), a global, parity-based industry network, driven by its members.

Safe and Local Supplier Approval (SALSA)[13]

In recent years, many of the UK's major buyers, including supermarkets, foodservice, catering suppliers, local authorities and health trusts, have seen local sourcing as a major objective. However, it is not always possible or appropriate for smaller food producers and processors to follow the BRC Global Standards, so SALSA was formed to deliver a robust and effective food safety certification scheme which is more suitable for small food producers and processors. SALSA is a non-profit organization set up by four UK food trade associations: the National Farmers' Union of England and Wales (NFU), the Food and Drink Federation (FDF), the British Hospitality Association and the BRC. This initiative is conducted by the Institute of Food Science and Technology, UK. To achieve SALSA certification, suppliers are audited for their capability to produce safe and legal food. The SALSA scheme is limited to those processors based in the UK and the Channel Islands.

CASE EXAMPLE   EU ban on imports of Indian mangoes[14]

On 26 March 2014, the European Commission declared that emergency measures were being taken to prohibit the import of some fruits and vegetables from India in order to tackle the significant shortcomings in the phytosanitary certification system of such products exported to the EU. This decision had to be taken owing to a high number of such consignments being intercepted on arrival in the EU and found to contain pests, mainly insects such as non-European fruit flies, that needed to be quarantined. The ban was put into effect from May 2014 to December 2015. When this message appeared in the media, it caused uproar in the UK, as the fruit affected by the ban was the Indian mango or, as Indians call it, 'Alphonso – the king of fruits'. The Alphonso mango season starts roughly from the month of May and lasts for about 10 weeks. The 10 weeks are worth almost £10 million to India–UK trade. From a consumer's perspective, this was an issue, as the UK Asian diaspora wait every year for the mango season to start. From a business perspective, this was a blow to the whole supply chain, as the supply chain was already preparing the mangoes for dispatch. This affected exporters in India and importers in the UK, as well as individual convenience stores that relied upon the extra footfall in the 10 weeks on account of customers coming in for mangoes. The importers created an online petition asking the UK government to try to get the ban lifted. Two local Leicestershire MPs raised the question in Parliament. The National Asian Business Association worked with the Department of Environmental Food and Rural Affairs (DEFRA) to organize a joint roundtable meeting, in June 2014, between the representatives of the UK and Indian governments and the businesses affected by the ban. This meeting was chaired by Lord de Mauley, Parliamentary Under-Secretary of State for Natural Environment and Science. It was agreed at the meeting that, if necessary, DEFRA would provide support (with training and technical assistance) to its Indian counterparts and exporters. The European Commission agreed to conduct an early inspection visit and a team of the Commission's Food and Veterinary Office visited India in September 2014 to inspect pack houses and verify improvement in plant health controls and certification systems. They found significant improvements in India's mango export system. The Food and Veterinary Office,[15] in its report, agreed that India had taken several measures to guarantee safe exports, including enhancement of capacity and number of inspecting staff, improvement in infrastructure and implementation of a standard operating procedure. It was announced on 21 January 2015 that the ban on the import of Indian mangoes into Europe had been lifted.

CASE EXAMPLE   The horsemeat scandal and food fraud[16]

In January 2013, the horsemeat scandal came to light when traces of horse DNA were found in products supplied to various UK supermarkets and millions of burgers were subsequently taken off the shelves by supermarkets, including Tesco, Lidl, Aldi and Iceland. As the story unfolded, it demonstrated the complexity of the meat supply chain in Europe, as the orders for meat were subcontracted almost seven times across a number of countries. No one had control over the chain and the fraud being committed passed unnoticed for some time. In the aftermath of the scandal, the UK government announced an independent review, to be led by Professor Elliott, to look into the causes of the systemic failure that enabled the horsemeat fraud. The review would investigate the roles and responsibilities of businesses throughout the food supply chain to consumers and how to support consumer confidence. The recommendations of the report focused on food crime and food fraud, and recommended that the government should set up a food crime unit. The report also discussed supermarkets' responsibility to pay a fair price to suppliers to deter fraud and asked for an intelligence-based monitoring system. The Business Standards Institution produced a revised version of PAS 96: Defending food and drink to safeguard food and drink against malicious tampering and bioterrorism. The Publicly Available Specification (PAS) was first published in 2008 as a guide to HACCP procedures and has subsequently been updated to include the introduction of the TACCP risk management methodology to help mitigate the risks. The GFSI also wants the inclusion of VACCP (Vulnerability Analysis Critical Control Point) as a part of its toolkit, along with HACCP and TACCP, to fight food fraud.

Summary

This chapter has discussed the various food regulations, standards and safety initiatives required in the supply chain to provide safe food to end consumers. The chapter provided a very high-level overview of the different mechanisms, and is a guide for food-sector organizations. The individual regulations and standards should be consulted when designing the food supply chains for specific products and categories. The chapter discussed the need for regulatory and certification systems based on the attributes of food products. It presented the different laws and regulation under four categories:

- food laws and regulation;
- reference standards;

- compatibility standards;
- private standards.

Notes

1 Rijpkema, W A, Rossi, R and van der Vorst, J G A J (2014) Effective sourcing strategies for perishable product supply chains, *International Journal of Physical Distribution & Logistics Management*, 44 (6), pp 494–510

2 FSA (accessed 24 February 2015) General food law [Online] https://www.food.gov.uk/enforcement/regulation/foodlaw

3 Codex Alimentarius (accessed 25 February 2015) About Codex [Online] http://www.codexalimentarius.org/about-codex/en/

4 WTO (accessed 24 February 2015) Understanding the WTO Agreement on Sanitary and Phytosanitary Measures, May 1998 [Online] http://www.wto.org/english/tratop_e/sps_e/spsund_e.htm

5 FAO (accessed 24 February 2015) 3. Important Food Issues [Online] http://www.fao.org/docrep/006/y8705e/y8705e03.htm

6 FAO (accessed 24 February 2015) The WHO International Health Regulations and the Promotion of Food Safety in International Trade, FAO/WHO Global Forum of Food Safety Regulators, Marrakech, Morocco, 28–30 January 2002 [Online] http://www.fao.org/docrep/MEETING/004/X6918E.HTM#P30_3207

7 Surak, J (accessed 24 February 2015) The Evolution of HACCP, Food Quality and Safety Magazine, February/March 2009 [Online] http://www.foodquality.com/details/article/807887/The_Evolution_of_HACCP.html?tzcheck=1

8 Henson, S, Holt, G and Northen, J C (1999) Cost and benefits of implementing HACCP in the UK dairy processing sector, *Food Control*, 10, pp 99–106

9 Ropkins, K and Beck, A J (2000) Evaluation of worldwide approaches to the use of HACCP to control food safety, *Trends in Food Science & Technology*, 11, pp 10–21

10 ISO (accessed 25 February 2015) ISO 22000 – Food safety management [Online] http://www.iso.org/iso/home/standards/management-standards/iso22000.htm

11 BRC Global Standards (accessed 24 February 2015) Home page [Online] http://www.brcglobalstandards.com/

12 The Consumer Goods Forum (accessed 24 February 2015) What is GFSI [Online] http://www.mygfsi.com/about-us/about-gfsi/what-is-gfsi.html

13 SALSA (accessed 24 February 2015) Home page [Online] http://www.salsafood.co.uk/

14 European Commission (accessed 24 February 2015) Daily News, 26 March 2014 [Online] http://europa.eu/rapid/midday-express-26-03-2014.htm

15 The Economic Times (accessed 24 February 2015) European Union lifts ban on import of mangoes from India, 21 January 2015 [Online] http://articles.economictimes.indiatimes.com/2015-01-21/news/58305774_1_safe-exports-four-vegetables-ban

16 Quinn, B (2013) Horsemeat Discovered in Burgers Sold by Four British Supermarkets, *The Guardian*, 2013 [Online] http://www.guardian.co.uk/world/2013/jan/16/horsemeat-burgers-supermarkets

The Guardian (2013) The Meat Industry [Online] http://www.guardian.co.uk/environment/meat-industry

Lawrence, F (accessed 24 February 2015) Horsemeat Scandal: The essential guide, *The Guardian*, 15 February 2013 [Online] http://www.guardian.co.uk/uk/2013/feb/15/horsemeat-scandal-the-essential-guide

The Global Post (accessed 24 February 2015) Agence France-Presse, World's Biggest Food Firms Embroiled in Europe Horsemeat Scandal, 19 February 2013 [Online] http://www.globalpost.com/dispatch/news/afp/130219/worlds-biggest-food-firms-embroiled-europe-horsemeat-scandal-2

BBC News (accessed 24 February 2015) Horsemeat Scandal: Retailers to give regular food test updates, 18 February 2013 [Online] http://www.bbc.co.uk/news/uk-21495300

The UK Government (accessed 24 February 2015) Food supply networks: integrity and assurance review [Online] https://www.gov.uk/government/groups/review-into-the-integrity-and-assurance-of-food-supply-networks

DEFRA, FSA and BSI (accessed 24 February 2015) PAS96: 2014 Guide to protecting and defending food and drink from deliberate attack [Online] http://www.food.gov.uk/sites/default/files/pas96-2014-food-drink-protection-guide.pdf

Food innovation 12

Innovation is a process through which ideas are generated, developed and implemented to formulate incremental improvements or radical products, processes and services that add value within the supply chain. Innovation is necessary both for finding solutions to future social challenges and to sustain business competitiveness. Within the food sector, innovation has been at the centre of activity. To meet the challenges of feeding an ever-growing population, with rising incomes and changing lifestyles, processes and product development have to be considered using novel ideas. These pressures modify where and how food products are grown, processed and distributed, with the additional requirement of being socially and environmentally compliant. The chapters in Part Two covered the operational challenges within food supply chains. This chapter focuses on the process of innovation and introduces concepts that are being increasingly used within the food sector. The chapter presents a number of innovations which have proved effective in food supply chains.

Classification of innovation methods

Consumer demand and changing needs drive the intent to create new product offerings and deliver these using sophisticated business models. Creating new product offerings is synonymous with innovation capability. Innovation can be classified using several different methods.[1]

Institutional innovations

These innovations bring about a change in institutional procedures, policies, standards, regulations and relationships with external organizations in order to encourage improvements in the performance of an institution to increase its competitive advantage.

Technological innovations

These innovations are the application of new ideas, scientific knowledge or technological practices to develop and market new products and services and/or improve production processes. These can be applied to other functions of the organization too.

Social innovations

These innovations are substantial improvements in ideas, organizations, goods and services in order to respond positively to social needs or purposes. These innovations are conducted for the well-being of individuals and communities.

Other classification systems

These classification systems are more general and can be used more widely, such as the following categories based on the OECD classification (2005):[2]

- *product innovation*: changes or additions to goods produced or services delivered;
- *process innovation*: changes to the way goods are produced or services are delivered;
- *marketing innovation*: changes in the method or conditions for marketing the goods, or changes in the placement or target of the goods or services;
- *organizational innovation*: changes in an organization's structure, activities or services, in its processes or methods, or in its relationship with other stakeholders (such as partnerships).

Innovation systems

Innovation systems may include a wide variety of sectors and functions that promote or implement innovation. A systems view is important in order to understand the interactions between the various agencies involved and to create a holistic flow of knowledge among the different participants. An innovation system consists of a wide array of public and private organizations, firms and individuals that demand and supply knowledge and technical, commercial and financial competencies. It also includes the rules and mechanisms by which these different stakeholders interact and relate with one another in social, political, economic and institutional settings.[3] Investment in agricultural science and technology, generally in the form of research and extension services, has proved to be highly valuable for improving crop yields and lessening poverty in developing countries.[3]

Food system and innovation

Scientific and engineering advances over the past century have revolutionized the way food is grown, distributed and sold. The advances have facilitated food processing for mass consumption. Food innovation has focused on creating safe, convenient and nutritionally enhanced food. However, this has also led to the manufacturing of long-shelf-life, fat-laden convenient food which is available on retail shelves. Processing and packaging innovations have led to increasing the life of a food product and made it possible to transport it across the globe. Logistics innovations in both storage and transport have created an opportunity where all types of food product can be made available across the globe. Innovative food-processing techniques developed through scientific advancement have resulted in improving the conversion of raw foodstuffs into safe consumer products of the highest possible quality. Some of the engineering techniques used by the food industry, including drying, milling, extrusion, refrigeration, heat and mass transfer, membrane-based separation, concentration, centrifugation, fluid flow and blending, powder and bulk-solids mixing, monitoring and control help to maintain the quality and safety of the food and fulfil consumer requirements.

Consumer perceptions

Introducing a new product to the market should be a consumer-led activity. It is important to understand the needs of the consumer before the product is developed. This also means that the 'newness' of the product or innovation is from the aspect of the consumer. If the consumer finds the product to be new or innovative and purchases it, the innovation exercise is deemed successful. Depending upon the position in the food supply chain and the entity involved in the transaction, the perception of newness will alter. Hence, what a distributor finds new or innovative may not be accepted by the end consumer. However, it is the end consumer as the culmination of the supply process and the entity that ascertains the value of the product that will determine its innovativeness. When McDonald's and Kentucky Fried Chicken first entered the Indian and Chinese markets with their worldwide offerings, they failed. Only when they realized that they had to innovate with their menus to suit consumer needs within the two countries were they successful in setting up shop. The McDonald's and KFC menus in India feature food items using paneer and rice, which are not available on their menus in other parts of the world.

CASE EXAMPLE   Indian curry in the UK

Indian curry has been available in the UK since the late 1700s. However, it entered the food supply chain, as we know it today, through restaurants and curry houses in the 1960s. The flavours and tastes that were new to consumers' palates needed modifying to get a product that was acceptable to an ordinary consumer who perhaps had not been introduced to these tastes before. This caused changes to the content of spice, salt and sugar and also led to some new products such as Chicken Tikka Masala (still claimed to be a dish first introduced in the UK). As the Indian curry houses gained consumers' approval, Western supermarkets worked with suppliers to create ready-to-eat curry meals for their stores. Innovation in the format of the packaging has changed the way curry is available on the retail shelf. From microwaveable ready-to-eat packaged curries to long-shelf-life vacuum-packed curries, innovation still continues to make curry available in various formats. This product was a new product within the retail supply chain and for the consumer, who now could enjoy curry at home without the need to go to a restaurant. Hence, the development processes used, the investments required, the challenge of introducing Asian food products to a Western market and the potential financial impact were no less important just because Asian foods had previously existed in Asia.

Product development in food supply chains

Success factors in the product development process

In research done by Stewart-Knox and Mitchell,[4] they found that the food industry preferred to innovate incrementally (modify or improve the existing product) rather than create radical innovation (a completely new product). They suggested that because food product development is a risky process, companies tried to follow a risk-averse approach to innovation. However, the reality is that there is a higher rate of product failure than success. They also found that if the retailer was involved in the product development process and also had an understanding of consumer needs, a greater rate of success was achieved. In the innovation literature, the food industry is typically classified as a sector with low research intensity, accounting for one of the lowest R&D-to-sales ratios of any industrial sector.[5] The pace of technological change in this industry, measured by the number of patented inventions, appears to be less dynamic than in other manufacturing sectors.[6] Beckeman and Skjolkebrand assessed the degree of innovation in the food industry, stressing the fact that 'very little innovation is taking place in the food industry'.[7]

Food industry innovations are often aimed at developing important replacement products, following a change in nutritional requirements, or following food additive regulations. They are generally new or improved consumer products and services, and can be focused in one area of food technology, for example process engineering, product formulation, food qualities or consumer needs. The process also has to combine technological innovation with social and cultural innovation in order to produce food that satisfies the consumer. Innovations may occur throughout all parts of the food chain, and a possible classification of food innovations is the following:

- new food ingredients and materials;
- innovations in fresh foods;
- new food process techniques;
- innovations in food quality;
- new packaging methods;
- new distribution or retailing methods.

Drivers and barriers to innovation in the food supply chain

In a study commissioned by the Department for Environment, Food and Rural Affairs (DEFRA) and conducted by Arthur D Little, the drivers and the barriers for innovation in the food sector were identified.[8] The study was titled 'Mapping current innovation and emerging R&D needs in the food and drink industry required for sustainable economic growth'. The report identified that within the food and drink machinery and automation sector, there are a number of excellent small businesses that still do not compete internationally.

The drivers for technological innovation are:

- consumer demand: making largely incremental developments to make products more convenient and attractive, healthier, more natural, better quality and, above all, less expensive;
- the increasing costs of doing business, owing to the rising and fluctuating costs of agricultural commodities and animal feed, and of utilities, including energy and water;
- regulatory drivers, such as food labelling requirements, which are sometimes difficult to meet.

Priorities for technological innovation

The priorities as presented in the report fall into four categories (Table 12.1).

Barriers to technological innovation

Delivering the technological innovations to address these challenges requires a number of barriers to be overcome:

1 Obtaining funding for technological innovation is the most significant barrier for companies large and small. In general, this is more an issue of access.

2 A shortage of appropriately skilled staff was the second most frequently cited barrier.

TABLE 12.1 Priorities for technological innovation, broken down into four categories

	Work to do	Innovations
Priority 1: working effectively at the farm gate interface	1 maintain and improve food quality and authenticity; 2 meet consumer demand for 'natural' foods; 3 respond to volatility in the cost of raw materials, as well as safeguarding food security. **Key challenge**: sourcing environmentally sustainable and resilient raw material.	1 further effort in plant breeding to enhance crop resilience and nutritional value; 2 the identification and sourcing of alternative raw materials with lower environmental impact; 3 the development of means to monitor and detect food quality and contamination online.
Priority 2: manufacturing healthy and differentiated food products	**Key challenge 1**: further reducing salt, sugar and fat content of processed products and including healthier components such as fibre; **Key challenge 2**: development of new products aimed at specific consumer groups, in particular personalized nutrition to support healthy ageing and lifestyles.	1 through technological innovation in areas such as: formulation engineering; improving understanding of sensory science and taste perception; and the identification of novel substitutes for salt and sugar; 2 improving the diagnosis and prediction of nutrition-related illness to help guide programmes of healthy eating; and the development of products targeted at reducing the risk of developing nutrition-related diseases.

TABLE 12.1   *continued*

	Work to do	Innovations
Priority 3: changing manufacturing and supply chain efficiency	1 improving energy and process efficiency in the food manufacturing environment focuses on reducing costs by minimizing processing steps and increasing throughput in order to reduce energy consumption, as well as seeking opportunities to reduce overall energy consumption. 2 water scarcity – especially the dairy industry.	1 new means of cooling the ambient factory environment; designing factories which are more energy efficient; and the development of new technologies for energy-intensive processing steps, such as freezing, chilling and cooking, as well as better use of low-grade heat. 2 reducing energy losses within the retail environment, particularly in chiller cabinets, without creating a barrier between the consumer and the product; and reducing the need for chilling throughout the food chain by improving supply chain efficiency. 3 technological innovation opportunities include: the development of low-water cleaning technologies; and identifying cheaper and more effective measures for water and effluent clean-up, and the recycling of non-potable water.
Priority 4: reducing and reusing waste materials	1 waste reduction and reuse is primarily driven by economic issues associated with maximizing efficiency and reducing operating costs. 2 finding new applications for off specification and residual products, particularly those arising from fruit and vegetable processing, dairy, and other primary processing applications.	1 innovation in packaging to prolong shelf life and reduce food spoilage and wastage is a key current priority. 2 smart packaging. 3 converting food-manufacturing and domestic waste to non-food materials; decontaminating waste streams for food or feed use; and improving connectivity with small-scale waste production, both within the supply chain and within individual businesses.

3 Food manufacturers tend to focus more on 'fire-fighting' short-term requests from retailers and consumers, rather than on a strategic long-term relationship.

4 The reluctance of consumers to move away from familiar products and buying habits, together with a reluctance to 'pay for new technology' and the perceived health and safety risks associated with novel food products, can be a barrier.

Innovations within food supply chains[9]

Some examples of innovations within the food sector that have enabled global food supply chains are these:

Chemically synthesized fertilizers, herbicides and pesticides that promote crop growth and protect crops from weeds, insects and other pests

These are very important to maintain food security for the present and future. However, the manufacture and use of these chemicals has to be monitored very closely. Modern fertilizers stem from a chemical engineering breakthrough pioneered in 1908 by Fritz Haber, who developed a process to synthesize ammonia by reacting hydrogen and nitrogen. In 1918, he was awarded the Nobel Prize in Chemistry for this discovery. The herbicidal activity of glyphosate, which is normally used as a pesticide, was first discovered in 1970 by Monsanto's John Franz, for which he received the National Medal of Technology in 1987 (the highest honour awarded to leading innovators in the United States by the US president). The research around producing high-yielding disease-resistant seeds has also been controversial, but with the objective of trying to meet future food security. Other recent innovations within the field of agriculture have been focused around the use of ICT for farm management, online connectivity and access to databases. The use of mobile phone apps (especially in Africa), enabling animal health workers and farmers to diagnose livestock illness accurately and find the most effective drugs to treat the disease, has been revolutionary. New cooperatives, food hubs and supply chain models (for example, Amul Cooperative in India) help small farmers to obtain access to markets and derive a livelihood from their produce.

Advanced food-processing techniques

These processing techniques add nutrients and improve the aesthetic appeal of the food. Processing can enable sourcing from across the globe, and long-distance logistics can extend the shelf life. Advanced processing can remove micro-organisms, reducing spoilage and food-borne illnesses. Modern food processing can also improve the quality of life for people with food allergies by treating the food to remove the allergens (for example, gluten-free, dairy-free and so on) and for diabetics (by reducing sugar content and providing sugar-free alternatives).

Modern-day packaging innovations

These include traditional metal cans, newer multilayer packages that allow foods to be heat-sterilized within the package, and packages with oxygen and carbon dioxide levels that slow ripening (for example, pineapple chunks) and spoilage.

Food preservation through sterilization

This is a key aspect of any food-packaging operation. The ability to sterilize foods to protect them against spoilage by oxidation, bacteria and moulds has been very useful. Some other techniques are high-temperature pasteurization and canning, refrigeration and freezing, chemical preservatives (using such compounds as sulfite, sodium nitrite, ethyl formate, propionic acid, sorbic acid and benzoic acid) and irradiation.

Aseptic packaging

This process allows many products once considered perishables, such as milk and juice, to be packaged, distributed, and stored for months or longer without the need for refrigeration, irradiation or chemical preservatives. During packing, both the food and the packaging are sterilized at high temperatures for very short periods. The sterile containers are then filled in a sterile atmosphere.

Advanced packaging options

Slowing the ripening process in fresh fruits and vegetables and protecting perishable foods against spoilage have helped source food from across the globe. One of the innovations that facilitated this is vacuum packaging, in which the food is first placed into a gas-impermeable bag and then the air within the bag is vacuumed out and the bag sealed. This process reduces the oxygen inside the bag, so that the microbes that spoil food cannot survive. Vacuum packaging has been further improved to create controlled-atmosphere packaging (CAP) and modified-atmosphere packaging (MAP). During CAP, oxygen and carbon dioxide levels inside the food packaging are controlled in order to limit fruit and vegetable respiration and reduce the amount of off-gas ethylene produced. In MAP, which is an advanced version of CAP, a customized blend of inert (non-reactive) gases (most often carbon dioxide and nitrogen) is pumped into the shipping container and the food package to replace oxygen in the 'head space'. This not only slows ripening, but also prevents many natural reactions that cause foods to spoil. In both scenarios, the outer packaging is such that it allows the gas generated through the slow ripening to escape, but does not permit oxygen to enter the package.

Other examples

Some of the other innovations in food processing have been the formulation of artificial sweeteners and artificial flavours, and fast-cooking foods and frozen/freeze-dried foods. Fast-cooking, or 'instant', foods, such as quick-cooking rice, canned soups, packaged bake mixes, and canned and frozen vegetables, are often prepared by hydrating and then pre-cooking the foodstuff, after which the treated products are dried to reduce the moisture content and prolong shelf life.

The advent of online grocery-buying mechanisms has revolution-ized the processing, packaging, storage and delivery of food products. In an era of instant buying from the home, food retailers and super-markets have had to change the way they do business and stock certain products. The advent of loyalty cards also helps the food supply chain to understand buying patterns and forecast demand to manage food inventories and thus reduce food waste.

Sustainable initiatives, food security, obesity challenges and nutri-tional requirements are pressing food-sector companies to rethink their processes and create solutions to solve these future problems. In a recent funding call by InnovateUK (an executive non-departmental public body, sponsored by the Department for Business, Innovation & Skills), £11m is being provided to obtain improved food supply chain efficiency. The agency will provide funding to improve the resource efficiency and resilience of the food and drink supply chain as part of the Sustainable Agriculture and Food Innovation Platform (SAF-IP).[10] The focus is for companies to develop innovative ways to:

- reduce the production of food waste;
- use resources such as energy, water and raw materials more efficiently;
- improve the productivity of food manufacturing and processing operations;
- improve the resilience of the food supply chain by making better use of resources and reducing environmental stresses on food systems.

This provides an important insight into the future of the food supply chains.

CASE EXAMPLE   Types of functional products[11-14]

From a product point of view, the following classification is proposed:

- foods fortified with additional nutrients (labelled fortified products), such as fruit juices fortified with vitamin C, vitamin E, folic acid, zinc and calcium;

- foods with additional new nutrients or components not normally found in a particular food (labelled enriched products), such as probiotics or prebiotics;

- foods from which a deleterious component has been removed, reduced or replaced by another with beneficial effects (labelled altered products), for example fibres as fat releasers in meat or ice cream;

- foods in which one of the components has been naturally enhanced (labelled enhanced commodities), for example eggs with increased omega-3 content.

CASE EXAMPLE   Detecting counterfeit whisky through the bottle[15]

The Food and Drink iNet supported a collaborative research and development project that allowed researchers to adapt a technique to detect counterfeit whisky without opening the bottle. The research used a technique which was originally developed from novel technology designed and built by the Space Research Centre, Leicester, for astronomical research. It relies on detecting the differences between the characteristics of light reflected from printed packaging for use in the pharmaceutical world. The research project was conducted by a team from the University of Leicester, Perpetuity Research and Consultancy International. Fake and adulterated whisky costs the industry an estimated £500 million in lost revenue every year. The outcome is an innovative process to detect counterfeit product without having to test it. Since news of the technology and its potential application was revealed, there has been interest from around the world. The project was crowned Food and Drink iNet Innovation Champion 2011 in recognition of the exciting potential for the technology in the food and drink sector.

Summary

This chapter has presented a discussion of innovation within the food sector. Innovation is represented as institutional, technological or social. The chapter also discussed the challenges with product design and consumer preferences and then presented a brief synopsis of the research commissioned by DEFRA in 2007 with regard to innovation in the food sector. Finally, the chapter presented some examples of current innovations in the food sector.

Notes

1 IICA (2014) Innovation in agriculture: a key process for sustainable development, Institutional position paper, San Jose, May

2 OECD (2005) *Oslo Manual: Guidelines for collecting and interpreting innovation data*, 3rd edn, European Communities, France (164 pp)

3 World Bank (2007) *Enhancing Agricultural Innovation: How to go beyond the strengthening of research systems*, World Bank, Washington, DC [Online] https://openknowledge.worldbank.org/handle/10986/7184

4 Stewart-Knox, B and Mitchell, P (2003) What separates the winners from the losers in new food product development? *Trends in Food Science & Technology*, **14**, pp 58–64

5 Bigliardia, B and Galat, F (2013) Innovation trends in the food industry: the case of functional foods, *Trends in Food Science & Technology*, **31** (2), pp 118–29

6 Christensen, J, Rama, R and von Tunzelmann, N (1996) Study on innovation in the European food products and beverages industry, European Innovation Monitoring System, EIMS Publication, 35, European Commission, Directorate General XIII, Luxembourg; Garcia Martinez, M and Briz, J (2000) Innovation in the Spanish food and drink industry, *International Food and Agribusiness Management Review*, 3, pp 155–76

7 Beckeman, M and Skjolkebrand, C (2007) Cluster/networks promote food innovations, *Journal of Food Engineering*, **79**, pp 1418–25

8 Arthur D Little (accessed 25 February 2015) Mapping current innovation and emerging R&D needs in the food and drink industry required for sustainable economic growth [Online] http://randd.defra.gov.uk/Default.aspx?Menu=Menu&Module=More&Location=None&Completed=0&ProjectID=18564

9 For a detailed account of chemical-engineering-based innovations, see American Institute of Chemical Engineers and Chemical Heritage Foundation (accessed 18 February 2015) Chemical engineering innovation in food production, 2009 [Online] http://www.chemicalengineering.org/docs/cheme-food.pdf

10 Sustainable Agri-Food Innovation Platform (accessed 24 February 2015) Home page [Online] https://connect.innovateuk.org/web/sustainable-agriculture-and-food-innovation-platform/2014-improving-food-supply-chain-efficiency

11 Kotilainen, L *et al* (2006) Health Enhancing Foods: Opportunities for strengthening the sector in developing countries, Discussion Paper 30, World Bank, Washington, DC

12 Sloan, A E (2000) The top ten functional food trends, *Food Technology*, 54, pp 33–62

13 Spence, J T (2006) Challenges related to the composition of functional foods, *Journal of Food Composition and Analysis*, 19, S4–S6

14 Christensen, J, Rama, R and von Tunzelmann, N (1996) Study on innovation in the European food products and beverages industry, European Innovation Monitoring System, EIMS Publication, 35, European Commission, Directorate General XIII, Luxembourg.

15 Food and Drink iNet (accessed 24 February 2015) Home page [Online] http://www.foodanddrink-inet.org.uk/case-studies?qfs=1&p=1

Sustainability challenges in food supply chains

13

This chapter presents a discussion of the sustainability challenges in the food supply chain. Sustainability is at the heart of all discussions within the business world. It pervades all levels of the operation and throughout the supply chain. The baseline for designing and running all operations must stem from the requirements to meet sustainability criteria. This is no longer a voluntary activity and organizations will have to meet a host of statutory regulations to achieve sustainability. The food supply chain is a very complex network of entities and spans a number of activities that are governed by statutory and market norms. If these are not met, the food supply chain will collapse. This chapter briefly looks at the idea of sustainability and then maps it across the different entities of the food supply chain. The aim is not to provide a detailed guide (this is not possible owing to the breadth of the various regulations and areas) but a synopsis of the things to consider within the sustainable food supply chain.

Sustainability – the origins of the idea

One of the first occurrences of the term sustainability associated with agriculture was in the 1980s when Fearnside[1] discussed 'the effects of cattle pasture on soil fertility'. In the following years, other authors adopted the term: for instance, Douglas[2] used it for a conference on agricultural sustainability and published a book chapter about agricultural sustainability, which gave the term 'sustainability', or its adjective 'sustainable', a new dimension: *the environmental perspective*. In 1983, the UN established the World Commission on Environment and Development (WCED) 4 as an independent expert commission based in Geneva. The purpose of this commission was the development of a viable long-term report about global environmentally friendly development extending to the year 2000 or even further. In 1987, Brundtland *et al*[3] eventually formulated the expression 'sustainable development' with the often-cited sentence: 'Humanity has the ability to make development sustainable to ensure that it meets the needs of the present without compromising the ability of future generations to meet their own needs.'

The WCED was officially dissolved at the end of 1987, after it released the 'Brundtland Report' (officially: 'Our common future') and continued in April 1988 as the Centre for Our Common Future, in Geneva; it was reactivated for the Rio conference in 1992. It was the Brundtland Report that started to coin the present common understanding of sustainability by clearly addressing three perspectives, namely 'economic and social systems and ecological conditions'.[4] The release of the Brundtland Report triggered a change of thinking in respect of the term sustainability. Its meaning as it was used before 1987 – the ability to sustain – changed to a triangle, which included the components economics, humanity and environment.

At the beginning of the 1990s, the first articles linking sustainability to the energy problematic were published. For instance, Parthasarathi[5] highlighted the necessity of a shift of energy sources, particularly for rural areas. As alternatives to conventional sources of electricity, Parthasarathi suggests photovoltaic and solar technology, as well as biomass-based systems. The studies in the early 1990s also focused on the predicted shortage of fossil fuels and the understanding that being sustainable in the generation and supply of energy means aiming for renewable energy production. Weizsäcker[6] had concerns about the waste of resources in developed countries and draws a scenario of how destructive it would be if the developing countries catch up to the natural resource per head consumption of the developed countries.

One of the most often quoted definitions of sustainability is the triple bottom line (TBL) model, introduced by Elkington, which divides sustainability into three bottom lines: a) economic prosperity;

b) environmental quality; and c) social equity.[7] Elkington chose his words very carefully when he came to define the term sustainability. He particularly used the established expression 'bottom line' to develop his model, a term widely used in financial terminology for evaluating a company's monetary success or failure.

Sustainable supply chains

In the academic literature, sustainable supply chain management is used synonymously with corporate social responsibility (CSR), green supply chain management (GSCM), environmental purchasing, value chain management and ethical purchasing. The terminology is vague and not precisely defined. Sustainable supply chain management is thus considered in this book to be the umbrella term that considers all three bottom lines together: economic, social and environmental. It is thus suggested that when designing the supply chain, all three bottom lines must be considered and how these interact with each other in the fulfilment process.

GSCM is often equated with sustainable supply chain management (SSCM). The principle of GSCM is prevalent in various different industries. Wang et al[8] find that it is important to implement three facets in order to achieve a green supply chain:

- green foods;
- green environment and equipment;
- green management and social responsibility.

Retailers and big brands are constantly in the public eye and under observation, not only by non-government organizations (NGOs), government institutions and shareholders, but also by their customers and stakeholders.[9] Styles et al[10] note that retailers are in a very good position to introduce and enforce supply chain eco-efficiency measures. The authors suggest environmental performance benchmarking of suppliers and third-party certification as efficient environmental initiatives. Consumer awareness is created by labelling products with the relevant environmental metrics. Anderson[11] discusses the value of localization of supply chains in working towards sustainability. It is found that the main benefit for local sourcing is the improvement to the environmental bottom line owing to the reduction in transport. Not only that, but local sourcing, which is demonstrated by the authors using the example of a food supply chain, can be beneficial for the local community.

Sustainable food supply chains

The UK Sustainable Development Commission[12-14] has combined many different stakeholder views to produce an internationally applicable description of 'sustainable food supply chains' as those that:

1 produce safe, healthy products in response to market demands and ensure that all consumers have access to nutritious food and to accurate information about food products;

2 support the viability and diversity of rural and urban economies and communities;

3 enable viable livelihoods to be made from sustainable land management, both through the market and through payments for public benefits;

4 respect and operate within the biological limits of natural resources (especially soil, water and biodiversity);

5 achieve consistently high standards of environmental performance by reducing energy consumption, minimizing resource inputs and using renewable energy wherever possible;

6 ensure a safe and hygienic working environment and high social welfare and training for all employees involved in the food chain;

7 achieve consistently high standards of animal health and welfare;

8 sustain the resource available for growing food and supplying other public benefits over time, except where alternative land uses are essential to meet other needs of society.

A lot of effort is required to make changes to the ways in which companies work to make supply chains more sustainable. Food businesses need to look closely at their operation (employee training and welfare, eco-efficiency, innovative 'cleaner' production and waste management) and at their own products (food quality, safety, labelling).

Measuring sustainability

Using the TBL concept as a base, measurement of sustainability can be done on three fronts:

- economic sustainability: financial measures (profitability, return on investment, etc);
- environmental sustainability: measuring the impact of businesses and processes (carbon emissions, packaging waste, fuel consumption, energy usage, etc);
- social sustainability: measures the social impact (labour conditions, pay scales, investment in the community, fair and ethical pricing, etc).

Large retailers will measure sustainability parameters as a part of their supplier selection programme and then review the parameters on renewal. One of the main concerns of businesses with sustainable implementation is the impact on costs. Also, it is difficult for a majority of companies to look at this strategically. Small and medium-sized enterprises will find it difficult to invest in sustainable operations; however, if they are a supplier to large multinationals, they will need to implement sustainability.

One of the methods that helps in measuring environmental performance is 'life-cycle analysis' (LCA).[15] This tool is used to model the environmental impact of a product over the lifetime of the product. ISO 14040 (2006)[16] standardizes the LCA process:

1 Define the goal and scope of the LCA.

2 Conduct a life-cycle inventory analysis (studying the environmental impact throughout the life cycle of a product).

3 Create an impact-assessment scoring sheet.

4 Interpret the results and identify the most important environmental impacts.

It is difficult to create full LCAs for a food product when mapping it from farm to fork, as there are too many processes and it is not clear which variables need to be considered in the analysis (for example, use of pesticides in farming, fertilizers and so on).[17] A new modification to the LCA tool was created by Sala *et al*,[18] which measured not only the quantitative environmental impact but also attributes of, for example, social policy. Sala *et al* took this idea further and created the 'Life-cycle Sustainability Assessment' methodology:

- *Ecological footprint*: indicates the quantity of land required to provide resources for a specific activity.

- *Carbon emissions*: greenhouse gas emissions from running processes.

- *Carbon footprint*: negative environmental impact associated with economic activities.

- *Food miles*: the distance travelled by a food product or the components of the product from source to consumption.

- *Eco-labelling*: Eco-labelling and social labelling are market-based mechanisms designed to demonstrate that products have been sourced with due regard for social and environmental consequences.[19] An eco-label may describe a product as 'environmentally friendly' or a social label may give some guarantee about the labour conditions under which the product was produced. However, Gadema and Oglethorpe[20] conclude that, even though most consumers in UK supermarkets are influenced by carbon footprint labels on products, voluntary labelling as currently practised does not improve the environmental impact of food products significantly.

Developing sustainability within food supply chains

Sustainable production

Sustainable production is about making sure that the ecosystem is not harmed when growing food. This also relates to animal welfare and soil conservation. Sustainability in agriculture will follow the three lines of thought – economic, environmental and social/ethical. Agriculture will be sustained and food will be produced in abundance in the future only if the sector survives, and this will happen if farmers and producers are economically sustainable. When farmers get the right price for their produce, access to finance and become better skilled in order to move up the value chain, they will be financially stable and able to innovate and grow the sector.

Environmentally, the sector is facing challenges on account of water shortage. Sustainable agriculture practices will make sure that water is conserved and farming techniques developed that use less water. Also, the use of energy has to be controlled. Ironically, a majority of small farms in the developing world will be in areas that are not electrified. The use of pesticides and fertilizers that are harmful to the ecosystem needs to be avoided, and organic farming techniques can be learnt to get better produce and maintain the environment. Crop rotation will also help to maintain the integrity of the soil.

Sustainability also relates to social/ethical practices, which will involve getting a fair price for the produce and creating communities that have access to schools, drinking water and so on. Processes that take animal welfare into account will also be important for the meat supply chain.

Diageo, a global drinks manufacturer, considers the following factors when discussing sustainable sourcing of agricultural produce:[21]

1 legal compliance: complying with national and sustainability-related regulations;

2 environmental impact reduction: reducing water use and pollution, preventing soil erosion, protecting biodiversity and reducing energy and carbon use;

3 socio-economic impacts: ensuring fair working conditions and health and safety, and eliminating child labour.

Sustainable processing

Sustainability in food processing or manufacturing focuses on a number of aspects. From an operational aspect, sustainable food manufacturing is about the level of resources utilized and the waste that is generated by the process. Most organizations, when considering sustainability within their manufacturing operations, will work towards reduction of water and energy use, reduction in greenhouse gas emissions and reduction in waste.[22]

The approach of Premier Foods,[23] a leading UK company with regard to sustainable food manufacturing, is to use fewer resources and generate less waste. The company focuses on the following six factors with regard to sustainable manufacturing:

1 Carbon footprint: The company works on reducing its carbon footprint by reducing carbon dioxide emissions from energy consumption in manufacturing, transportation and logistics operations and waste. It follows the greenhouse gas protocol.

2 Energy consumption: The company actively maps out energy use within manufacturing and has created energy reduction action plans.

3 Packaging design: The company has built joint plans with the Waste Resources Action Programme (WRAP) to reduce food waste, improve packaging design for recyclability and reduce product and packaging waste.

4 Transport: Although not directly connected to manufacturing, it can still be considered as an extension of the process. The company works towards reducing food transport miles. It works actively with third-party logistics providers (3PLs) and hauliers to achieve its objectives.

5 Waste: Reducing waste generated through processing and waste generated on site (paper, plastics, metal cans, etc).

The company also works on reducing excess production of food and food waste in general.

6 Water: The company has a commitment to use less water in the operations and is also a signatory to the Federation House Commitment (FHC2020) on water reduction. Water management and alternative sources of water conservation and harvesting should be considered.

Unilever[24] operates a similar strategy and has included the following four initiatives:

1 reducing the environmental impact of new production facilities – either new factories or new production lines;

2 reducing the impact of all existing factories;

3 making its global and regional purchasing more efficient;

4 embracing new technologies.

Sustainable logistics and retail

Sustainability practices within the logistics and retail environments are focused on reduction of energy use and subsequently reduction of carbon emissions. The Carbon Trust[25] suggests that the retail sector should focus on reducing energy consumption by focusing on:

- Lighting: Work towards cutting energy costs by improving the lighting in the retail environment. This will help to reduce the carbon footprint and improve the working environment for your staff.

- Refrigeration: Make the refrigeration systems more efficient by utilizing them efficiently or upgrading and replacing equipment.

- Energy management: Monitoring energy use across the operation and developing action plans and training for staff.

Retailers will also work towards waste reduction and water conservation within their environments.

Sustainable or green logistics is about cutting down on energy use (fuel consumption) and reducing carbon emissions. The environmental effects of retail logistics are:[26]

1 greenhouse gas emission: carbon dioxide released in the atmosphere due to the burning of fossil fuels;

2 pollutants from vehicle exhaust;

3 noise pollution;

4 waste generated from packaging that is required to ease transportation.

Food retailers and logistics companies will need to reconsider and map routes to reduce energy consumption, and this will include thinking of cleaner multimodal transportation, for example using railways and waterways where possible. The development of port-centric logistics has helped to reduce road miles travelled by containers and increased the use of distribution centres (DCs) at the ports as the main points of distribution. There is also a need to utilize vehicle capacity effectively in order to reduce vehicles' empty running. The logistics sector is currently trying out alternative fuels and also training its employees to reduce fuel consumption by driving effectively.

Sustainable sourcing

Sustainable sourcing ensures that, to the best of the food supply chain's ability, products or goods purchased have no, or a limited, negative impact on the communities and ecosystems from which they are sourced.[27] The definition put forth by IGD discusses the impact of the food supply chain on the environment and society. There is no clear-cut definition as such on sustainable sourcing, as people tend to use various terms within the domain. Green purchasing, responsible purchasing, green procurement and ethical purchasing are all terms used for the same process, which is about sourcing and purchasing raw material for the downstream supply chain. Complexity arises from the source and how the material is obtained. For example, palm oil sourced from the Far East has environmental impacts of deforestation, leading to a threat of extinction of orangutans. So a harmless purchasing decision to buy palm oil for your manufacturing operation can trigger a process in which forests are razed to make way for land to grow more palm trees; thus, the impact of the decision, perhaps not known or not projected at the time of purchase, makes the process highly complex and one that requires immediate attention as a management activity. The TBL concept may appear to be a very simple approach, but it has sufficient strength as a framework to make us think when we set about our management tasks. In the context of this book, sustainable sourcing is defined as an activity that meets the TBL objectives of the organization. This is very simplistic and there is a lot of debate as to how many organizations can in reality achieve the triple objective, with people often citing the horsemeat scandal or the plight of the smallholders in developing countries. The focus here is not to demonstrate that this is a perfect framework, but more a framework that prods the person taking the role of the buyer to think about priorities and take responsible decisions. The criteria for a sourcing strategy can be based on the UN Global Compact 10 framework, which was discussed in Chapter 8. Some of the factors to consider under sustainable sourcing are:

1 *Economic sustainability*: this is applicable for both the buyer and the supplier. The CSR commitment of the buyer organization will steer it to be economically sustainable (which means making sufficient returns to stay in business), as it affects shareholders, employees and local society. However, the other side of the coin makes it important that it treats its suppliers fairly so that they stay in business too. Driving down prices to make profits but eventually closing down the supplier network is not a sound strategy. Hence, the UN, WTO, FAO, UNIDO and other such organizations advocate strengthening the economic status of the agriculture sector in the developing world in order to maintain the supply for the present and for the future.

2 *Environmental sustainability*: this is about working on initiatives through the sourcing strategy to make sure that the supplier network is not harming the environment. This can happen on two counts: the buyer drives down prices, which

creates a situation where the supplier takes shortcuts (not treating waste, because it is costly, and instead letting it escape into water bodies, harming the ecosystem); or the supplier, of its own accord, in order to make more profit, behaves unethically and uses certain chemicals (as seen in the Chinese milk case study), commits to deforestation in order to obtain more land, or does not care about carbon emissions and use of resources as it thinks that it is not monitored on these grounds. It is true that most organizations will have a sustainable sourcing policy, but they may not have stringent measurement processes. They will know about a breach only when the issue turns into a crisis.

3 *Social/ethical sustainability*: this is about working on initiatives that provide benefits to the supplier network and to society in a fair and ethical way. A fair price for produce, a living wage, good and safe working conditions, absence of child and forced labour, skilling local communities and increasing the capability of the supplier base are some of the ways in which buyer organizations can help through their strategic sustainable sourcing policies.

Most large organizations will have a sustainable sourcing policy which will not only be based on commitment and intent but will be framed around many legal regulations, statutory certifications and a host of voluntary self-certification schemes, which are helpful as they provide the framework for sustainability but also prove to the consumer base that the company is actively working on these initiatives. For a detailed look at a sustainable sourcing policy and operational guide, please see Unilever's sustainable sourcing programme for agricultural raw materials.[28,29]

CASE EXAMPLE   Various initiatives within food supply chains

The governments of various countries, the UK (DEFRA), European Union, United Nations, World Trade Organization, Food and Agriculture Organization, United

States Department for Agriculture and the ILO, among others, have initiatives that promote food sustainability and good agriculture practices. There are many initiatives that have been started by NGOs and collaborative partnerships between food-sector companies to help with specific areas of food sustainability and create voluntary and industry-led certifications. Some of these initiatives are:

- EurepGAP;

- GlobalGAP;

- Common Code for the Coffee community;

- Sustainable Agriculture Initiative Platform;

- Roundtable on Sustainable Palm Oil;

- United Nations Millennium Development Goals;

- Fairtrade Foundation;

- Ethical Tea Partnership;

- Forest Stewardship Council;

- Marine Stewardship Council;

- Ethical Trading Initiative;

- International Cocoa Initiative;

- Carbon Trust Foundation.

This is not an exhaustive list, but it provides an insight into the activities being conducted on various fronts across the food supply chain.

CASE EXAMPLE   Just Eggs – recycling egg shells to make filler for plastics[30]

Egg shells are a waste by-product of the egg-processing industry. Egg-processing companies have to bear the cost of sending these egg shells to be disposed of at landfill sites, costing thousands of pounds and creating waste. This case study is about 'Just Eggs', an egg-processing company based in Leicester, UK. This company processes around 1.3 million eggs per week, creating 10 tonnes of egg shells. The cost of disposing of these egg shells was £30,000 per year.

The challenge was to transform this waste and reduce the costs to the company. The Food and Drink iNet, UK, funded a Collaborate to Innovate project involving researchers from the Department of Chemistry, a company – Integrated Food Projects, and a number of egg-processing SMEs in the East Midlands of the UK.

This project is working on extracting glycosaminoglycans (GAGs), proteins which are found in egg shells, to convert into fillers for manufacturing plastics and also to use within biomedical applications. The aim is to reuse proteins and calcium carbonate from the egg shells to transform into packaging material (even turning this into packaging for fresh eggs). This case highlights that there are opportunities for innovating within the food supply chain to reduce food waste and transform it into a new product – helping the sustainability agenda and creating further economic benefits.

Summary

This chapter has introduced the origins of the term sustainability and discussed how this related to supply chains. The sustainable supply chain is a very important area of work both in the practitioner world and in academia. The chapter gave a brief synopsis of what this is and then applied it to the food sector. The activities within the food supply chain were considered individually from the aspect of sustainability, and the chapter discussed how sustainability is achieved within these activities. Finally, a few case examples were provided to wrap up the discussion.

Notes

1 Fearnside, P M (1980) The effects of cattle pasture on soil fertility in the Brazilian Amazon: consequences for beef production sustainability, *Tropical Ecology*, **21** (1), pp 125–38

2 Douglas, G K (1984) Agricultural sustainability in a changing world order, in *Agricultural Sustainability in a Changing World Order*, Westview Special Studies in Agriculture, Science and Policy, Chap. Conclusions: Sustainability for Whom?, pp 271–75, Westview Press, Boulder, CO

3 Brundtland, G H *et al* (1987) Our Common Future, Technical Report, World Commission on Environment and Development (WCED)

4 See note 3.

5 Parthasarathi, A (1990) Science and technology in India's search for a sustainable and equitable future, *World Development*, **18** (12), pp 1693–701

6 Weizsäcker, E U von (1991) Sustainability: a task for the north, *Journal of International Affairs*, **44** (2), p 421

7 Elkington, J (1998) *Cannibals with Forks: The triple bottom line of 21st century business*, The Conscientious Commerce Series, New Society Publishers, Gabriola Island, BC, Canada

8 Wang, Y-F *et al* (2013) Developing green management standards for restaurants: an application of green supply chain management, *International Journal of Hospitality Management*, **34** (1), pp 263–73

9 Wolf, J (2014) The relationship between sustainable supply chain management, stakeholder pressure and corporate sustainability performance, *Journal of Business Ethics*, **119** (3), pp 317–28

10 Styles, D, Schoenberger, H and Galvez-Martos, J-L (2012) Environmental improvement of product supply chains: proposed best practice techniques, quantitative indicators and benchmarks of excellence for retailers, *Journal of Environmental Management*, **110**, pp 135–50

11 Anderson, M (2008) Rights-based food systems and the goals of food systems reform, *Agriculture and Human Values*, **25** (4), pp 593–608

12 DEFRA (2002) The Strategy for Sustainable Farming and Food: Facing the Future, 51 pp, DEFRA Publications, London

13 Smith, G (2008) Developing sustainable food supply chains, Philosophical Transactions of the Royal Society B, **363**, pp 849–61

14 See note 12.

15 Oosterveer, P and Sonnenfeld, D A (2012) *Food, Globalization and Sustainability*, Earthscan Routledge, London

16 ISO (accessed 24 February 2015) ISO 14040:2006 [Online] https://www.iso.org/obp/ui/#iso:std:iso:14040:ed-2:v1:en

17 Andrews, E *et al* (2009) Life cycle attribute assessment: case study of Quebec greenhouse tomatoes, *Journal of Industrial Ecology*, **13** (4), pp 565–78

18 Sala, S, Farioli, F and Zamagni, A (2012) Life cycle sustainability assessment in the context of sustainability science progress (part 2), *International Journal of Life Cycle Assessment*, **18** (9), pp 1689–97

19 Food for thought: Corporate social responsibility for food and beverage manufacturers, Prince of Wales International Business Leaders Forum

20 Gadema, Z and Oglethorpe, D (2011) The use and usefulness of carbon labelling food: a policy perspective from a survey of UK supermarket shoppers, *Food Policy*, **36** (6), pp 815–822

21 Diageo (accessed 24 February 2015) Sustainable Agricultural Sourcing Guidelines, November 2011 [Online] http://neostaging.ccreport2010. diageoreports.com/media/3689/Agricultural_Sourcing_Guidelines_ v1.1.pdf

22 Food Industry Sustainability Strategy, 2006 DEFRA

23 Premier Foods (accessed 24 February 2015) Sustainable Manufacturing [Online] http://www.premierfoods.co.uk/sustainability/sustainable-manufacturing/our-approach/

24 Unilever (accessed 24 February 2015) Eco-efficiency in manufacturing [Online] http://www.unilever.com/sustainable-living-2014/reducing-environmental-impact/eco-efficiency-in-manufacturing/index.aspx

25 Carbon Trust (accessed 24 February 2015) Retail and distribution [Online] http://www.carbontrust.com/resources/guides/sector-based-advice/retail-and-distribution

26 Mckinnon, A and Edwards, J (2014) The greening of retail logistics, in *Logistics and Retail Management*, ed J Fernie and L Sparks, Kogan Page, London

27 IGD (accessed 24 February 2015) Sustainable sourcing within the food chain, 22 December 2008 [Online] http://www.igd.com/Research/ Sustainability/Ethical-social-issues/3722/Sustainable-sourcing-within-the-food-chain/

28 Unilever (accessed 24 February 2015) Our Strategy [Online] http:// www.unilever.com/sustainable-living-2014/reducing-environmental-impact/sustainable-sourcing/our-strategy/

29 Unilever (accessed 24 February 2015) Unilever Sustainable Sourcing Programme for Agricultural Raw Materials: Scheme rules, 1 March 2014 [Online] http://www.unilever.com/images/Scheme-Rules-30-sep_tcm13-338425.pdf

30 Food and Drink iNet (accessed 24 February 2015) Egg Shell Recycling [Online] http://www.foodanddrink-inet.org.uk/case-studies/resources-environment-egg-shell-recycling-collaborate-to-innovate

Food sector and economic regeneration

14

The food sector is an important part of any national economy as it has a product that will never fail to have a demand. This product in any form will be valid as the population on our planet increases on a daily basis. However, a need and a want have different connotations and as the food sector creates more innovative products and varieties, it works hard on the wants of the consumers. The food sector has realized that margins are greater for the wants and not the needs of the end consumers. Hence, certain products are marketed and sold not as staple products but more of a lifestyle choice (for example, Starbucks coffee). During the recent economic downturn it was evident that the food industry (although it may have had to deal with increased costs) did not face any demand challenges. On the other hand, when consumers did not have disposable income to spend on material goods, they spent more on food (as a small luxury – takeaways, chocolate bars and so on).

Although large food companies and their supply chains are organized, the global food sector is largely unorganized in nature, ranging from a one-person food service to off-licences to food/grocery retail environments. The food sector (along the supply chain) employs a considerable number of people providing the necessary economic activity. Recognizing the potential of the food sector (mainly food processing), the governments of various countries such as India, Thailand, Malaysia and Brazil have started focusing on creating the necessary infrastructure to facilitate this industry. For infrastructure and capital investment, the impetus should come from appropriate government policy, wherein there is a long-term view for the sector. This chapter will consider some of these activities and the challenges involved in implementing them.

Infrastructure development for the food sector

Logistics infrastructure

As nations compete with each other to get a share of the global economy, the food sector has been identified in developing countries as one sector that can help the lives of millions of people living below the poverty line. As the majority of the producers live in rural areas of developing countries, the development of logistics infrastructure is key to the growth of the food sector. Logistics infrastructure is required to create efficiencies of scale and to reduce the excessive post-harvest food loss. As the food-processing industry increases its capacity and generates products for the organized retail environment, the importance of effective, safe and efficient logistics is paramount. A major quantity of food produced in the developing world is lost after harvest owing to too few warehouses (to store the harvest), lack of road/rail (to deliver the harvest to the next stage of the chain) and a lack of cool chains. The need to develop sustainable solutions for all processes requires governments and the logistics industry to develop policies and practices that will lead to sustainable movement and storage of goods. The integration of transportation networks to create optimized and efficient movement of goods and reduce carbon emissions has led many governments to think of using rail as a transport mode of choice rather than roads. However, in developing countries, road building in rural areas will take preference over rail infrastructure, as connectivity to individual villages through roads (the last mile) is required. The integrated nature of the infrastructure will therefore use the road networks to access the rail networks, making roads the main mode of goods transportation in some countries. In some countries the use of waterways and coastal routes may have a wider impact. The building of dedicated rail-freight corridors within Thailand and

India has taken precedence in the infrastructure-building process. This affects the agriculture industry, as the movement of agri-produce for export will require connectivity from the farm to the port, which will include a network of roads and rail with connectivity to the port also becoming a major hurdle in some countries. Some governments have planned warehousing and logistics cities along the freight corridors. The following is a synopsis of the logistics plans for India:[1]

1 Dedicated rail-freight corridors: initially two planned corridors between Delhi–Kolkata and Delhi–Mumbai, and a plan for three other routes.
2 Coastal freight corridors: along major coastal regions in the west and east of the country through integrated connectivity that includes last-mile rail and roads, trans-shipment hubs and ports.
3 National expressways: construction of major expressways by 2020 to increase connectivity, with the aim of reducing lead-times and increasing operational efficiency.
4 Last-mile roads: links to connect ports and railway terminals to production and distribution centres.
5 Multimodal logistics parks: situated along transport corridors with warehousing and distribution facilities.
6 Roads to connect villages to the main network.

These plans are important for India's growth in the food sector with the advent of mega-food parks, intensive farming, higher levels of food processing and the changing retail environment with the entry of organized food retailing.

Food clusters and enterprise zones

Broadly, the food-processing cluster consists of enterprises whose principal activities are the growing, harvesting, processing and/or distribution of food.[2] The food processing cluster will include:

• Producers: farmers who are the input to the processing chain.
• Farmer processors: these utilize their produce to create value-added products and attempt to differentiate them from those in the marketplace.

- Food processors: these enterprises are not engaged in farming, but they use farm products as raw materials.

The cluster will also include other supporting organizations:

- suppliers to the processing companies – packaging etc;
- accounting and law firms;
- engineering and process-design firms;
- marketing and design firms that promote and package products;
- distribution firms;
- research and development centres;
- educational institutions: skills in farming and food processing.

In Europe, the European Food Cluster Initiative[3] has been designed to bring together expertise across the European regions by establishing European clusters of coordination in order to enhance regional research, capacity building and regional economic development with significant impact at local level.

Food parks and hubs

In Europe, an initiative to create location-specific agricultural clusters called agroparks, which bring together agro-food production and related economic (processing) activities, is under way. Agroparks aim to increase sustainability by higher resource productivity, better utilization of agriculture produce, utilization of waste products and by-products of the agriculture process, and the deployment of new technologies. Agroparks link various food and non-food-related businesses, to enable close material flow cycles, creating more sustainable production and better economic benefits (InnovatieNetwerk).[4]

In India, the mega food park concept aims to provide a similar mechanism to agroparks, but focused more on the entities in the agrichain. The primary objective of the scheme is to facilitate establishment of an integrated value chain with processing at the core and supported by the requisite forward and backward linkages in the supply chain, with access to appropriate infrastructure such as cold chains, preservation facilities, pack houses and so on. The UK has also been moving towards developing food parks.

The basic infrastructure requirements for food parks, as seen from India and the UK, are:

1 Basic amenities required in the premises will be: power generation and power distribution (or availability – depending upon the size of the park), water, telecommunications, internet connectivity and waste handling.

2 The availability of food-grade premises for production is an ever-present barrier for manufacturers. 'Standard' business units can be converted to conform to food and environmental health standards, but this can be expensive and incurs ongoing costs to maintain them. These costs inhibit manufacturers' growth by drawing cash away from investment opportunities. The food park will have modern and cost-amenable food-grade premises that conform to the highest food standards, including BRC Grade A, and meet the latest environmental health legislation. The park should have various-sized units to enable start-up and growing manufacturers to fulfil their production requirements.

3 Logistics connectivity to the markets and other multimodal facilities.

4 Facilities to conduct food-based and bioengineering research.

5 Warehouses and cold storage facilities.

6 Food testing laboratories: quality control and standardization are important for the preparation of high-quality foods by local industries. This will also provide service to SMEs and micro-SMEs, which will not have the funding capability to have their own laboratories.

7 For large parks with exporting companies, it will be useful to incorporate the provision of certification.

8 Access to knowledge and skills training through agencies in the park or proximity to educational establishments.

9 Business centre facilities: access to training rooms, new product development kitchens and food training facilities, meeting rooms.

Food hubs

A 2010 report[5] by the US Department of Agriculture (USDA) Economic Research Service noted that one of the main constraints to the entry and expansion of local foods is the 'lack of distribution systems for moving local foods into mainstream markets'.[6] This need has created an emerging local collaborative model called the 'food hub'. USDA's working definition of a regional food hub is 'a business or organization that actively manages the aggregation, distribution and marketing of source-identified food products, primarily from local and regional producers to strengthen their ability to satisfy wholesale, retail and institutional demand'.[7] Food hubs are being used increasingly as a way for a group of producers to access local markets for their agricultural produce. Within a rural environment, food hubs represent a strategy for producers, particularly small and mid-sized producers, to market their production locally. One of the main constraints to the entry and expansion of local foods is the lack of distribution systems for moving local foods into mainstream markets. Food hubs help connect rural producers as directly as possible to rural, suburban and urban markets, with assistance in marketing their produce and creating pooled distribution. Food hubs can help in creating local employment.[8]

Training and skills[9]

As the food industry grows and supply chains move internationally, the level of automation and subsequently the demand for skilled manpower has increased. As with many sectors, the food sector is struggling to recruit skilled manpower. This has an adverse effect on the sector and could affect growth. The food industry employs a variety of managerial and professional workers:

- operational managers;
- food-manufacturing employees;
- engineers, scientists, and technicians;
- food scientists and technologists;
- sales and retail professionals.

The food industry should partner with educational institutions to design and develop skills and training programmes from both the vocational and higher education aspects.

Moving up the value chain

Agro-processing is an activity that is helping smallholder farmers in many developing countries to produce products locally from local farm produce. For this to work well and to help it grow into a more successful, profitable agricultural sector, smallholder farmers need better linkages and access to markets, technology and information. The farmers need access to information and mechanisms that help them plan and sustain their businesses despite the risks of weather conditions and volatile prices. Investment is needed in rural areas to create significant improvements in basic infrastructure and services, access to water and better governance. The farmers need legal empowerment and protection of their rights and support in forming farmers' organizations and cooperatives to give them more bargaining power.[10]

In a study conducted for the State of North Carolina in the United States[11] on the economic feasibility of the North Carolina Food Processing and Manufacturing Initiative, the importance of an economic innovation ecosystem for the development of a sustainable value-added food-manufacturing cluster was recognized. As prices in commodity markets stay volatile, the return to the producer from production is minimal. As the chain adds value to the raw material produced, the returns increase. Hence, the future of the agriculture sector and especially the rural smallholder sector will depend on initiatives to create value-added food production chains. As the producer integrates vertically to add value, a higher return will be received, helping to increase the economic sustainability of the production process and individual livelihoods. The strategy of first determining what consumers require from the food products and then creating those products will provide a better economic model.[12] Product differentiation and value addition are the future. The producers will consider themselves to be a part of the chain, understanding the significance of their activity when they realize the consumption pattern of their product. Although this may be easier to put into context within a rural developed world, it is extremely difficult to envisage the thought process prevailing within a rural developing economy. It does not mean that this cannot happen in the developing economy. Producers will need to be trained and skilled to think economically, the social structures (the most difficult to break) will need to be handled, and infrastructure and finance will need to be provided until the upheaval has settled down.

The value-added supply chain will require a significant level of coordination between the entities in the chain for vertical integration. Within smallholder production environments, individual producers may not have sufficient levels of produce to create vertically integrated value-added businesses. In these cases, horizontal collaboration involving consolidation or pooling of produce, either to make one value-added business or having one producer acting as a buyer for the produce of the other smallholders, may happen. There is scope for creating cooperatives for value addition or entrepreneurs. Apart from skills and training related to farming methods and improving yield, skills development within areas such as contracting, processing, marketing, licensing and so on will help. However, different models for value-added chains need to be created for the developed and developing worlds, taking into consideration environmental factors.

Linking farmers to markets and group formation[13]

Strong links to markets for poor rural producers are essential for generating economic growth in rural areas and reducing hunger and poverty by accessing markets to sell their produce for a fair price. However, this is not possible just by accessing markets. Logistics infrastructure, safe storage facilities, roads and affordable transportation are required to deliver the produce to the market. Farmers will also need access to the latest technology, internet connectivity and accessibility to hardware. It will help farmers to know in real time about weather conditions, market prices and demand patterns. It is also important to understand the dynamics of the supply chain and the distribution of power and control among the various actors. This means understanding the influence that supply chain entities can have over the quantity, quality and prices within the chain. As the supply chains form, whether led by large multinational food companies or through locally formed cooperatives, the terms and conditions of the business will have to be adhered to. As value chains grow and move internationally, they become better organized and more highly integrated and coordinated (as depicted by the entry of multinational food retailers in developing countries). As the supply chains get organized, the relationships among the entities tend to become more codified and institutionalized. Food safety, traceability and quality are paramount and this needs support from collaborating partners.

CASE EXAMPLE Food infrastructure in India and new mega food parks[14,15]

In 2014, the new government in India, under the leadership of Prime Minister Narendra Modi, launched a campaign to reduce post-harvest food loss through helping producers create food-processing opportunities. The government's immediate focus is to bring down wastage in fruits and vegetables by stepping up food processing. The government expects processing in fruits and vegetables to go up from the current low level of 2 per cent to 6 per cent in the next five years. The government expects that if the wastage is turned into processed food, the farmer can get a better price and does not have to throw away the yield. Processing of surplus yield into long-shelf-life products has the potential to set up a new industry and increase local employment opportunities. This also creates further opportunities for skills training where unskilled people can be trained, creating economic regeneration of the region through increased economic activity. The government has set aside $350 million for the food-processing sector to implement this initiative and, as an incentive, reduced the Central Excise duty from 10 to 6 per cent for the sector. The government has approved 17 food parks and 20 cold-chain projects across the country. A mega food park provides various facilities to food processors, farmers, retailers and exporters, thus helping the fast growth of food-processing industries.

Srini Mega Food Park

The Srini Mega Food Park at Chittoor in Andhra Pradesh is the first mega food park in India. The park facilitates end-to-end food processing with forward and backward linkages. The food park is equipped with a central processing centre and primary processing centres. The park provides state-of-the-art food-processing infrastructure designed according to global standards. The park is supported by the government (the Ministry of Food Processing Industries and the Andhra Pradesh Infrastructure Investment Corporation) and supports the complete agri-value chain. The park sprawls over 147 acres and provides world-class facilities for pulping, individual quick freezing (IQF), bottling, Tetra Paking, modular cold storage, warehousing and advanced testing laboratories. It enables basic and supply chain infrastructure and cluster farming, and is backed by field collection centres, self-help groups and individual farmers. It will set up sourcing support and aims to become a major food-processing centre.

CASE EXAMPLE   Rubies in the Rubble[16,17]

Jenny Dawson started Rubies in the Rubble, a small food-processing company that makes handmade chutneys and jam. She recently opened a commercial kitchen at the New Spitalfields fresh fruit and vegetable market in east London so that she could be on site to pick up high-quality produce that would otherwise go to landfill or compost because it stayed unsold at the end of the day. As it is produce that was going to be thrown away, she can pick up the leftovers free of charge, which means her raw material cost for the fruits is zero. The business works on very close relationships with the fruit and vegetable traders in the market.

Every year, millions of tonnes of fresh fruits and vegetables are discarded in the UK and across the world, as perfectly good produce cannot be sold as the fruits and vegetables, although of good quality, are not aesthetically sound. They are too small, too large, too ripe or too ugly to fit aesthetic criteria or last long enough to sit on a shop shelf for a week.

Jenny picks this produce and transforms it into chutneys and jams, which is a value-adding process, and has generated a successful enterprise. The company now works directly with growers and distributors of fresh fruit and vegetables in the UK. Waste occurs at multiple levels in the supply chain, and for multiple reasons and also according to the season. The company is able to produce seasonal flavours from raw material that would otherwise have been wasted. It has also generated employment for two other people and demonstrates how moving up the value chain can be economically sound. The products are sold online and at London's Borough Market. The products are also available at gourmet food shops across the UK and are also sold in Waitrose.

CASE EXAMPLE   Development of smallholder agro-processing in Africa[18]

The Sasakawa Africa Association (SAA) works to improve post-harvest handling, storage and processing of agricultural produce in Africa. It works with smallholder farmers and small agro-processors to reduce post-harvest losses. This helps to increase their income and improve their livelihoods. It works on a number of themes, in which theme 2 focuses on strengthening the competitiveness of smallholder farmers. There are four activities involved in tackling post-harvest loss:

- improving post-harvest handling and storage technologies;

- development of agro-processing enterprises;

- development of post-harvest private service providers;

- promoting supply and maintenance of post-harvest and agro-processing machinery.

As part of the activity of developing agro-processing enterprises, the team works with poor families to create off-farm employment through agro-processing. Farmer groups run by women farmers are supported in setting up processing to manufacture food products from locally sourced crops. These products are sold locally and in larger cities. The food products are prepared using household recipes, but the women are assisted by experts in improving the nutritional aspects of the food and food safety. They are educated in understanding consumer needs and modifying the recipes to appeal to consumers. As the products are popular among consumers, this initiative has led to additional income for the families and resulted in a sustainable agro-processing unit.

The SAA team also focuses on training the women to think of adding value to the crops, so that the raw produce is not wasted and some of it will have an extended shelf life. For example, the team teach the women parboiling of rice, extraction of oil from groundnuts, milling for flour and producing condiments from soybeans.

Summary

This chapter has presented a discussion of how the agricultural supply chain and sector is an important sector for any country. The chapter discussed the requirement for good infrastructure and logistics facilities to get benefit from the agribusiness sector. The chapter also considered the various initiatives in the United States, Europe and Asia with regard to the development of food parks, food clusters, food hubs and agroparks, with the aim of supporting the food-processing sector and creating economic regeneration. The discussion then looked at ways to support poor smallholder farmers in developing countries in moving them up the value chain. The initiatives currently being used in the developing world are types of agro-processing techniques which help farmers to process their produce, which helps in two ways: (1) it reduces post-harvest food loss and (2) it helps the farmer generate some extra income to support the family. Finally, the chapter used a few case examples to highlight the points discussed in the chapter.

Notes

1 McKinsey & Company: Building India: Transforming the nation's logistics infrastructure

2 Clusters of Creativity: Innovation and Growth in Montana, A Report to the Montana Governor's Office of Economic Opportunity on The Food Processing Cluster, 2003

3 Food Cluster Initiative (nd) So, What Is the Initiative? [Online] http://www.foodclusterinitiative.eu/what

4 Wubben, E F M and Isakhanyan, G (2011) Stakeholder analysis of agroparks, *International Journal of Food System Dynamics*, 2 (2), pp 145–54; Food Dynamics [Online] www.fooddynamics.org; InnovationNetwork [Online] http://www.innovatienetwerk.org/en

5 USDA Agricultural Marketing Service, Farmers Markets and Local Food Marketing, 2010.

6 Martinez, S *et al* (2010) Local Food Systems: Concepts, impacts, and issues, USDA, Economic Research Service, Economic Research, Report Number 97, May

7 Barham, J *et al* (2012) Regional Food Hub Resource Guide, U.S. Department of Agriculture, Agricultural Marketing Service, Washington, DC, April

8 Matson, J, Sullins, M and Cook, C (2013) The Role of Food Hubs in Local Food Marketing, USDA Rural Development Service, Report 73, January

9 FICCI STUDY on Rising Skill Demand: A Major Challenge for Indian Food Industry

10 Riccardi, A and Nwanze, K Y (accessed 19 February 2015) G8 Summit: Putting Food on the Table Through Investing in Small Farmers, *Huffington Post*, 16 May 2012 [Online] http://www.huffingtonpost.com/andrea-riccardi/g8-summit-small-farms_b_1522601.html

11 NC State University College of Agriculture and Life Sciences and North Carolina Department of Agriculture & Consumer Services (accessed 19 February 2015) The North Carolina Food Processing and Manufacturing Initiative: An Economic Feasibility Study, December 2014 [Online] http://harvest.cals.ncsu.edu/ckfinder/userfiles/files/The%20North%20Carolina%20Food%20Processing%20and%20Manufacturing%20Initiative%20%20-%20An%20Economic%20Feasibilty%20Study(1).pdf

12 See note 11.

13 IFAD (accessed 25 February 2015) Access to Markets: Making value chains work for poor rural people, 2012 [Online] http://www.ifad.org/pub/market/market_e.pdf

14 Times of India (accessed 20 February 2015) Govt to Approve 17 food parks; Rs 2,000 crore investment expected: Food processing minister, 22 September 2014 [Online] http://timesofindia.indiatimes.com/business/india-business/Govt-to-approve-17-food-parks-Rs-2000-crore-investment-expected-Food-processing-minister/articleshow/43162088.cms

15 Srini Food Park [Online] http://www.srinifoodpark.com/html/overview.html

16 Rubies in the Rubble [Online] http://www.rubiesintherubble.com/our-mission/

17 *The Guardian* (accessed 20 February 2015) Tackling Food Waste Through a Social Enterprise Model, 22 August 2012 [Online] http://www.theguardian.com/sustainable-business/tackling-food-waste-social-enterprise-model

18 Sasakawa Africa Association (accessed 20 February 2015) Theme 2: Post-harvest & Agroprocessing [Online] http://www.saa-safe.org/wwd/theme2.html

Food security and future challenges

15

In his most well-known work called *An Essay on the Principle of Population*, Thomas Malthus in 1798[1] argued that increases in population would eventually diminish the ability of the world to feed itself. He also said that populations expand in such a way as to overtake the development of sufficient land for crops.[2] Although this was said over 200 years ago and no one would have paid any attention to it, the state of the world today, the push towards food sustainability and predictions of population growth make the statement a very big challenge. Similarly, the World Economic Forum's Global Risks Report (2015) identifies that food shortage is one of the biggest risks to society.[3] Food security is high on the agenda of every government and many activities are conducted by both government and non-government organizations to understand the challenge and find solutions to alleviate it. The first outlook is for the next 15 years and after that for 2050. Hence, as much as there is work being done on the ground with smallholder farmers and other producers, this long-term view will require policy making both in terms of alleviating operational difficulties in production and, most importantly, within the area of technology, bioengineering and food waste. Food trade has always been a bone of contention between nations, as national food security takes precedence over market dynamics and trade. The world needs to take a more holistic and cohesive view of the challenge and find common solutions. This chapter presents a discussion on the future challenges we face with regard to food security. The factors affecting future food availability and access are studied, along with specific food security challenges. The chapter presents some solutions for the future.

Food security

The Food and Agriculture Organization[4] has defined food security as existing 'when all people at all times have access to sufficient, safe, nutritious food to maintain a healthy and active life'. Food security can be handled at different levels:

- individual or household food security;
- regional food security;
- national food security;
- global food security.[5]

Although most governments and national companies would be interested only in the national view on food security, this chapter will consider it from the aspect of meeting global food demand. Food security can be considered using the following themes:

1 Availability: volume of food and its reliability.

2 Access: ability to avail oneself of the food.

3 Affordability: who can afford to pay for the food? To what level of income will the food be accessible to the people?

4 Nutrition and quality: what does the food contain and does it provide the necessary quality and purpose?

5 Safety: the food needs to be safe to eat.[6]

In order to make food available, accessible and affordable for all to eat and meet the demand in 2050, we need to understand the drivers behind this challenge.

Drivers of change affecting food security

The UK Government Office for Science published a report titled 'The Future of Food and Farming'[7] in which it discussed very comprehensively the project that it had undertaken to investigate the future of food sustainability, with a long-term view as far as 2050.

The report considers the future demand for food and the supply issues. It comprehensively studies the supply issues from both a developing and developed country perspective. The study has identified five challenges:

Challenge A: balancing future demand and supply sustainably;

Challenge B: addressing the threat of future volatility in the food system;

Challenge C: ending hunger;

Challenge D: meeting the challenges of a low-emissions world;

Challenge E: maintaining the biodioversity and ecosystems of the world while feeding the world.

These are all very important challenges; however; this chapter will focus on Challenge A from a food security perspective. This also means that the demand and supply issues of food availability need to be studied before finding out how to balance the demand and supply of food in the future.

Factors affecting the future of the food supply chain

World population and the demand for food

Based on United Nations Population Division projections, policymakers will assume that today's population of about seven billion is most likely to rise to around eight billion by 2030 and probably to over nine billion by 2050.[8] Most of these increases will occur in low-income countries. Factors affecting population size will include GDP growth, educational attainment, access to contraception and gender equality; possibly the single most important factor is the extent of female education.[9] Population growth will also combine with other transformational changes, such as rural to urban migration in developing countries, and will put enormous pressure on cities to cope with extra demand for food, water and energy.

Changing consumer demand patterns

As developing countries increase their standard of living and salaries in China, India, Brazil and other countries start increasing, a growing number of consumers with middle and higher incomes will increase their food consumption, especially of meat and dairy products and fruits, vegetables and processed and fast foods, because they can now afford these items. As a result, consumption of rice is expected to decline in favour of wheat, both directly in wheat-based bakery products and indirectly via meat consumption.[10]

Highly processed food tends to be cheaper within the retail environment on account of economies of scale and the use of cheap ingredients for manufacturing, but processed foods are dearer than fresh foods. However, with the move towards more sedentary lifestyles, the reduced nutritional quality of consumer's diets can increase the risk of obesity and pose other significant social challenges.

Meat production is a resource-intensive process. A rise in the demand for meat will increase the demand for grain, as more grain will be required for animal feed.[11,12] An increase in demand for fish will require aquacultures to be equipped with the capacity to increase farming. Increased grain production will require scarce land and water, and input materials will be required to produce more grain. Another effect of rising incomes involves increasing consumer concerns over food safety, the environment, health, animal welfare and fair trade. The change in demographics within the developing countries (this will be roughly 25–30 per cent of the population) will create a different perspective towards the growing concentration of greenhouse gases in the atmosphere, biofuels and other non-food use of biomass, global warming, water scarcity and soil productive quality.

Governance of food supply systems

The globalization of markets has shaped the global food system owing to the movement of food products from one end of the globe to the other. The extensive movement of people for jobs or other migration has created a demand for food products which normally would not have been available easily. The opening up of national boundaries, proliferation of the internet and ICT, and reduction in transaction costs have facilitated trade between countries. Demand for varied but cheap food and in large quantities suggests that supply chains have to be very efficient, but also have to be safe.

In 2008, Brazil became the third-largest world exporter of agricultural products after the United States and the European Union, exporting $55.6 billion worth of goods.[13] China and India have built huge capacity and invested in large public stockholdings and public distribution systems with agricultural policies that remain inward-facing. There has been a trend for consolidation in the private sector, with the emergence of a limited number of very large transnational companies in agribusiness, in the fisheries sector and in the food-processing, distribution and retail sectors. Production subsidies, trade restrictions and other market interventions already have a major effect on the global food system, and how they develop in the future will be crucial. International food supply chains are subjected to food politics within the auspices of the WTO's Agreement on Agriculture and the tussle between nations regarding import tariffs and subsidies. The food supply chain will also need to deal with food safety regulations, the SPS Agreement and so on. However, this is not a problem and does not affect global food security. It will also be interesting to study how many governments take decisions collectively or individually, or whether they always act in their national interests and all decisions are based around that.

Climate change

Climate change and the uncertainty it brings is one of the most important aspects of the analysis and can change the working of the global markets and agriculture production. In many places, but particularly in poorer countries, climate change will act as a multiplier of existing threats to food security.[14]

Climate change has the potential to affect all four dimensions of food security:[15]

- Availability: climate change will affect food production owing to changes in ecological conditions; production/cultivation of certain plants is likely.

- Stability: as weather conditions become more variable, extreme events will increase in frequency and severity. This will lead to greater fluctuations in crop yields and livestock numbers and reduce food supply stability and security.

- Access: climate change may lead to supply shortages and hence food price increases.

- Use: the impact of climate change on the reduction of food production will create medical issues as malnourished people will be susceptible to diseases. If more people fall ill, this will lead to a decline in productivity, an increase in poverty and subsequently reduced ability to purchase sufficient food, and so the cycle continues.

Agriculture systems will need to be innovative to deal with climate change. For example, some of the innovations are: development of low-emission farming; drought, heat or salt-resistant crop varieties; innovative ways to irrigate crops; and new ways to manage soil.[16]

Competition for resources

Water scarcity

The usage of water has grown at twice the rate of population increase in the past century and quite a few nations find it increasingly difficult to meet water demand and deliver sustainable water services.[17,18] The problem of water scarcity is experienced worldwide. Water is the most precious commodity and it can cause friction between nations when they have common waterways. There have been instances when one nation has stopped water flowing to another nation, and this has created an international issue. Agriculture is both a cause and a victim of water scarcity. Food production affects water availability through land degradation, fertilizer runoff and disruption to groundwater. It also affects water quality. Water is key for food security and the strategies for nations should be to collaborate on sharing and distributing water across the globe.

Energy demand[19]

Energy demand is projected to increase by 45 per cent between 2006 and 2030 and could double between now and 2050. Energy prices are projected to rise and to become more volatile in the future. The food supply chain (from farm to fork) is an energy-intensive chain and a lot needs to be done to reduce energy at all points in the chain. Most corporates and large companies will have a mapped scenario or objective to try to reduce energy within the supply chain. This was discussed in Chapter 13.

Availability of land[20]

Overall, relatively little new land has been brought into agriculture in recent decades. Although global crop yields grew by 115 per cent between 1967 and 2007, the area of land in agriculture increased by only 8 per cent and the total currently stands at approximately 4,600 million hectares.[21] Land will be lost to urbanization, desertification, salinization and rises in sea levels. Soil degradation is an issue and good land is lost due to processes that erode soil (for example, the wrong type of crop). In addition, with an expanding population, there will be more pressure for land to be used for other purposes. While some forms of biofuel can play an important role in the mitigation of climate change, they may lead to a reduction in land available for agriculture.

Availability of supply

Intensification of agriculture through the use of increased pesticides, fertilizers and advanced irrigation methods created high-yielding scenarios in certain countries.[22] Intensification, however, did not increase the land mass but created additional productivity on the same land mass. There is a debate regarding 'intensification', as some believe that it is the way forward, whereas others feel that intensification kills the potential of the land over the long term and producers should be using traditional methods, such as organic farming and crop rotation, to manage their farms. The future land mass will be obtained via deforestation as people in developing countries cut down forest to make way for agricultural land. Increasing pressure from biofuel crops is particularly strong and will impact on agricultural supply. The pressure to grow biofuel crops to make alternative fuel looks easy, but it will have ramifications in terms of how the market structures work. Farmers getting a good demand for these crops will not grow any other crops, thus destroying the land in the long run. This will also affect the supply of food grains. The barriers to growth are limited resources, lack of physical infrastructure and capital, poorly functioning distribution and marketing systems and so forth. Good agricultural practices and farm management techniques need to be studied by small businesses to increase their efficiency and productivity.

Societal

Lack of access to food is a national political problem, and could lead to protests, demonstrations, looting and theft if the supply chain fails and subsequently the retail environment shuts down. There will be instances where the retailer may have stock in the system and may survive the supplier problem. Globalization of the food environment is creating alliances among large food businesses to support and create opportunities for farmers and smallholders to get access to training, funding and so on. This has been done through the G8, but there are people who are not sure about the work that the alliance does. Smallholders in the developing world will need access to clean water, schools for children, a decent living wage, skills and training, and financial instruments that will be useful for growing the business.

Balancing demand and supply sustainably

The 'Future of Food and Farming' report[23] considered the challenge of balancing demand and supply of food in the future and identified certain factors or levers that can make this happen:

1 Improving productivity sustainably using existing knowledge and technologies: different foods will require different levels of resource for their production. It is important to understand the

products and their impact on greenhouse emissions, soil erosion, requirement for fertilizers and so on. To increase productivity levels in line with increasing the supply, inefficient processes will need to be identified, including the pockets of waste in the system. This is a coordinated task. However, when modifying variables it will be essential to see what the actual outcome of the changes will be. A better use of scientific skills, knowledge and technology will be essential to increase production of food. Efficient production methods can be tested to find out which ones will be able to create increased supply without increasing carbon emissions. Some of the ways to increase skill sets and productivity are:

- *Extension services*: networks and access to ICT in rural communities can help farmers to access the correct information both from the perspective of running a business sustainably and also making it economically strong.

- *Improving access to markets*: to link farmers to the markets, identify market opportunities, consumer requirements and work within groups to understand food safety and environmental sustainability.

- *Land rights*: strengthening the land rights of individuals within developing economies can provide the motivation to consider it as a business and invest in it for the long term.

- *Infrastructure*: logistics infrastructure (access roads, multimodal connections, ports) and ICT systems are among the basic requirements to improve the potential of smallholder farms and low-income people in developing countries.

2 New technology and science can create processes and seeds that will increase yield and thus increase sustainable production.

3 Reducing waste: this is essential on both the supply side and the demand side. The loss of post-harvest produce within the developing world is very high owing to lack of infrastructure in handling harvested food. These losses are a direct impediment to balancing supply and demand. There is extensive food waste at the retailer end (owing to mismatch of forecast and actual demand) and a lot of food waste in the consumers' homes. These points have a direct impact on food sustainability and availability.

4 Improving governance of the food system: since the horsemeat scandal, governance of the food system with regard to food safety and quality has become more stringent and this will have to be conducted properly for the benefit of consumers. Global governance from agencies such as the WTO will be done at a higher level of activity.

5 Influencing demand: campaigns, school visits and advertising are some of the ways in which demand can be influenced so that consumers will try different things. This will help reduce the burden on some products.

CASE EXAMPLE Partners in Food Solutions[24,25]

Partners in Food Solutions (PFS) is a consortium of leading global food companies – General Mills, Cargill, Royal DSM and Bühler – working in partnership with the United States Agency for Development (USAID) to help improve food security and nutrition, in order to enrich lives around the world.

PFS is a non-profit organization and works on a model that links volunteers from the four consortium companies with small farmers and small businesses in the developing world. These small businesses are agro-processors and millers which are trying to move up the value chain. The volunteers provide expertise to these farmers to grow their business and also strengthen the supply chain for the companies involved. Since its start, 700 skilled employees from these companies have acted as volunteers on 350 individual projects totalling about 60,000 hours of work. This has helped 600 food companies in Kenya, Zambia, Tanzania, Malawi and Ethiopia impacting about 738,000 farmers (within the supply chain). The four companies each take a lead on specific areas; for example, Cargill takes the lead on vegetable oils, General Mills on blended flours, Royal DSM on fortification of staple foods and Bühler on process engineering.

The work done with small farmers and businesses focuses on improving the capacity and efficiency of the processors and the quality of the products. The volunteers also help with product safety and regulations and nutrition requirements and, in general, improve the skills of the farmers and processors to help them manage their business.

CASE EXAMPLE   Coca-Cola and water conservation[26]

Water conservation is Coca-Cola's key principle and activity. It has realized that water is key to its sustainability. Water is used to make all the drinks under the Coca-Cola brand and water is used in agriculture to produce the ingredients required by Coca-Cola. It is essential to use less water and try to return the water that is used. Coca-Cola has a very ambitious goal: 'Our goal is to return to communities and nature an amount of water equivalent to what we use in our beverages and their production by 2020.'

The company is focusing on three areas:

- Reducing the water use ratio. In 2011, Coca-Cola used 293.3 billion litres of water to make 135 billion litres of product (beverage). This is not a good sign; however, these figures cover the whole Coca-Cola system, which included 300 independent bottling plants.

- Recycling water used in the manufacturing processes and returning it to the environment (water bodies) after carefully treating it.

- Replenishing water in communities and nature through the support of healthy watersheds and community water programmes.

As the performance of the supply chain was not very good, Coca-Cola worked with its partners to jointly develop a Water Efficiency Toolkit, which contains more than 60 practices that Coca-Cola bottling partners can implement within their plants, communities, or basins where they operate.

Coca-Cola has partnered with the World Wildlife Fund (WWF) through the Water+ commitment and will help challenge the forces that impact fresh water. WWF and Coca-Cola are working together to conserve some of the world's most important places, spanning Asia, Africa and the Americas. The partnership is working through basin-wide engagement and comprehensive policy support to solve freshwater challenges in the regions of the Mesoamerican Reef, the River Yangtze, the river basins of the Amazon, Koshi, Mekong, Rio Grande/Bravo and

Zambezi; the catchments of the Great Barrier Reef; and watersheds in the Amur-Heilong, Atlantic Forests and Northern Great Plains.

Coca-Cola is also working on improving agriculture, climate, packaging and water efficiency impacts with efforts in:

- *Climate protection*: reduction in product-specific CO_2 by 25%, making comprehensive carbon-footprint reductions across the manufacturing processes, packaging formats, delivery fleet, refrigeration equipment and ingredient sourcing.

- *Renewable packaging*: Coca-Cola will work with WWF to assess the environmental and social performance of plant-based materials for potential use in its PlantBottle™ packaging. This will enable the company to meet its goal of using up to 30% plant-based material for all its PET plastic bottles by 2020.

- *Sustainable sourcing*: Coca-Cola will work to source its key agricultural ingredients sustainably, including cane sugar, beet sugar, corn, tea, palm oil, soy, pulp and paper fibre, and oranges. The company has established Sustainable Agriculture Guiding Principles and will work with WWF to implement the guidelines throughout the Coca-Cola system for these commodities.

- *Water efficiency*: Coca-Cola will improve its water use efficiency per litre of product produced, through operational advancements throughout the Coca-Cola system.[27]

Coca-Cola has engaged in 509 diverse, locally focused community water projects in more than 100 countries. Each project works towards set objectives, such as providing or improving access to safe water and sanitation, protecting watersheds, supporting water conservation and raising awareness on critical local water issues. In India, Coca-Cola set a goal to replenish more than 100 per cent of the water it uses in its manufacturing operations nationally. In fact, it replenished more than 130 per cent of the water it uses in India through supporting projects across the country. Projects include providing safe water access and sanitation in schools, building rainwater-harvesting structures, restoration of ponds, checking dams and interventions focused on improving water use efficiency in agriculture. Similar projects and goals have been set across the Coca-Cola system, with strong results.[28]

CASE EXAMPLE   International wheat initiative to improve wheat security[29-31]

Wheat is one of the world's most important staple crops. It plays a crucial role in the global agricultural economy and in global food security. Wheat accounts for an estimated 20 per cent of calories consumed throughout the world and hence it is important from the aspects of world hunger and poverty. A new multinational initiative, the International Wheat Yield Partnership (IWYP), was launched at the Borlaug summit on wheat for food security, held in Mexico on 25 March 2014. The initiative was formed to address the rising demand for wheat around the world and to help raise global wheat yields and develop new wheat varieties that are better adapted to meet the world's changing needs.

The partnership builds on commitments made by agriculture ministers from the G20 nations in 2011 to coordinate worldwide research efforts in wheat genetics, genomics, physiology, breeding and agronomy. Drawing on transparent collaboration and data sharing, the network's goal is to increase wheat's genetic yield potential by 50 per cent over the next 20 years.

The IWYP brings together members of the UK's Biotechnology and Biological Sciences Research Council (BBSRC), USDA, USAID, the International Maize and Wheat Improvement Center (known by its Spanish acronym, CIMMYT), the International Center for Agricultural Research in the Dry Area (ICARDA) and Syngenta, as well as representatives from Canada, Australia, the UK, China, Argentina, Brazil, Turkey, Germany, India, Mexico, France, Japan and Ireland. To date, the network partners have committed $50–75 million over the next five years.

Summary

This chapter discussed the topic of food security. It presented the challenges that the world may face with regard to food security and then focused on one to discuss within the chapter. Balancing demand and supply of food is crucial for the future and the chapter discussed the various factors that are affecting food sustainability and security. A brief discussion regarding possible solutions was also presented. Finally, the chapter ended with a few case examples highlighting initiatives in food security.

Notes

1 Malthus, T R (1798) *An Essay on the Principle of Population*, J Johnson, London

2 BBC History (accessed 24 February 2015) Thomas Malthus (1766–1834) [Online] ttp://www.bbc.co.uk/history/historic_figures/malthus_thomas.shtml

3 World Economic Forum (2015) Global risks, 2015 Insight Report

4 FAO (1996) *Rome Declaration on World Food Security* and *World Food Summit Plan of Action*, World Food Summit, 13–17 November 1996, Rome

5 DEFRA (2006) Food Security and the UK: An Evidence and Analysis Paper, Food Chain Analysis Group, DEFRA, London, December

6 See note 3.

7 Government Office for Science (accessed 25 February 2015) Foresight. The Future of Food and Farming, Final Project Report, Government Office for Science, London [Online] https://www.gov.uk/government/uploads/system/uploads/attachment_data/file/288329/11-546-future-of-food-and-farming-report.pdf

8 World Population Prospects: The 2012 Revision, United Nations, Department of Economic and Social Affairs, Population Division, Population Estimates and Projections Section

9 See note 6.

10 Sjauw-Koen-Fa, A (2010) Sustainability and Security of the Global Food Supply Chain, Rabobank Netherland – Economic Research Department of Rabobank, The Netherlands, pp 6–9, 16

11 Schuman, M (accessed 20 February 2015) A future of price spikes, *Time*, 14 July 2011 [Online] http://www.time.com/time/business/article/0,8599,2083276,00.html

12 von Braun, J (2008) Supply and Demand of Agricultural Products and Inflation – How to Address the Acute and Long-Run Problem, IFPRI, Prepared for the China Development Forum, Beijing, 22–24 March

13 See note 7.

14 Dyer, G (accessed 20 February 2015) Climate Change and Security: Risks and Opportunities for Business, Lloyd's, 2009 [Online] http://www.lloyds.com/~/media/Lloyds/Reports/360/360%20Climate%20reports/Climatechangeandsecurity_200904.pdf

15 Ludi, E (accessed 20 February 2015) Climate change, water and food security, Overseas Development Institute, 2009 [Online] http://www.odi.org.uk/sites/odi.org.uk/files/odi-assets/publications-opinion-files/4116.pdf

16 Lloyd's (2013) Feast or Famine: Business and Insurance Implications of Food Safety and Risk, Lloyds, London

17 Pegram, G (accessed 20 February 2015) Global Water Scarcity: Risks and Challenges for Business, Lloyd's, 2010 [Online] http://www.lloyds.com/~/media/Lloyds/Reports/360/360%20Climate%20reports/7209_360_Water_Scarcity_AW.pdf

18 FAO Water (accessed 20 February 2015) Water Scarcity [Online] http://www.fao.org/nr/water/topics_scarcity.html

19 Shen, Y *et al* (2008) Projection of future world water resources under SRES scenarios: water withdrawal, *Hydrological Sciences*, **53**, pp 11–33; Chartres, C (2008) Invest in water for farming, or the world will go hungry, SciDev.Net: Science and Development Network, 10 July

20 See note 6.

21 FAOSTAT (2010) Rome: FAO. Available: http://faostat.fao.org/site/291/default.aspx

22 Jones, A *et al* (accessed 25 February 2015) Resource Constraints: Sharing a finite world. The evidence and scenarios for the future, January 2013, Institute and Faculty of Actuaries [Online] http://www.actuaries.org.uk/research-and-resources/documents/resource-constraints-sharing-finite-world-evidence-and-scenarios-fu; Anglia Ruskin University (accessed 25 February 2015) Global Resources & Risk [Online] http://ww2.anglia.ac.uk/ruskin/en/home/microsites/global_sustainability_institute/our_research/resource_management.html

23 See note 7.

24 Partners in Food Solutions (accessed 20 February 2015) [Online] http://www.partnersinfoodsolutions.com/who-we-are

25 Technoserve (accessed 20 February 2015) Partners in Food Solutions, USAID and TechnoServe Expand Partnership to Improve Food Security in Africa, 18 October 2012 [Online] http://www.technoserve.org/press-room/detail/partners-in-food-solutions-usaid-and-technoserve-expand-partnership-to-impr

26 Coca-Cola (accessed 20 February 2015) Using Water Wisely: A sustainable water policy to protect Coca-Cola's main ingredient [Online] http://www.coca-cola.co.uk/environment/water-conservation-reducing-our-water-use.html

27 Coca-Cola Journey (accessed 20 February 2015) Renewing Our Partnership. Expanding Our Impact, 1 January 2012 [Online] http://www.coca-colacompany.com/stories/converging-on-water-an-innovative-conservation-partnership#TCCC

28 MarketWatch (accessed 20 February 2015) Coca-Cola Replenishes 108.5 Billion Liters of Water Back to Communities, 5 June 2014

[Online] http://www.marketwatch.com/story/coca-cola-replenishes-1085-billion-liters-of-water-back-to-communities-2014-06-05

29 BBSRC (accessed 20 February 2015) International Wheat Yield Partnership to help meet growing wheat demands, 26 March 2014 [Online] http://www.bbsrc.ac.uk/news/food-security/2014/140326-pr-international-partnership-wheats-potential.aspx

30 *The Guardian* (accessed 20 February 2015) Global food security: could wheat feed the world? 1 April 2014 [Online] http://www.theguardian.com/global-development-professionals-network/2014/apr/01/international-wheat-yield-partnership-food-security

31 Food Security Portal (accessed 20 February 2015) New International Wheat Initiative Aims to Improve Global Wheat Yields, 3 January 2013 [Online] http://www.foodsecurityportal.org/new-international-wheat-initiative-aims-improve-global-wheat-yields

ADDITIONAL READING

Anderson, J C and Narus, J A (1990) A model of distributor firm and manufacturer firm working partnerships, *Journal of Marketing*, 54 (January), pp 42–58

Arthur D Little (2013) Mapping Current Innovation and Emerging R&D Needs in the Food and Drink Industry Required for Sustainable Economic Growth, May, DEFRA, London

Bonfield, P (2014) A Plan for Public Procurement: Enabling a healthy future for our people, farmers and food producers, DEFRA, London

Bourlakis, M and Weightman, P W H (2004) *Food Supply Chain Management*, John Wiley & Sons, Chichester

Brody, A *et al* (2008) Innovative food packaging solutions, *Journal of Food Science*, 73 (8), pp R107–R116

Bukeviciute, L, Dierx, A and Ilzkovitz, F (2009) The Functioning of the Food Supply Chain and Its Effect on Food Prices in the European Union, European Economy Occasional Papers 47, May

Burch, D and Lawrence, G (2007) *Supermarkets and Agri-Food Supply Chains: Transformations in the production and consumption of foods*, Edward Elgar, Cheltenham

Cattaneo, O (2013) Aid for Trade and Value Chains inn AgriFood, OECD and WTO

Chandrasekaran, N (2014) *Agribusiness Supply Chain Management*, CRC Press, Baton Rouge, FL

Cox, A (1999) Power, value and supply chain management, *Supply Chain Management: An International Journal*, 4 (4), pp 167–75

Cox, A, Sanderson, J and Watson, G (2000) *Power Regimes Mapping the DNA of Business and Supply Chain Relationships*, Earlsgate Press, Stratford on Avon

Dahl, R (1957) The concept of power, *Behavioural Science*, 2, pp 201–15

Dani, S, Backhouse, C and Burns, N (2004) Application of transactional analysis in supply chain networks: a potential holonic mediating tool, *Proceedings of the Institution of Mechanical Engineers, Part B: Journal of Engineering Manufacture*, 218 (5), pp 571–80

DEFRA (2006) Food Industry Sustainability Strategy, DEFRA, London

DEFRA (2011) Guidance on the Application of Date Labels to Food, September, DEFRA, London

DEFRA (2014) Food Statistics Pocket Book 2014, DEFRA, London

Deloitte (2013) The Food Value Chain: A challenge for the next century, Deloitte Touche Tohmatsu, London

Department for International Development (2005) Growth and Poverty Reduction: The role of agriculture, A DFID policy paper, DFID, London

Desai, P, Potia, A and Salsberg, B (nd) Retail 4.0: The future of retail grocery in the digital world, McKinsey & Co,

Diamond, A and Barham, J (2012) Moving Food Along the Value Chain: Innovations in regional food distribution, US Department of Agriculture, Agricultural Marketing Service, Washington, DC, March

Dubinsky, A J and Gwin, J M (1981) Business ethics: buyers and sellers, *Journal of Purchasing and Materials Management*, **17** (4), pp 9–16

Dwyer, F R, Schurr, P H and Oh, S (1987) Developing buyer–seller relationships, *Journal of Marketing*, **51** (April), pp 11–27

Eastham, J and Sharples, L (2001) *Food Supply Chain Management: Issues for the hospitality and retail sectors*, Routledge, London

Fellows, P (2009) *Food Processing Technology: Principles and Practice*, 3rd rev edn, Woodhead Publishing Series in Food Science, Technology and Nutrition, Woodhead Publishing, Cambridge

Food Industry Innovation Forum (2012) Food Industry Innovation & Profitability: The next ten years, 2011 Forum Report, Food Industry Innovation Forum, Manchester

Forum for the Future (2007) Buying a Better World: Sustainable public procurement, Forum for the Future, London

Gebresenbet, G and Bosona, T (2012) Logistics and supply chains in agriculture and food, in *Pathways to Supply Chain Excellence*, ed A Groznik, InTech, Rijeka, Croatia

Giovannucci, D *et al* (2012) Food and Agriculture: The future of sustainability. A strategic input to the Sustainable Development in the 21st Century (SD21) project, United Nations Department of Economic and Social Affairs, Division for Sustainable Development, New York

Gradl, C *et al* (2012) Growing Business with Smallholders: A guide to inclusive agribusiness, German Federal Ministry for Economic Cooperation and Development, Bonn, Germany

GS1 (2012) GS1 Global Traceability Standard, GS1 Standards Document, Business Process and System Requirements for Full Supply Chain Traceability, Issue 1.3.0, November, GS1, London

Harland, C M (1996) Supply chain management: Relationships, chains and networks, *British Journal of Management*, **7** (Special Issue March), pp S63–S80

HM Government (2013) A UK Strategy for Agricultural Technologies, Department for Business, Innovation and Skills, London

HM Government (2014) Elliott Review into the Integrity and Assurance of Food Supply Networks: Final Report, A National Food Crime Prevention Framework, July, DEFRA, London

Humphrey, J and Memedovic, O (2006) Global Value Chains in the Agrifood sector, UNIDO working paper, UNIDO, Vienna

IGD (2013) Developments in Click and Collect (drives) for Groceries, Special Analysis, April, IGD, Watford

IICA (2014) Innovation in Agriculture: A key process for sustainable development, Institutional Position Paper, San Jose, May

Jap, S D (2001) Perspectives on joint competitive advantages in buyer–supplier relationships, *International Journal of Research in Marketing*, 18, pp 19–35

KPMG (2013) The Agricultural and Food Value Chain: Entering a new era of cooperation, KPMG Global Life Sciences, London

Lamming, R C, Cousins, P D and Notman, D M (1996) Beyond vendor assessment: the relationship assessment project, *European Journal of Purchasing and Supply Management*, 2 (4), pp 173–81

Lemke, F, Goffin, K and Szwejczewski, M (2003) Investigating the meaning of supplier–manufacturer partnerships: an exploratory study, *International Journal of Physical Distribution & Logistics Management*, 33 (1), pp 12–35

Lorange, P and Nelson, R T (1987) Uncertain imitability: an analysis of interfirm differences in efficiency under competition, *Bell Journal of Economics*, 13, 418–38

Mahalik, N P and Nambiar, A N (2010) Trends in food packaging and manufacturing systems and technology, *Trends in Food Science & Technology*, 21, 117–28

Mangan, J et al (2011) *Global Logistics and Supply Chain Management*, 2nd edn, John Wiley & Sons, Chichester

Marsh, K and Bugusu, B (2007) Food packaging: roles, materials and environmental issues, *Journal of Food Science*, 72 (3), pp R39–R55

Mattsson, B and Sonesson, U (2003) *Environmentally-Friendly Food Processing*, Woodhead Publishing in Food Science and Technology, Woodhead Publishing, Cambridge

Murray, S (2007) *Moveable Feasts: The incredible journeys of the things we eat*, Aurum Press, London

National Audit Office (2006) Smarter Food Procurement in the Public Sector, Report by the Comptroller and Auditor General, HC 963-1, March, National Audit Office, London

NSF International (2014) The 'new' phenomenon of criminal fraud in the food supply chain, 4 September, Long Hanborough, Oxon, UK

Parfitt, J, Barthel, M and Macnaughton, S (2010) Food waste within food supply chains: quantification and potential for change to 2050, *Philosophical Transactions of the Royal Society B*, **365**, pp 3065–81

Pollock, C (2013) Feeding the Future: Innovation requirements for primary food production in the UK to 2030, Joint Commissioning Group, TSB

Pond, W G, Nichols, B L and Brown, D L (2009) *Adequate Food for All: Culture, science, and technology of food in the 21st century*, CRC Press, Boca Raton, FL

Pottier, D and Locchi, L (2009) *Assuring Safety in the Food Chain: A European Research Priority*, Publications Office of the European Union, Luxembourg

Pullman, M and Wu, Z (2011) *Food Supply Chain Management: Economic, social and environmental perspectives*, Routledge, London

Rackham, N (2001) The pitfalls of partnering, *Sales & Marketing Management*, **153** (4), p 32

Ratnasingam, P (2000) The influence of power on trading partner trust in electronic commerce, *Internet Research: Electronic Networking Applications and Policy*, **10** (1), pp 56–62

Robson, I and Rawnsley, V (2001) Co-operation or coercion? Supplier networks and relationships in the UK food industry, *Supply Chain Management: An International Journal*, **6** (1), pp 39–47

Rodrigue, J-P (2014) Reefers in North American Cold Chain Logistics: Evidence from Western Canadian Supply Chains, The Van Horne Institute, University of Calgary

Rodrigue, J-P, Comtois, C and Slack, B (2013) *The Geography of Transport Systems*, 3rd edn, Routledge, London

Roekel, J V, Willems, S and Boselie, D M (2002) Agri Supply Chain Management: To stimulate cross-border trade in developing countries and emerging economies, 19 August, World Bank Paper, World Bank, Washington, DC

Rosin, C, Stock, P and Campbell, H (2012) *Food Systems Failure: The global food crisis and the future of agriculture*, Earthscan, London

Schiefer, G and Deiters, J (2013) *Transparency in the Food Chain*, Universität Bonn-ILB Press, Germany

Seth, A and Randall, G (2005) *Supermarket Wars: Global strategies for food retailers*, Palgrave Macmillan, Basingstoke

Smith, B G (2008) Developing sustainable food supply chains, *Philosophical Transactions of the Royal Society B*, **363**, 849–61

UNIDO (2009) Agro-Value Chain Analysis and Development: The UNIDO approach, A Staff Working Paper, UNIDO, Vienna

USAID (2011) The Logistics Handbook: A practical guide for the supply chain management of health commodities, USAID, Deliver Project, Task Order 1, Arlington, VA van der Vorst, J G A J *et al* (2007) Quality Controlled Logistics in Food Supply Chain Networks: Integrated decision-making on quality and logistics to meet advanced customer demands, 14th Internal Annual EUROMA conference, 17–20 June, Ankara, Turkey

Vorley, B and Fox, T (2004) Global Food Chains: Constraints and opportunities for smallholders, OECD DAC POVNET, Agriculture and Pro-Poor Growth Task Team, Helsinki Workshop, 17–18 June

Walmart (2013) Food Safety Requirements for Processors, Walmart, Bentonville, AR

Welch, R W and Mitchell, P C (2000) Food processing: a century of change, *British Medical Bulletin*, 56 (1), pp 1–17

Whipple, J M and Frankel, R (2000) Strategic alliance success factors, *Journal of Supply Chain Management*, 36 (3), pp 21–8

Williamson, O E (1975) *Markets and Hierarchies*, The Free Press, New York

World Bank (2007) *Enhancing Agriculture Innovation: How to go beyond the strengthening of research systems*, World Bank Publications, Washington, DC

INDEX

00207051

CPSIA information can be obtained at www.ICGtesting.com
Printed in the USA
BVOW08s1135050615

403396BV00007B/169/P